THE *AMITY* PAPERS, 1690

The Siege of Limerick and Franco-Irish Mercantile Networks

Records of Social and Economic History is a British Academy Research Project.

The British Academy, established by Royal Charter in 1902, is the national academy for the humanities and social sciences, promoting, sustaining, and representing advanced research. As an academy composed of senior scholars throughout the UK, it gives recognition to academic excellence and achievement, and plays a leadership role in representing the humanities and social sciences nationally and internationally. As a learned society, the British Academy facilitates the research of individuals and groups of scholars.

More information can be found at www.thebritishacademy.ac.uk.

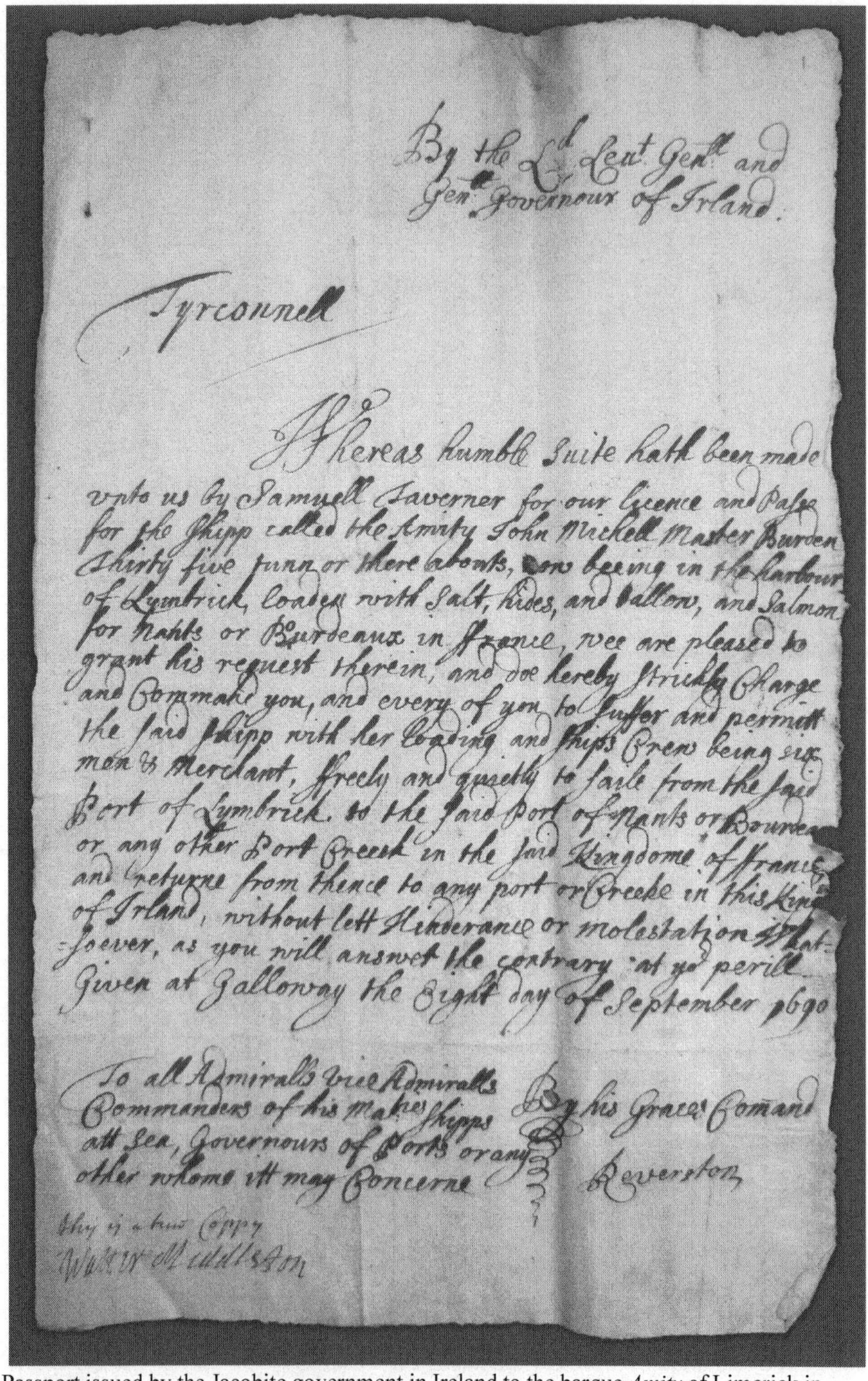

By the Ld Lieut Genll and Genll Governour of Irland.

Tyrconnell

Whereas humble Suite hath been made unto us by Samuell Taverner for our licence and Passe for the Shipp called the Amity John Mickell Master Burden thirty five tunn or there abouts, now beeing in the harbour of Lymbrick, loaden with Salt, hides, and tallow, and Salmon for Nants or Bourdeaux in France, wee are pleased to grant his request therein, and doe hereby strictly Charge and Commande you, and every of you to suffer and permitt the said shipp with her loading and Shipps Crew being six men & Merchant, freely and quietly to saile from the said Port of Lymbrick to the said Port of Nants or Bourdeaux or any other Port Creek in the said Kingdome of France and returne from thence to any port or Creeke in this Kingdome of Irland, without lett Hinderance or molestation whatsoever, as you will answer the contrary at yor perill Given at Galloway the Eight day of September 1690

To all Admiralls Vice Admiralls Commanders of his Maties shipps att Sea, Governours of Ports or any other whome itt may Concerne

By his Graces Comand
Reverston

this is a true Coppy
Walter Middleton

Passport issued by the Jacobite government in Ireland to the barque *Amity* of Limerick in September 1690 authorizing its trading voyage to France (TNA, HCA 32/1851/19).

RECORDS OF SOCIAL AND ECONOMIC HISTORY
NEW SERIES 68

THE *AMITY* PAPERS 1690

The Siege of Limerick and Franco-Irish Mercantile Networks

EDITED BY

THOMAS M. TRUXES

JOHN SHOVLIN

Published for THE BRITISH ACADEMY
by OXFORD UNIVERSITY PRESS

Oxford University Press, Great Clarendon Street, Oxford OX2 6DP

First edition published in 2025

British Library Cataloguing in Publication Data
Data available
Library of Congress Cataloguing in Publication Data
Data available

Typeset by the editors
Printed in Great Britain by CMP Books, Poole, Dorset

ISBN 978-0-19-726789-9 (hardback)
ISBN 978-0-19-897228-0 (ebook)
ISBN 978-0-19-897229-7 (online)

To our parents, with gratitude

Margaret and 'Dewey' Truxes

Collette and Frank Shovlin

Foreword

In the last twenty years or so historians have increasingly come to value the evidence to be found in bundles of letters seized from captured merchant ships during wartime and now preserved in the UK's National Archives. Usually the letters evidence, through personal connections, the struggles of overseas trade and communication in a period of significant growth, notably Europe's deepening engagement with the wider world. Such 'prize papers' were mainly a function of the frequency of Britain's resort to martime warfare in the seventeenth and eighteenth centuries, a period of its growing naval reach and power. By contrast, one important feature of the 'Amity Papers' is that they were seized during what was not only a European war but also a civil war across Britain and Ireland centring on dynastic and religious issues. That war was most intense in Ireland, the scars of which are still felt. Many of the letters reproduced in this valuable edition note the progress of the war there, in Limerick on Ireland's west coast especially, as well as offering a window into complex and valuable connections between the city and France, including strong mercantile ones.

The Records of Social and Economic History is pleased to add this volume to its list. The series has published many volumes of mercantile correspondence, each shedding distinctive light on the significant challenges of overseas trade in past centuries. The 'Amity Papers' are particularly to be placed alongside Professor Truxes' two previous volumes in the series, published in 2001 and 2013. As then, he has undertaken great labours, in this case working in partnership with Professor Shovlin, accurately to reproduce the originals and to provide in detailed footnotes all of the information necessary to make best use of them. They have been helped in this through the efforts of several members of the RSEH Committee: Professor Craig Muldrew, Professor Vanessa Harding, our outgoing General Editor, and, especially, her successor, Dr Richard Ansell. At the British Academy, Portia Taylor and Geetha Nair have, as always, been very helpful with the production process. I am very grateful to all of these colleagues.

November 2024

Julian Hoppit
Chair, Records of Social and Economic History Committee

Contents

Maps

Preface

The documents published in this volume were discovered in 2016 by Amanda Bevan of The National Archives of the United Kingdom at Kew, who brought them to the attention of Thomas M. Truxes. Seized from an Irish ship, the *Amity* of Limerick, by an English naval vessel in October 1690, the letters had lain unread for over three centuries among the 'Prize Papers' of the High Court of Admiralty (now part of the collections of The National Archives). A historian of Atlantic trade at New York University, Truxes immediately recognised the historical significance of the documents. With the assistance of archivists at Kew, he was able to assemble the remaining evidentiary traces of the condemnation proceedings of the *Amity*, and to piece together the story of its owners, its crew, and the men and women whose letters – primarily bound for France – the ship was carrying. To bring these extraordinary sources to the attention of historians and a broader public, Truxes partnered with his NYU colleague, John Shovlin, to transcribe all seventy-four documents, translate the six French and two Dutch letters, and contextualise the collection.

The *Amity* left Limerick just weeks after the first siege of the city during the Williamite War (1689–1691), fought in Ireland between supporters of the deposed Catholic King James II and the Protestant William III. The siege of Limerick was the only major Jacobite victory of the war. Written predominantly by merchants, the letters aboard the *Amity* document the experience of civilians during the siege of August 1690. They describe vividly the terrors of bombardment, resentment at military requisitioning, and the death and suffering of loved ones. They equally capture the elation experienced by many civilians at the breaking of the siege. This is the first collection of documents to present life in Limerick largely from the perspective of civilians trapped in the city. But it also contains letters written by Jacobite officers – many of them leading figures in James II's armies.

Beyond the dramatic events of the summer of 1690, the *Amity* papers offer new perspectives on early modern Irish trade, especially in wartime. The letters connect two closely intertwined, yet distinct, trading networks, linking Ireland to France and to England. The first was composed mostly of Catholic merchants with family and business connections in the French cities of Nantes, La Rochelle, Rouen, and Saint-Malo. The second was a Quaker network with close ties to London. The two groups worked together to continue the trade to France from Limerick, despite the insecurities caused by privateers, the depredations of the English and French navies, and the restrictive policies of the Jacobite government. Historians have done much in recent decades to illuminate early modern Irish connections with continental Europe. Less well-known is the place of Quakers in the commercial life of cities such as Limerick in this period. No documents hitherto published bring into such sharp relief the situation of Quakers in Limerick during the siege and their attitudes toward the war and the Jacobite cause. Extensive annotations in this edition identify and situate most of the individuals mentioned in the letters along with their authors and those to whom they were addressed. An introduction sets the documents in context and explores their principal themes.

The British Academy's Records of Social and Economic History is the ideal series in which to publish the letters, and this was possible with the support of Julian Hoppit, Chair of the RSEH committee, and the generous assistance of his publications team: academic specialists Craig Muldrew, Vanessa Harding, and especially Richard Ansell, together with senior production editor Portia Taylor.

In the course of working on this project, Truxes and Shovlin accumulated many debts to individuals and institutions. We would like to express our thanks to the UK National Archives at Kew for permission to publish the documents and, particularly, for the guidance of archivists Amanda Bevan and Randolph Cock of the 'Prize Papers' project. Thanks as well to The National Archives for permission to reproduce the *Amity's* passport as a frontispiece, and to James Harte at the National Library of Ireland for permission to use Thomas Phillips' 1685 map of Limerick as a cover image. The five maps that accompany the introduction were prepared by cartographer Bill Nelson of Accomac, Virginia, while Emmet Truxes of ASTVDIO in Santa Monica, California, assisted in the preparation of graphic images.

The editors have benefited from the generosity of many colleagues in the scholarly community. Sandrine Tromeur shared her research on the Irish community in seventeenth-century La Rochelle, and John Bergin provided access to a rare Limerick customs document. Thanks, as well, to Mary Ann Lyons for assistance with the Irish trading community at Saint-Malo and to Thomas O'Connor and Liam Chambers for their help with the Irish Jesuit College at Poitiers. For translating the Dutch letters, the editors are grateful to Wim Klooster and Timo McGregor, as well as to Emma Scoble for assistance transcribing. J. J. Lee and Kevin Kenny, directors of Glucksman Ireland House NYU, provided support for this project from the outset. Closer to home, the editors wish to thank their patient and supportive wives (An-Ming Sze Truxes and Kristel Smentek), and acknowledge the debt they owe their parents – to whom this book is dedicated.

November 2024

Thomas M. Truxes, NYU
John Shovlin, NYU

Note on Weights, Measures, Money, and their Corresponding Abbreviations

A wide array of weights, measures, and monies are mentioned in the papers aboard the *Amity*, often in abbreviated form, especially in letters written by merchants. Original symbols of weight, measure, and money have been reproduced in the transcriptions, within the constraints of modern typography and the legibility of the symbols in the original documents.

Weights and Measures

Measures of cloth, especially linen, are common in the documents. The width of fabrics in this period was standardised; the length in the *Amity* documents is generally specified in *aunes*, the rough French equivalent of an English ell, and defined as three feet (*pieds*), eight inches (*pouces*) by the *Dictionnaire de l'Académie française* (1694). However, like all French weights and measures, an *aune* would have varied somewhat by region, each province having its own custom. In the documents aboard the *Amity*, merchants most often use an *arroba*, '@', to abbreviate *aune*. In the case of linens, the value of which depended on quality, they also specified what appears to be a measure of the fineness of the cloth using a symbol we reproduce as '§' together with a number (e.g. 'fine Lineing of aboutt 24§ p^{r} @.' [10]).

Liquids such as wine or brandy, semi-solids like butter and tallow, and also fish, were transported in casks of various sizes. The largest cask size was the tun which, depending on local custom, held roughly 200 to 250 imperial gallons (approximately 900–1,100 litres), and was most commonly used for wine. Tuns were also used to reckon the overall cargo capacity of a ship, to gauge the volume of bulky items, such as wheat, which was shipped in sacks rather than casks, or to refer to the aggregate volume of goods stored in smaller casks. Tuns could be abbreviated 'tts', usually in superscript. Brandy was transported in pipes (half-tun casks), or in smaller barrels such as the quarter cask. The generic term 'cask' – also referred to as a hogshead (abbreviated 'hox^{tts}') – held a quarter tun. Salmon was transported on the *Amity* in tierces, a smaller cask holding one-sixth of a tun. In letter 33, there is reference to a firkin of spermaceti. Firkins were small barrels, varying in size depending on the commodity, but representing a quarter of the corresponding full barrel size.

The most common measure of weight in the documents is pounds, often abbreviated to a superscripted 'l' or 'li' (with the l sometimes crossed, making it look like a t), all referencing the Latin *libra*. Merchant writers also reckoned mass in hundredweight (112lbs) and, more rarely, in quarter hundredweight (28lbs), or quarters. Hundredweight could be spelled out, or abbreviated with a superscripted 'Cl', with the l usually crossed. (For reasons discussed below, the crossed l is transcribed in the documents as a simple l.) In cases where it was important to specify the distinction between the net weight of the contents of a cask and the gross weight, writers specified the 'tare' weight, that is, the weight of the empty cask. In some cases, writers used the '£' symbol, more typical of money, to refer to weight, for example '£400^{Cl}' to refer to four hundredweight. This is consistent with the occasional use of 'li', even in the same letter, to refer to both money and weight.

Money

In England, France, and Ireland in this period, prices in trade were reckoned in monies of account: in France, using *livres tournois*, each composed of 20 *sols*, made up of 12 *deniers*; in England and Ireland, reckoned in pounds, shillings, and pence, with 20 shillings to the pound, and 12 pence to the shilling. The Irish pound was officially valued at twelve-thirteenths of sterling, but actual exchange rates would have reflected market conditions and varied somewhat from this standard. Writers sometimes indicate that the pounds they refer to are sterling, most often using the abbreviations 'sterl' or 'ster', but they otherwise assumed this would be clear from context. If balances from Continental trade were remitted to London – as was often the case – the exchange would have been to sterling, and the balances would have remained in sterling for Irish merchants to draw upon in future transactions. *Livre tournois* is never spelled out in the documents but abbreviated to *livres*, or more commonly 'lt' (usually in superscript) or occasionally 'lt tur'. Two different abbreviations are generally used to refer to English and Irish pounds, the familiar '£', placed either before or after the numeral, or a superscripted 'l' (often crossed, making it look like a t) or 'li'. All such abbreviations refer to the Latin *libra*. To avoid confusion with the French 'lt', these symbols appear in the transcriptions as a simple 'l' or 'li'. Occasionally, writers used both symbols together, a '£' before the numeral and 'li' superscripted after.

Actual coins in circulation did not correspond closely to the monies of account. In England, for example, no coin corresponded to the pound (the gold guinea, at 21 shillings, came closest). In France, the principal large denomination coins were the silver *écu* (often translated into English as 'crown'), and the gold *louis* (informally known as a *pistole*). The value of these coins fluctuated relative to the *livre tournois* as the metallic content of the latter was set by royal decree and changed frequently during the reign of Louis XIV (r. 1643–1715). In all three countries, foreign coins circulated widely. The Jacobite regime introduced a temporary base metal currency in Ireland, to be redeemed in silver when James II was restored. The *Amity* writers refer to this as 'brass money', and make clear that it traded at a steep discount relative to silver, which is sometimes described as 'white money'.

Abbreviations

ADC-M	Archives Départementales de la Charente-Maritime (La Rochelle)
Add MSS	Additional Manuscripts
ADM	Admiralty
AMLR	Archives Municipales de La Rochelle
Aylward Papers	'The Aylward Papers, 1672–1717', in the Arundel Castle Archives, Chichester, West Sussex (Francis W. Steer [ed.], *Arundel Castle Archives: Interim Handlists*, Nos. 1–12 [Chichester, 1968])
B	Amirauté de La Rochelle
D'Alton, *Army List*	John D'Alton, *Illustrations, Historical and Genealogical, of King James's Irish Army List, 1689*, 2nd edition enlarged, 2 vols. (London, 1861)
DIB	*Dictionary of Irish Biography,* online edition (2021), at www.dib.ie
GG	Cultes, instruction publique, assistance publique
HCA	High Court of Admiralty
IND	Public Record Office, Indexes of Various Series
Lenihan, *Limerick*	Maurice Lenihan, *Limerick: Its History and Antiquities, Ecclesiastical, Civil, and Military, from the Earliest Ages* (Dublin, 1866)
Mulloy, *Franco-Irish Correspondence*	Sheila Mulloy, *Franco-Irish Correspondence: Dec. 1688–Feb. 1692*, 3 vols. (Dublin, 1984)
ODNB	*Oxford Dictionary of National Biography*, online edition (2004–), at www.oxforddnb.com
OED	*Oxford English Dictionary*
OLJ	*The Old Limerick Journal*, 28 (Winter 1990)
SP	State Papers
TNA	The National Archives, Kew (United Kingdom)

Calendar of Documents

1. Thomas Burton [address unknown], 'For Mrs Ellen Lee, at Kilrush', 9 April 1690. No. 44a

2. Petition of Samuel Taverner, Limerick, 'To his Grace the Duke of Tyrconnell Lord Deputy Gen^{ll} & Gen^{ll} Governor of Ireland', 2 August 1690. No. 4

3. Morrish Moore, Henry Trant, Grechus and Ambrose Moore, Tralee, 'To the Hon^{rble} Sr Patricke Trant K^{t} and Barronett' [place unknown], 19 August 1690. No. 69

4. To His Grace The Duke of Tyrconnell Ld Lieut Genl and Genl Governor of Ireland. The Humble Petticon of Christmas Smith of Traly in Kierry Merchant', n.d. No. 68

5. Passport for ship *Amity* from the Duke of Tyrconnell, Galway, 8 September 1690. No. 1

6. Robert Woulfe, Limerick, 'To m^{r} James Molley Mer^{t} recomended to m^{r} John new porte, Merchant In the recurrance in Brest', 3 September 1690. No. 21

7. James Missett, Limerick, 'To m^{r} Andrew Missett, Merc^{nt} In Rochell', 9 September 1690. No. 59

8. John Martin, Limerick, 'To Mr Andrew Gerraldin, Marchantt, In Nantes', 15 September 1690. No. 49

9. Robert Woulfe, Limerick, 'To m^{r} Patrick Rirdan, Merchant In Nantes', 18 September 1690. No. 20

10. Francis Rice, Limerick, 'ffor m^{r} James Rice, merchant In Rouen', 20 September 1690. No. 40

11. Slane, Limerick, 'for m^{r} James Rice merchant In Rouen', 20 September 1690. No. 41

12. Samuel Taverner, Limerick, 'To Patrick Rirdan, Merchants In Nants', 20 September 1690. No. 3

13. Samuel Taverner, Limerick, 'To The Widdow Lee, and Sons Lee and Lucar, Merchants in Nantes', 20 September 1690. No. 43

14. Samuel Taverner, Limerick, 'To Joseph Reade, In Nants', 20 September 1690. No. 50

15. Samuel Taverner, Limerick, 'To Francis White, Merchant In St Mallows', 20 September 1690. No. 62

16. Samuel Taverner, Limerick, 'To Lancellot Glanvill at Franc: Whites, Merchant In St Mallows', 20 September 1690. No. 63

17. Christmas Smith, Limerick, 'To mr Abraham Loyd Merchant In Bristol', 20 September 1690. No. 66

18. Christmas Smith, Limerick, 'For Mr Bartholomew Nagle, Merchant in Parris In France', 20 September 1690. No. 67

19. Robert Hannan, Limerick, 'To mr John Degrave, Merchant In London', 23 September 1690. No. 39

20. Samuel Taverner, Thomas Pearce, & Zachary Holland, Limerick, orders to Capt. John Mitchell, present, 24 September 1690. No. 2

21. Samuel Taverner, Thomas Pearce & Zachary Holland, Limerick, orders to Capt. John Mitchell, present, 24 September 1690 [copy of Document 20]. No. 76

22. Zachary Holland, Limerick, 'To Mr Patricke Rirdan, Merchant In Nants', 24 September 1690. No. 5; bill of lading, 25 September 1690. No. 8

23. Zachary Holland 'To Mr Tho & Joseph Carpentter, at the Blackamores head In Alderman burre, London', [?] September 1690. No. 71

24. Zachary Holland, [Limerick], to unknown, n.d. [Damaged document] No. 79

25. Thomas Pearce, Limerick, 'To Patrick Rirdan, Marchant In Nants', 24 September 1690. No. 6

26. William Dorrington, Limerick, to 'Monsieur Wauchope, Brigadier des Armie du Roy de D'anglete A St Jarmin en Laye,' 24 September 1690. No. 10

27. Francis Wauchop [place unknown] to 'Monsieur [John] Wauchope, Bregadier des Arme du Roy Dangletere att St Germin en Lay', 24 September 1690. No. 11

28. Robert Rirdan, Limerick, 'To Robert Rirdan and Pat: Rirdan, merc^{t} In nantes', 24 September 1690. No. 22

29. John Rirdan, Limerick, 'To m^{r} Patrick Rirdan, Merchant In Nantes, france', 24 September 1690, No. 15; bill of lading, 23 September 1690, No. 17; duplicate bill of lading, 23 September 1690. No. 77

30. John Rirdan to Pat Rirdan [Nantes] [n.d., but probably enclosure in above letter]. No. 16

31. John Rirdan, Limerick, 'To m^{r} Andrew Gerraldin, Merchant, In Nantes, france', 24 September 1690. No. 48

32. Thomas Pearce, Limerick, 'To John & Edmund Gold, Marchants In Rochelle', 24 September 1690. No. 58

33. Thomas Pearce, Limerick, 'To Joseph Scriven, linnen draper in watling street, London', 24 September 1690. No. 74a

34. Thomas Pearce, Limerick, to Capt. Thomas Flaxon, [place unknown], 24 September 1690. No. 74b

35. James Craven, Limerick, 'To the Widdow Lee and sonns John Lee & Luckar March^{ts}, In Nantes', 24 September 1690. No. 23; bill of lading, 24 September 1690. No. 24

36. Nicholas Skyddy, Limerick, 'To Mr Pat^{rk} Riordane, In Nants', 25 September 1690 [damaged document]. No. 9

37. Nicholas Skyddy, Limerick, 'To m^{r} Christian Skiddy att the Convent of the Ellizabeths In Nantes', 25 September 1690. No. 12

38. Nicholas Skyddy, Limerick, 'For Captn Skiddy, [Nantes]', 25 September 1690. No. 14

39. E. Connell, Limerick, to Capt Connell [place unknown], 25 September 1690. No. 13

40. Thomas Creagh, Limerick, 'To Mr Patrick Rirdane In Nantes', 25 September 1690. No. 18

41. Thomas Creagh, Limerick, 'To Madam Lee and sonn Jo^{h} and Lucor, Merc^{ht} In Nantes', 25 September 1690. No. 19

42. Thomas McNemara, Limerick, 'for Messieurs Clerke and Quinn, Merc^{ts}, In Lisborne', 25 September 1690. No. 32

43. Robert Hannan, Limerick, 'To mr Patrick Rirdan, Merchant In Nantes', 25 September 1690. No. 33

44. John D'herbe, Limerick, to 'Monsr Jean Stalpaert, March^{t} a Nantes', 25 September 1690. No. 51

45. John D'herbe, Limerick, to 'Monsr Phillippe van Tours, March^{t} a Bruges', September 1690. No. 52

46. Samuel Taverner, Limerick, 'To John & Edm^{d} Gould, Merchants In Rochelle', 25 September 1690. No. 57; bill of lading, 25 September 1690. No. 78

47. Samuel Taverner, Limerick, 'To Patrick Rirdane, Merchant In Nants', 25 September 1690. No. 7

48. Samuel Taverner, Limerick, 'To Prudence Taverner at Joseph Scriven, Linen draper at the ragged staff and beare In watling street In London', 25 September 1690. No. 73

49. James Cravin, Limerick, 'To James Cravin, Junr, Merchant [London]', 25 September 1690. No. 70

50. Zachary Holland, Limerick, 'To m^{r} Jos: Holland, Merch^{t} In Minehead', 25 September 1690. No. 72

51. Robert Talbot, Limerick, 'To Patrick Cusacke, Chester', 26 September 1690. No. 47

52. Adam Cusack, Limerick, 'To Mr Mathew Rooth, or in his absence to Dr Patrick Cusacke att m^{r} Gregory ffitzgerra^{lds}, March^{t} in Nantes', 27 September 1690. No. 45

53. Adam Cusack, Limerick, 'To the Reverend ffather in God Dr Patrick Cusack in Nantes or elsewhere', 27 September 1690. No. 46

54. Robert Hannan, Limerick, 'To Madam Lee and Company, Merchants In Nantes', 28 September 1690. Nos. 30 and 31

55. Robert Hannan, Limerick, 'To m^{r} James Hannan, Studint In Potyers', 28 September 1690. No. 34

56. Robert Hannan, Limerick, 'To m^{r} James Power, In Rochell', 28 September 1690. No. 35

57. Robert Hannan, Limerick, 'To Sr Daniel Arthur Kn^{t}, In Paris',' 28 September 1690. No. 36

58. Robert Hannan, Limerick, 'To the R^{t} R^{d} father in God John Ld Bisp. of Lymerick & Killaloe, In Paris', 28 September 1690. No. 37

59. Robert Hannan, Limerick, 'To m^{r} James Rice Francis, Merchant In Rouen', 28 September 1690. No. 38

60. Robert Hannan, Limerick, 'To Madam Lee & Company, Merchants In Nantes', 28 September 1690. No. 42

61. Robert Hannan, Limerick, 'To m^{r} James Power, Merchant In Rochell', 28 September 1690. No. 61

62. Ellen Lee, Kilrush, 'For Her Loveinge Husband Nicholas Lee in Nance In Franc', 28 September 1690. No. 44

63. Ducorail, infantry major, Limerick, to unknown, 28 September 1690. No. 54

64. Nicholas Gerraldin, Jr, Limerick, 'To ye Widdow Lee & Comp^{e} In Nantes', 1 October 1690. No. 25

65. Nicholas Gerraldin, Jr, Limerick, to Madame Gerraldin at 'Monsr Nicolas Gerraldin, Lejeune, Merch^{t} a s^{t} malo', 1 October 1690. No. 28

66. Laughlin Cleere, Limerick, 'To m^{rs} margaret Walsh, alias Cleere, In s^{t} Malo', 1 October 1690. No. 29

67. Pierre Charié, Limerick, to his wife, care of Pierre Charié de Senaserre, in the river of Nantes, 2 October 1690. No. 53

68. Guillaume Nau, Limerick, to his mother in Pornic, 2 October 1690. No. 64

69. Thomas Pearce, Limerick, 'To Joseph Scriven, linnen draper in Watling street, London', 6 and 7 October 1690. No. 5

70. Thomas Girard, Limerick, to his wife in Saint-Malo, care of de La Riviere, surgeon, Champs au vers, Saint-Malo, 9 October 1690. No. 27

71. René Lelieur, Limerick, to his father and mother in Saint-Malo, care of Dupremorin, merchant at Saint-Malo, 9 October 1690. No. 26

72. Jacques Mahon, Scattery Island, to Jacques Souchay and François Bouchaud, bankers, Nantes, 12 October 1690. No. 56

73. Zachary Holland 'To Mr Tho & Jos Carpenter, at the Blackamores head In Alderman burr^{e}, London', 7 December 1690 (TNA, HCA 30/15).

74. Thomas Pearce, Limerick, 'To Joseph Scriven, In London', 18 December 1690 (TNA, HCA 30/15).

Introduction

In October 1690 a small Irish trading vessel, the 35-tun barque *Amity*, sailed from Limerick bound for the Bay of Biscay.[1] It was wartime. Limerick had just withstood a brutal siege by forces loyal to William of Orange, the new king of England. The *Amity* became a casualty of the conflict when it was captured off Milford Haven in Wales by an English warship, the 36-gun HMS *Nonsuch*.[2] Blown off course, and overpowered, the Irish vessel offered no resistance. With a prize crew aboard, Captain Robert Sincock sent the *Amity* into port where its crew and master, John Mitchell, were interrogated and the ship's papers examined in preparation for condemnation proceedings at the High Court of Admiralty in London. If condemned, the vessel and its cargo would be forfeited as a prize of war, with the proceeds of its sale to be divided between the Crown and the captain and crew of the *Nonsuch*.[3]

In addition to several petitions, a handful of customs documents, and Mitchell's orders, the ship carried over sixty letters – fifty bound for destinations in France, the rest for English towns and cities or other Continental ports.[4] Bundled together by officers of the Prize Court in January 1691, they were rediscovered in spring 2016 in the British National Archives at Kew. These

[1] TNA, IND 1/9013, p. 13.

[2] TNA, HCA 32/1851/19.

[3] For the English Prize Court and its procedure, see E.S. Roscoe, *A History of the English Prize Court* (London, 1924), vii, 1–50; Francis Deák and Philip C. Jessup, 'Early Prize Court Procedure: Part One', *University of Pennsylvania Law Review and American Law Register*, 82:7 (May 1934), 677–94, and 'Part Two', *University of Pennsylvania Law Review and American Law Register*, 82:8 (June 1934), 818–37; Richard Hill, *The Prizes of War: The Naval Prize System in the Napoleonic Wars, 1793–1815* (Stroud, 1998), 5–11.

[4] Sixteen destinations in all are mentioned: eleven in continental Europe, including nine in France, and four in England. Among letters sent to France, Nantes was the most important destination with twenty-eight. Other western ports include Saint-Malo, Brest, La Rochelle, and the small port of Pornic, near the mouth of the Loire estuary. Three letters were addressed to Paris and two to Saint-Germain-en-Laye, where the Jacobite court was exiled. Others were intended for Rouen, and Poitiers. Eleven were destined for English towns and cities: eight for London and one each for Bristol, Minehead, and Chester. One was sent to Lisbon and one to Bruges. A single letter, anomalous because the addressee, Ellen Lee, was in Ireland (1), was presumably enclosed with her letter to her husband Nicholas (59). All but seven of the letter writers wrote in English. Two letters (43, 44) were written in Dutch to addressees in Bruges and Nantes by John d'Herbe, a merchant, while six, from as many different writers, were composed in French (62, 68, 69, 70, 71, 72). These are transcribed in the original language and translated into English in the following section.

Map 1. Ireland

'Seventy foure Ship-papers' are reproduced in this volume, opening a window on a world long gone, and a dramatic moment in Irish and British history.

The seizure of the *Amity* took place at the height of the struggle fought on Irish soil in the wake of the 1688 Glorious Revolution between the forces of the deposed King James II and his successor William III. At stake was control of the Three Kingdoms of England, Scotland, and Ireland. Unsurprisingly, the war is a major preoccupation of the letter writers, especially the siege of Limerick, lifted just weeks before the *Amity* sailed. While six of the letter writers were soldiers, and these letters offer a distinctive, professional perspective on the siege and the war, the large majority were civilians. Their letters reflect the terrors of bombardment for residents of Limerick trapped in the city; the loss of goods or livelihoods through military requisitioning or plunder; the frustrations of trying to make a living in a city at war; the elation of victory; and the inevitable anti-climax after the siege was lifted as civilians faced a future of uncertainty, insecurity, and possibly hunger. The appetite for small consumer pleasures unobtainable at such a moment is palpable – hats, stockings, soap, fine paper, and other minor luxuries. We are not aware of another source that so vividly captures the perspectives of civilians who lived through those terrifying and exhilarating events.

Yet it is not only the siege and its aftermath to which the *Amity* papers give access. A majority of the letter writers were merchants – at least twenty out of the thirty-six in total. Several others were seamen serving on merchant vessels. Linked to the same milieu were the only two women among the writers. Mrs E. Connell hoped to recall her husband, a Captain Connell, from France, while Ellen Lee's husband, Nicholas, was a member of an Irish merchant family in Nantes. This mercantile and maritime world – a world that spread far beyond Limerick, yet remained tightly connected to the city – is also brought to light in the ship's papers.

Two networks, distinct though closely intertwined, bound most of the letter writers and their correspondents. The first, mostly Catholic, linked Limerick to the western ports of France – the destination of the *Amity*. Of Irish merchants in France we gain a revealing snapshot: they were concentrated in Nantes, La Rochelle, Saint-Malo, and Rouen, in many cases long-settled there; they managed Irish trade with the Continent, organising cargoes of European (and often American) goods for Irish markets. They had links with students in Irish colleges, priests pursuing education or a career in France, and Irish soldiers, whose numbers had declined sharply since the 1650s but would rebound in 1691 at the war's end. Irish historians are quite familiar with this Franco-Irish trading world – a little less so, perhaps, with the second network revealed in the letters, which was Quaker.

At least thirty of the letters carried aboard the *Amity* were written by Quakers, while as many as twenty of the recipients were likely also Friends. The ship's owners, Samuel Taverner, Thomas Pearce, and Zachary Holland, were Quakers – as, indeed, the name of the vessel proclaims. (The owners changed its original name – the *Ann and Mary* – when they acquired it.[5]) The Society of Friends was

[5] Deposition of Captain John Mitchell to the High Court of Admiralty, 13 October 1690, TNA, HCA 32/1851/19. For a copy, see Appendix IV in this volume.

founded in England in 1652 and quickly spread to Ireland.[6] There, most converts were drawn from among other dissenting Protestants, some of them soldiers in Cromwell's armies.[7] Quaker beginnings in Limerick date to the summer of 1655 when a mission to the town, despite being ejected, convinced a few – notably Richard Pearce, the father of Thomas Pearce. (The circumstances of Richard's death on 7 October 1690 are recounted in his son's letter to a relative in London [69]). Despite suffering considerable disabilities under the Commonwealth and Restoration governments, the Limerick Friends opened a first meeting house in 1671 on Creagh Lane, and in the same year a small burial ground on Peter Street. In the following decades, the community would grow to about seventy.[8]

If the letters are any guide, the Quaker merchants of Limerick did not specialise in a different area of business from their Catholic counterparts. Their vessels carried the same goods on the same routes as other Limerick traders, and the letters show that they shared the same, mostly Catholic, correspondents in French ports. Yet Limerick's Quaker merchants were much less firmly implanted in France: they lacked the density of connections to religious and military life enjoyed by Irish Catholic mercantile networks. Commercial, familial, and religious ties bound them, rather, to London, which had the largest concentration of Quakers in the Atlantic World. These links with coreligionists allowed them to channel flows of credit, remittances, and information through the English capital – and to find refuge for family members there in time of war.

Beyond illuminating their trading activities and networks, the *Amity* papers offer hints about how Quakers positioned themselves vis-à-vis the Jacobite cause in Ireland, and in relation to the Williamite forces invading Ireland and besieging Limerick. Quakers had been among the principal beneficiaries of James II's policies of religious toleration. Leading Limerick Friends, including one of the owners of the *Amity*, Samuel Taverner, rose to high office for the first time in the city. The congeniality of the Jacobite regime, and the massive destruction caused by the Williamite War, made at least some of Limerick's Quakers resistant to these revolutionary changes.

The Williamite War and the Siege of Limerick

In 1688, James II, king of England and Ireland, and a Catholic, had been deposed in the Glorious Revolution by his own subjects, some fearing the establishment

6 The first Irish meeting was established at Lurgan, Co. Armagh, in 1654. Albert Cook Myers, *Immigration of the Irish Quakers into Pennsylvania, 1682–1750, with Their Early History in Ireland* (Swarthmore, PA, 1902), 16.

7 Myers, *Immigration of the Irish Quakers*, 32–7.

8 Hiram Wood, *History of the Quakers of Limerick 1655–1900* (Cratloe, 2020); Seán Spellisy, *The History of Limerick City* (Limerick, 1998), 274–6.

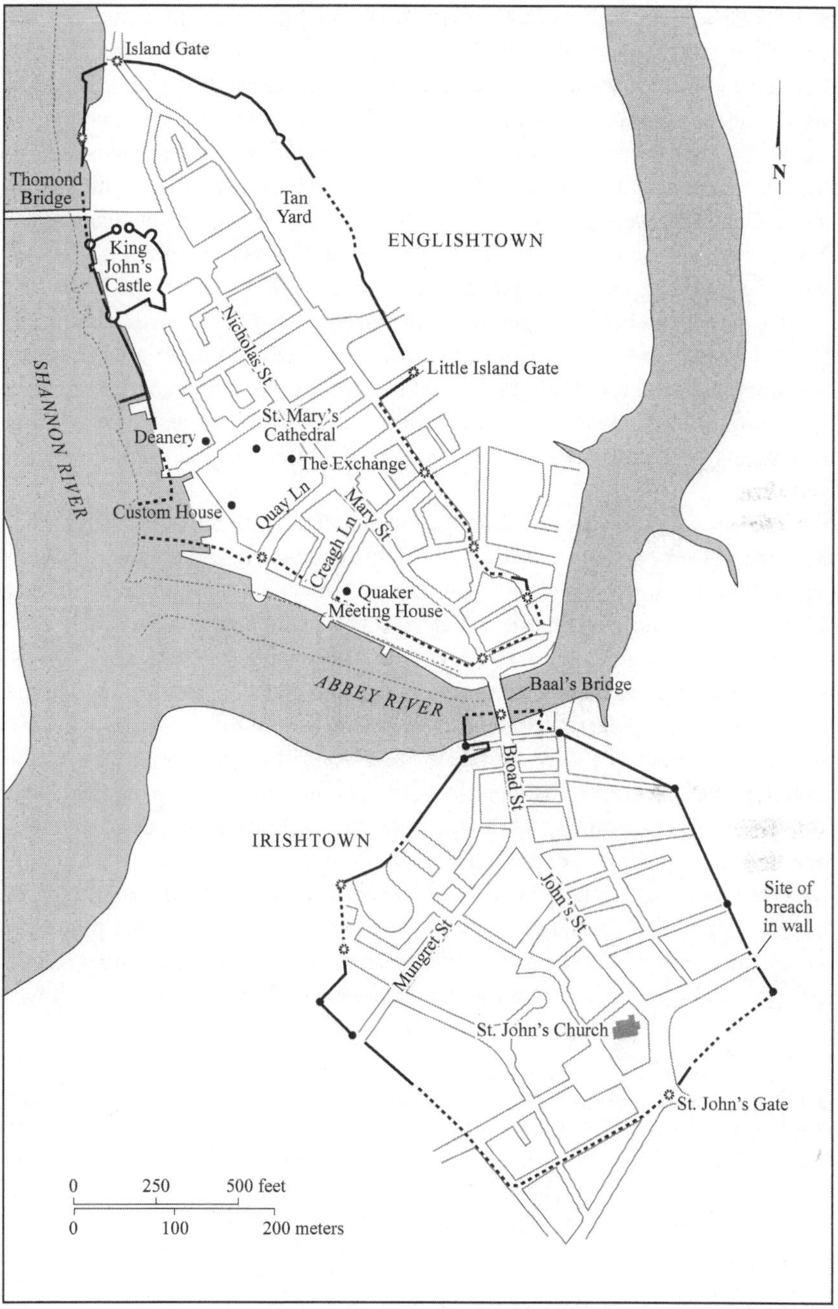

Map 2. Limerick City in 1690

of a Catholic dynasty, wholesale changes to religious arrangements, and the redistribution of power, others with political and economic designs for England opposed to those of the king.[9] The plotters invited James' Protestant daughter, Mary, and her husband, Prince William of Orange, the Dutch stadholder, to invade England. William took charge of the government after James fled to France, where he was welcomed by Louis XIV, whose expansionist ambitions on the Continent were opposed by a coalition of mostly Protestant states under William's leadership. The path for James' return to power lay through Ireland where he could expect the support of Catholics eager to regain the lands and privileges that had been stripped from them in the wars of the seventeenth century. He landed at Kinsale, Co. Cork, in March 1689, a month after William and Mary accepted a formal offer of the crown. Although French aid would be forthcoming, accomplishing his goal hinged primarily on the defeat of William by a mostly Irish army deficient in weapons, ammunition, and military experience.[10]

The Jacobites, as James' followers are known, suffered early reverses at the siege of Derry and at Enniskillen. Still, the country remained largely in their hands. William, having sent supplies and reinforcements to Ireland, including Dutch, Danish, and German troops, arrived at Carrickfergus on 14 June.[11] Soldiers and materiel were likewise arriving from France to bolster James' forces. In the summer of 1690, the two armies manoeuvered for position astride the road to Dublin. The Jacobites took up positions south of the River Boyne, not far from Drogheda, the only significant barrier blocking William's path to the capital.[12] The two armies collided on 1 July (12 July in the Gregorian calendar adopted in 1752), leading to a rout of James' forces. In panic, the defeated monarch fled south to Cork, boarding a ship for France three days later.[13]

Assuming that the Jacobite cause had been crushed, William issued a proclamation on 7 July offering generous terms to common soldiers but pointedly not to their officers or James' political supporters.[14] Waterford surrendered without a fight on 23 July, and the nearby fortress of Duncannon on 26 July.[15]

[9] J. R. Jones, *The Revolution of 1688 in England* (New York, 1972); Steve Pincus, *1688: The First Modern Revolution* (New Haven, CT, 2009).

[10] Harman Murtagh, 'The War in Ireland, 1689–91', in W. A. Maguire (ed.), *Kings in Conflict: The Revolutionary War in Ireland and Its Aftermath, 1689–1750* (Belfast, 1990), 62.

[11] John Childs, *The Williamite Wars in Ireland, 1688–1691* (London, 2007), 205.

[12] Murtagh, 'War in Ireland', 72.

[13] J. G. Simms, *Jacobite Ireland, 1685–91* (London, 1969), 152–4.

[14] Simms, *Jacobite Ireland*, 160.

[15] Simms, *Jacobite Ireland*, 163; Childs, *Williamite Wars*, 239.

Yet the Boyne had not destroyed the Jacobite army.[16] The deposed king's followers regrouped at Limerick, strengthening the town's defences in anticipation of the siege that would surely come.

It was a city 'inferior to none in Ireland but Dublin', wrote a well-travelled visitor in the 1680s – 'and not to very many in England', said another.[17] Located at the head of the Shannon estuary with the advantage of a safe harbour sixty miles inland from the Atlantic, the town benefited from a large and productive hinterland that included not only County Limerick but South Clare, North Kerry, and South Tipperary.[18] Before the influx of Jacobite soldiers, Limerick's population stood at roughly 5,000 within the walls, with perhaps as many again in its liberties and suburbs. In 1706, when it would not have been substantially different in size, the city, including its liberties, had a population of nearly 12,000, with perhaps 4–5,000 of these residing within the walls.[19] Limerick had a distinctive hourglass shape. To the north was Englishtown, situated on King's Island in the River Shannon, and linked to the Clare side of the river by Thomond Bridge. It was joined by Baal's (or Ball's) Bridge to Irishtown on the Limerick side of the Abbey River, a branch of the Shannon. Within the city walls were landmarks, such as the 'triple-towered' castle begun in the reign of King John, St Mary's Cathedral with its 'large high square steeple containing 6 tuneable Bells', an exchange dating from 1674, and numerous three and four-storey buildings, many constructed of stone or wood. The city's busy commercial life was reflected in inns, counting houses, warehouses, and workshops, even 'a fair Tan yard in the ruines of an Abbey'. But more numerous were the thatched-roof dwellings of the mass of the population.

As Limerick braced for the inevitable, civilians – those with the means to do so – sought refuge outside the city. 'Aboute a fortnight before the siege, shipping presenting hence for ffrance', Nicholas Skyddy told his brother in Nantes, 'severall went on them of the Natives of this Cittie' (38). But flight presented its own risks. As Thomas Pearce told his brother-in-law Joseph Scriven, 'though some have gon[e] of[f] well others have endured much hardships n^{t} to be exprest' (33).

[16] Murtagh, 'War in Ireland', 75–8.

[17] Evelyn Philip Shirley and James Graves (eds.), 'Extracts from the Journal of Thomas Dineley, Esquire, Giving Some Account of His Visit to Ireland in the Reign of Charles II', *Journal of the Kilkenny and South-East of Ireland Archaeological Society*, New Series, 4:1 (1862), 38; Robert H. Murray (ed.), *The Journal of John Stevens, Containing a Brief Account of the War in Ireland, 1689–1691* (Oxford, 1912), 149.

[18] Shirley and Lenihan (eds.), 'Extracts from the Journal of Thomas Dineley', 428.

[19] David Dickson, *The First Irish Cities: An Eighteenth-Century Transformation* (New Haven, CT, 2021), 32; J. G. Simms, 'The Restoration, 1660–85', in T. W. Moody, F. X. Martin, and F. J. Byrne (eds.), *A New History of Ireland. III, Early Modern Ireland, 1534–1691* (Oxford, 1976), 448; Eamon O'Flaherty (ed.), *Limerick: Irish Historic Towns Atlas*, No. 21 (Dublin, 2010), 5; D. A. Fleming, *Politics and Provincial People: Sligo and Limerick, 1691–1761* (Manchester, 2010), 55–6.

Limerick was no stranger to attack, having endured a siege as recently as 1651 when Henry Ireton, commanding Oliver Cromwell's forces, took the city. As Jacobite soldiers converged on Limerick in July 1690, officers commandeered shelter, displacing individual residents and families without discrimination. 'Wee are sadly opprest with Soldiers & officiers whoe scarsly allow our Sealves an ordinary bed to ly on', John Rirdan complained to his brother in France. Displaced citizens scrambled for what was left, sometimes 'In the Garrat & atther times In the shope & Celler' (29). Food likewise became scarce and expensive.

Several writers alluded to the requisitioning of goods by the two armies. Rirdan explained that most of the wine his brother Patrick had just shipped to Limerick on the *Amity* had either been sold for devalued 'brass money' or 'forced from us at the Kings rate by officiers' (29) – a reference to price fixing by the authorities. At the height of the siege in August 1690, Thomas McNemara ordered his ship *Catherine* to return to La Rochelle without off-loading in Limerick. He feared the confiscation of the vessel and cargo if the Williamites took the city, or perhaps just the cargo if the Jacobites prevailed (7). At her property in Kerry, Mrs E. Connell described requisitioning most vividly. She lost her whole crop of both corn and hay to soldiers: 'ye kings hors cap^{n} came & did not Leave me one hand full of one nor ye other; & y^{n} ye enemy Came at theire heels'. Thankfully, she had taken the precaution of sending nearly all her cattle and sheep to the mountains. In the county, she reported, nobody was secure from plunder by Williamite forces: 'both porestants & Catholiques; they were all a Like to ye forrainers that were in that army'. Connell thought she had been relatively fortunate because the wheat, oats, and malt stored in the house from the previous year, though requisitioned by the Jacobites, had not been 'sent to ye stores till ye Enymy Came'. William's forces were not interested in it: they 'did not take above two barell of wheat from me & halef a barrell of malt not any oats' (39).

In advance of the enemy's arrival, Jacobite forces poisoned standing water, burned crops they could not seize, and devastated a wide area encircling the city.[20] The most audacious Irish stroke to parry the Williamite attack was Patrick Sarsfield's raid on William's heavy artillery and supply train lumbering across Ireland. In a daring night-time strike on 13 August, Sarsfield, at the head of a cavalry force of 500, attacked the main body of the train at Ballyneety, seven miles from Limerick. Its escort was shattered, two out of eight heavy guns were destroyed together with all the gun carriages and a vast quantity of stores and ammunition including 12,000 pounds of gunpowder.[21] The excitement generated in Limerick by the raid was still palpable weeks later in letters the *Amity* carried.

[20] P. A. Lucas, 'Irish Armies in the Seventeenth Century' (unpublished Ph.D. dissertation, University of Manchester, 1982), 230.

[21] Piers Wauchope, *Patrick Sarsfield and the Williamite War* (Dublin, 1992), 126–44.

'I beleive yow hard of Great searsfields feates, whome God Allmightÿ I hope will preserve for the Good of our Nation', wrote Adam Cusack to his brother, a priest in France (53). Nicholas Skyddy admired how 'that Brave Heroe' had led his men 'wth such Expedition & soe very secrett that att 2 a Clock in a morning ... he did Surprise those that guarded the traine of Artillerie the fairest of the biggness that was in Christendom, & after haveing putt 500 horse & Dragoones to the sworde bursted 7 pieces of the gunns wth manny a thousand bumbs & a very greate quantitie of Powder' (38). Although historians have argued that the raid was not as decisive a blow as it appeared at the time, it certainly raised Irish morale and deprived the enemy of powder and ammunition that would tell when it came to the siege.[22]

The fate of Limerick would depend mostly on the spirit of its citizens and the determination of the roughly 14,000 troops available for its defence.[23] The Jacobites could expect little help from their French allies. Declaring the city indefensible, the French withdrew to Galway where they prepared to board troop ships for home.[24] 'It is unnecessary for the English to bring cannon against such a place as this', wrote the comte de Lauzun, the French commander. 'What you call ramparts might be battered down with roasted apples'.[25] Lauzun's dismissive remark may have reflected disdain for the fighting capacity of the Irish, but his misgivings were widely shared.[26] Richard Talbot, duke of Tyrconnell, James II's viceroy in Ireland, and other members of the peace party within the leadership, saw little hope against the Williamite juggernaut. They were eager to come to an accommodation and salvage what they could. Yet stronger voices prevailed, including a few remaining French officers. Despairing the outcome, Tyrconnell departed for the safety of Galway.[27] When, on 9 August, William demanded that the city surrender, the order was rejected by the marquis de Boisseleau, the French officer commanding Limerick's defences.[28]

Both parts of Limerick were walled, but Englishtown was inaccessible without control of the Clare bank of the river, then in Jacobite hands. With marshy ground and the guns of Englishtown covering the western approaches

[22] On this point, and for an excellent discussion of the siege, see Pádraig Lenihan, 'Ballaí Luimnigh: The Sieges of Limerick', in Liam Irwin and Gearóid Ó Tuathaigh (eds.), *Limerick: History and Society* (Dublin, 2009), 129–58.

[23] Lucas, 'Irish Armies', 353–4.

[24] See Murray (ed.), *Journal of John Stevens*, 163; Simms, *Jacobite Ireland*, 159.

[25] Simms, *Jacobite Ireland*, 163; Murray (ed.), *Journal of John Stevens*, 101n2.

[26] Murtagh, 'War in Ireland', 62.

[27] John Todhunter, *Life of Patrick Sarsfield, Earl of Lucan, with a Short Narrative of the Principal Events of the Jacobite War in Ireland* (London, 1895), 80–81.

[28] Alexandre de Rainier de Droue, marquis de Boisseleau (1650–98). See John T. Gilbert, *A Jacobite Narrative of the War in Ireland, 1688–1691* (New York, 1971), 113.

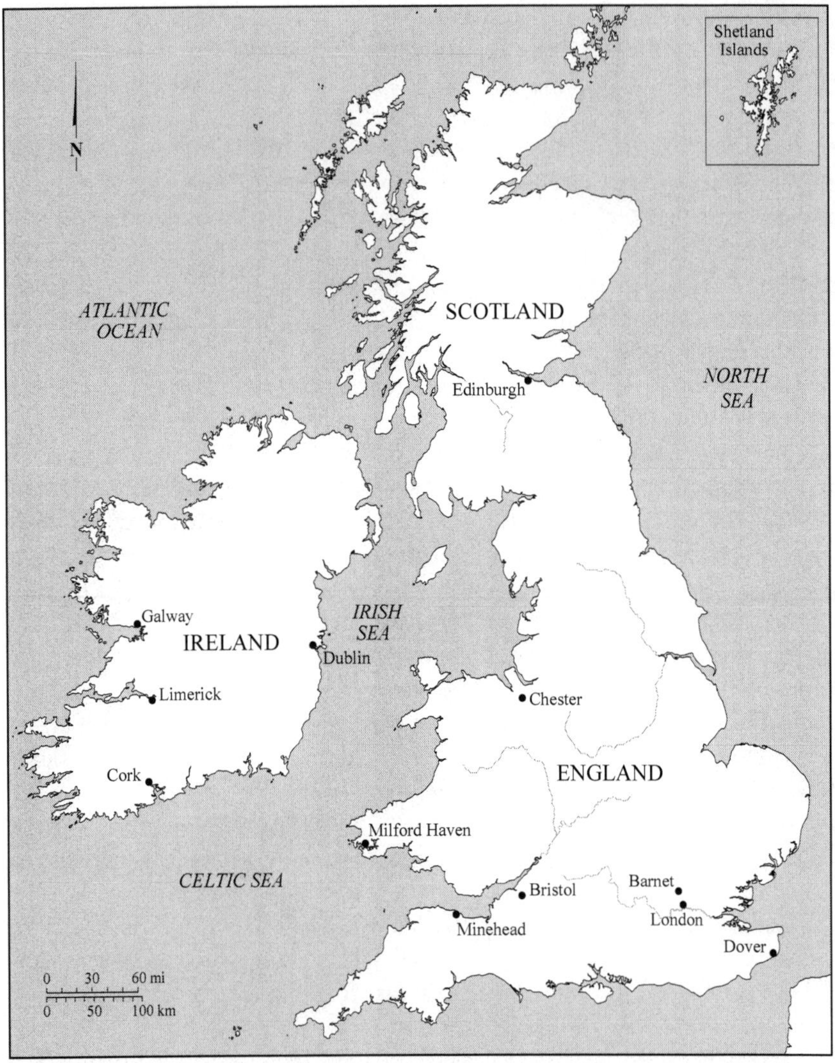

Map 3. The British Isles

to Irishtown, William's forces focused their attack on its eastern flanks, where the Jacobites had hastily dug a palisaded ditch and additional redoubts and outworks. The army arrayed against Limerick was smaller than at the Boyne, about 25,000 men, and much smaller than was typical of a besieging force in seventeenth-century warfare. But on 16 August, the guns salvaged from Sarsfield's raid finally arrived on site, and the following day William's troops began work on the trenches.[29] The defenders were soon pushed back from their advanced positions, and the besieging force positioned its artillery within range of the city walls.[30]

Then began ten days of intense bombardment. Between August 17 and 21, William's artillery concentrated on a point near St John's Gate.[31] On August 22, the besiegers unleashed their fury on those within the walls. 'That night we threw good store of Bombs and Carcasses [incendiaries] into Town', wrote a Williamite officer, 'which disturb'd the Enemy very much, most of them having never seen such things before'. This was just the beginning. The following night, the shelling 'set part of the Town on fire, which burnt all that night'.[32]

For those huddling within the city walls, the bombardment was terrifying. 'Bullets, red hot balls, Karkasses bums & smale shot came in ye towne in an exceeding manner both day & night', wrote Thomas Pearce (33). The enemy 'placed 4 batterries within a muskett shott of the wall with 6 peeces of Cannon on each of them and Continued batterring the towne and walls for the space of three or fower days haveing fiered noe less than 15 hundred Shotts every day untill they Made a breach', wrote Adam Cusack (53). '[T]hey fired from 4 in ye morning till 8 att night', Robert Woulfe told his correspondent in Brest, 'incessantly for 10 days & everie night wth oute intermission throwinge theire fire bales bumbs & Carcasses to ye greate terro^r^ of our woomen & Children' (6). Though the physical damage was extensive, the loss of life was relatively small. Because the town was open to the north (away from William's guns), many escaped the worst of the bombardment.[33] Still, there were many close calls. 'Tho wee had a great bomb & severall lardge Cannon balls fallen in our house', wrote Alderman Robert Hannan to his son in Poitiers, 'Your Mother & B^rs^ are all well' (55). Even ships in the harbour faced the inferno. 'Many a ffierballe have passed over the vessell', said John Martin, a ship captain recently arrived from Nantes, 'and some with in six feett off her with small shot in abondance' (8).

By 25 August, the shelling had at last torn a breach in the walls. The next day, wrote a Williamite officer, 'we widened the breach we had made the day before ... and beat down part of the enemies Pallisados on the Counterscarp' (the outer wall of the ditch the defenders had dug to protect the city walls).[34] A

[29] Gilbert, *Jacobite Narrative*, 114.

[30] Simms, *Jacobite Ireland*, 168.

[31] Lenihan, 'Ballaí Luimnigh', 137–40.

[32] [George Warner Story], *A True and Impartial History of the Most Material Occurrences in the Kingdom of Ireland During the Two Last Years* (London, 1691), 126–7.

[33] Lucas, 'Irish Armies', 400; Lenihan, 'Ballaí Luimnigh', 138–9, 144–5.

[34] Samuel Mullenaux, *A Journal of the Three Months Royal Campaign of His Majesty in Ireland, Together with a True and Perfect Diary of the Siege of Lymerick* (London, 1690), 29.

Williamite force stormed the breach at around 3:30 in the afternoon on 27 August. Emboldened and perhaps ignoring orders to halt at the counterscarp, the besiegers pushed into the city. Some of the Irish defenders panicked, but their flight was halted by dragoons blocking the bridge into Englishtown, and they rallied. Others, massed behind a retrenchment Boisseleau had built to block access from the breach, delivered a withering fire on the attackers. 'The Irish forces advanced on every side', wrote the Duke of Berwick, the natural son of James II, 'and charged the enemy afterwards in the streets with so much bravery, that they beat them back as far as the top of the breach'.[35] Meanwhile, Williamite sappers failed to dig themselves in on the counterscarp. After hours of hard fighting, the Williamites were driven back, losing over 2,300 in the day's fighting, compared to Jacobite losses of about 400.[36]

The defence of Limerick was the worst defeat suffered by William's forces and the most significant victory of the Jacobites in the course of the war – a fact recognised at the time. Many of the *Amity* letter-writers comment on the courage and spirit of the city's defenders. 'I doubt nott but y^{w} have an acc^{t} how bravely our men behaved themselfes before this towne', wrote James Missett to his brother Andrew in La Rochelle (7). Having breached the walls, the enemy was 'most Couragiously repulsed by oure owne Irish boys', affirmed Woulfe (6). '[O]ure men ... did soe bravlÿ & manfully sett appon them both in the breatch & pallisades that they were forcd to give way', wrote Skyddy, 'men such as feow could be parralleld unto for vallour & endureing of greate fatigues' (38). 'I assure you ye Ireshe behaved them sellves during ye sidge more leike Lyones then men', Francis Rice told his brother James in Rouen (10). Several viewed the successful defence as redemption for the Boyne – 'our rout of Drogheda', as more than one called it (7, 38). '[O]uer Irish have behaved themselves gallantly', wrote Cusack, 'and hope they have regained their Creditt' (53).

Though strategically less important than the Boyne, in terms of casualties Limerick was a more serious defeat for William than the earlier battle had been for James. The loss of so many men, heavy rain, and shortages of gunpowder and ammunition led him to accept that his force was too small and ill-equipped to take Limerick by assault. After lifting the siege, William departed for England. His army withdrew into winter quarters. For the people of Limerick, it was a time of both hope and anxiety. 'Wee are in greatt hopes of retreiveing ye Kingdom next sumer', Francis Rice told his brother, and 'now begin to fortefie this Cittie againste ye next Campan' (10). But without French troops and military supplies there was little hope the Jacobite cause could endure. Fresh supplies would eventually arrive, but no additional troops. More than a year of

[35] James Fitzjames, *Memoirs of the Marshal Duke of Berwick*, 2 vols. (London, 1779), 1:70–71.

[37] Simms, *Jacobite Ireland*, 169–70; Fitzjames, *Memoirs*, 1:71; Lenihan, 'Ballaí Luimnigh', 144–5.

war lay ahead. Boding ill for the Jacobite cause, in September and October a Williamite expeditionary force led by the Earl of Marlborough (on his way to becoming one of the great generals of his age), captured Cork and Kinsale in a three-week campaign.[37]

Ten days of shelling and the fighting at the breach had left Limerick in shambles. There were 'Housses ruined and a Lardge breach Made on ye walls eastward of the Cittadell', wrote John Rirdan (29). The catastrophe left disease and hunger in its wake. 'Wee are scarsce of Bread[;] all the Corne of the Countery burned', he wrote, and 'Depend of y^{r} supply for our Subsistance' (29). Connell remarked that the Jacobite forces had 'destroyed all ye corn every where within 8 mile of ye town; nay all ye County of Clare & galway so as we are Like to have famine in this Country'. Scarcity was worsened by the behaviour of troops now free to roam outside the city. 'When ye sieg was raisd ye kings souldiers geting out of Lymerick plunderd ye whole country within sixe mile of ye town', Connell reported (39). Nicholas Skyddy feared that the enemy planned to drive resisters across the Shannon and 'pein uss upp in the Countie of Clare and Province of Connaught wch will cause a greate ffamen amongst uss through scarsitie of bread' (38). Malnutrition and the collapse of even minimal standards of health took their toll. 'Manie of our Nabo^{rs} are hackin away wth the Country decease', wrote Zachary Holland – a reference typically to dysentery (50).

For the light it sheds on the situation in Limerick after the siege and the state of mind of a citizen, one letter deserves special notice. It was sent by Samuel Taverner, one of the owners of the *Amity*, to his wife, Prudence, who found refuge at the home of Joseph Scriven, a Quaker linen draper resident on Watling Street in London. Strikingly intimate, Samuel tells his wife he is 'over Joyed to hear of thy welfare wch is my harts desire ... and that wee may have the Sweet felicity of Enjoying one another, once againe'. He desires no longer to be separated from his wife regardless of the dangers. 'I thinke all ye hardships and hazards that this uncertaine world, can impose on us shall never separate us more but will take our chance toogether[.] Let what will happen wee wil bee fellow sharers in prosperity, and adversity, and Leave all to providence'. After a digression into practical matters, the letter takes a more amusing turn. 'I know not what will be done with Johny Craven', Samuel writes, admitting that he had sent him to London 'to bee ridd of him, not imagining twould bee thy hard fortune to bee perplexed with him'. This Johny Craven was a son of James Craven, a leading Limerick Friend and one of Taverner's colleagues among the city aldermen. Whether Prudence forgave Samuel for burdening her with this

[37] Frederick Joseph Riegler, 'Anglo-Irish Catholics, the Army of Ireland, and the Jacobite War' (unpublished Ph.D. dissertation, Temple University, 1983), 565.

nuisance we will never know. Sadly, the letter ends on a note that brings us back to the brutal realities of life in Limerick after the siege: 'people dyes heare fast', Samuel tells his wife, listing at the bottom of the letter the names of thirty-nine of those lost (48).

Yet for all the suffering and death brought by the siege, absent from the letters is any strong sentiment of bitterness or hatred toward the attackers. For most they were simply 'the enemy', though Woulfe chose the more pointed 'ye Rebells' (6). William is almost always referred to as the 'Prince of Orange' – a title that, while respectful, denies his claim to the throne. For John Rirdan, more grimly, he was 'the usurper'. Rirdan also emphasised the foreignness and cruelty of the enemy forces – the fact that William was served by Dutch, German, and Danish soldiers, 'who spares neither adge nor sex but ruines all' (29). He also dwelt on the religious divide in Ireland. '[T]he Ennemy is Every wheare amongst us', he fretted, 'not one protestant In the Countery but are In armes with them' (29). There was talk in the letters of wanton acts committed by enemy troops. '[Y]^{e} Enemy stript Nick Rice & som Einglish gentle women that were with him in hospitall stark naked', reported E. Connell (39). Some were prepared to believe even worse of the Williamites. When they lifted the siege, about 300 of the most grievously wounded of the enemy's troops were massacred by their own comrades, Skyddy claimed: 'burnt ... alive moste barbarousely' to 'save carriage' (38). While this sounds fanciful, in fact a fire set to destroy what was left of the Williamite camp (to prevent supplies falling into Jacobite hands) spread accidentally to hospital tents, consuming the sick and wounded.[38]

Such dark musings are rare in the letters. The writers' harshest words were reserved not for William or his allies but for those Jacobite leaders imagined to be corrupt, treacherous, or cowardly. The peace party was characterised in the darkest colours by Robert Woulfe: '[S]uch pernicious Vermin I feare wee have some wch is ever fatall to our Contrie' (6). Skyddy echoed this view: 'I neede not tell yo^{w}', he wrote to his brother, 'the designes that were lay^{d} to betray the whole Kingdom' (38). Such remarks likely reference the opposition to Tyrconnell within the Jacobite camp; at one point before the siege there was even talk of arresting him and drafting Berwick to take his place.[39] Robert Hannan complained to his son that an opportunity had been missed to send the Jacobite army in pursuit of the retreating Williamite forces – a strategy pressed by Sarsfield and Berwick but resisted by Tyrconnell and the comte de Lauzun (55).

Did Limerick's Quakers have a different perspective on the siege and the Jacobite cause? The letter of Thomas Pearce to his cousin Joseph Scriven in London offers clues. Pearce identifies as one of the 'English' community in

[38] Lenihan, 'Ballaí Luimnigh', 147.

[39] Wauchope, *Patrick Sarsfield*, 117–22.

the city (whether Old English or more recent settlers is unclear). '[M]any fell on both sides', he tells Scriven, 'but as I remember but one or two of ye English inhabitants lost, though ye bullets, red hot balls, Karkasses bums & smale shot came in ye towne in an exceeding manner both day & night for ye last two weekes'. Subsequent to the lifting of the siege, Pearce adds, '[S]everall of *our English* have lately died' [emphasis added]. 'English' does not equate with 'Williamite.' Several of the English inhabitants of Limerick, Pearce says, 'I think were wounded & lost their lives at ye breach y^{t} adventerd to p^{r}serve them from ye Cruielty of ye foriners'. These 'foreigners', Pearce was prepared to believe, 'intended to put all to ye sword for ye plunder sake'. Pearce goes on to say that one 'Ed Taverner' was among the English killed. He leaves ambiguity about whether Taverner fell in the defense of the city or in the bombardment, though it would be startling if an individual presumptively a Quaker fought in the siege. A final remark Pearce makes in the same letter is worth noting: 'Irland looks as if it would be a new plantation such is ye great ruen here aways' (33). The equation of plantation with 'ruin' seems more closely aligned with a Jacobite perspective than with a Williamite one.

Having suffered under the governments of Cromwell and the Restoration, Quakers had good reason to welcome the accession of James II, who favoured religious toleration. Quaker beliefs challenged widely shared conventions. Aside from rejecting war and refusing to serve in armies or militias, they held that women were spiritually equal to men and permitted women to preach and to act as missionaries. They refused to acknowledge social rank. Quaker men kept their hats on regardless of the company and used the informal 'thee' and 'thou', instead of the more elevated 'you', with social superiors. Under the Commonwealth, Limerick Quakers were oppressed by the Cromwellian governor Colonel Henry Ingolsby – worried no doubt that their creed of non-violence might win more recruits among the garrison.[40] They refused to take oaths, and therefore to sit on juries. The same refusal would keep them out of the professions, craft guilds, and higher civic office under the Restoration. When the Anglican church was reestablished, they refused to pay tithes or church rates. Under Charles II, some historians argue, nonconformists enjoyed de facto toleration in Ireland.[41] If so, the benefits to Quakers were limited. During his reign, 780 were imprisoned in Ireland.[42] The Limerick community suffered harassment

[40] *To the Parliament of England, who are in Place to do Justice, and to Break the Bonds of the Oppressed a Narrative of the Cruel and Unjust Sufferings of the People of God in the Nation of Ireland Called Quakers* (London, 1659), 5–7.

[41] Sandra Maria Hynes, 'Changing Their Path: Quaker Adaptation to the Challenge of Restoration, 1660–1680', in Coleman A. Dennehy (ed.), *Restoration Ireland: Always Settling and Never Settled* (Aldershot, 2008), 87.

[42] John Rutty and Thomas Wight, *A History of the Rise and Progress of the People Called Quak-*

and prosecutions through the 1670s and 1680s. James Craven, for example, had 55 yards of linen cloth distrained from him in 1675, presumably for non-payment of tithes or church rates.[43]

The accession of James II greatly improved Quaker fortunes, and some Friends were grateful to the new king and may have sympathised with the Jacobite cause. In March 1686, James granted a general pardon and release to imprisoned nonconformist subjects, about 1500 of whom were Quakers.[44] The number of Friends imprisoned in Ireland fell to twelve during James reign.[45] In April of 1687, he issued a Declaration of Indulgence that suspended laws penalising non-conformity. In some cities, Quakers were invited to assume high civic office. Three became aldermen in Limerick in 1687: Samuel Taverner, and James and William Craven.[46] James' willingness to extend toleration to dissenters is usually read as tactical – toleration for non-Anglicans would benefit Catholics too. Most nonconformists were wary of political alliance with the king because they feared he would reestablish Catholicism and because, to do so, he appeared willing to sideline parliament, or pack it with his supporters. Quaker leaders voiced less suspicion of James. The king was famously close to William Penn, who served him as an informal advisor. The Quaker theologian Robert Barclay affirmed after the monarch's fall that 'I love King James, that I wish him well ... I have been and am sensibly touched with a feeling of his misfortunes'.[47] Penn repeatedly defended the king in print in 1687 and 1688, was suspected of Jacobitism under the new regime of William and Mary, and was arrested several times on suspicion of Jacobite plotting, though after a period in hiding he escaped prosecution.[48]

We see at least an opportunistic attitude to the Jacobite cause in some of the Quaker letters. Samuel Taverner's correspondence exhibits a frank willingness to work the levers of James II's government in Ireland – along with connections at the Jacobite court in France – in the interests of business. In his petition to the Duke of Tyrconnell asking for the king's intercession to recover the *Diligence*, a ship captured by French privateers, Taverner identified himself as 'one of those

ers in Ireland, from the Year 1653 to 1700 ... Afterwards Revised, Enlarged, and Continued to the Year 1751, 2nd edn (London, 1800), 345.

43 Wood, *History of the Quakers of Limerick*, 21.

44 S. H. Mayor, 'James II and the Dissenters', *Baptist Quarterly*, 34:4 (1991), 180–90, at 182; Scott Sowerby, 'William Penn and James II', in Andrew R. Murphy and John Smolenski (eds.), *The Worlds of William Penn* (Brunswick, NJ, 2019), 172.

45 Though considerable value in goods and money was still taken from them. Rutty and Wight, *Rise and Progress of the People Called Quakers in Ireland*, 345.

46 Wood, *History of the Quakers of Limerick*, 23.

47 Mayor, 'James II and the Dissenters', 182.

48 Sowerby, 'William Penn and James II', 172, 181.

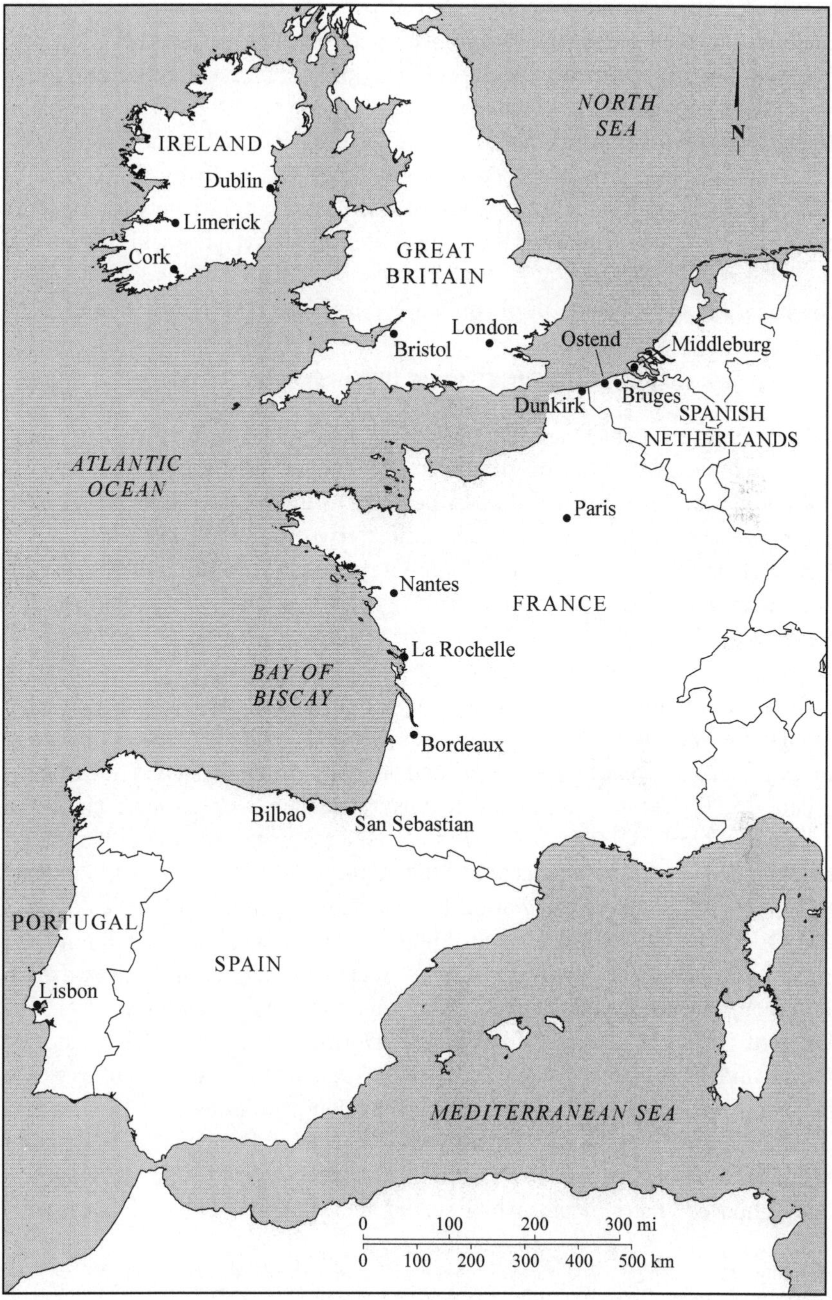

Map 4. Western Europe

called a Quaker', as if his religion were a badge of friendliness to the Jacobite regime, or would be so understood. The petition parades Taverner's loyalty: 'yor Pet^{r} who allways demeaned himself a loyall Subject, and has beene serviceable in this kingdom by importing of Goods necessary for the subsistence of his Mat^{ies} Army, and who delivered the same for the Kings use at the Kings rates' (2). Such was the formula of petitions. But in a letter to Patrick Rirdan, Taverner reveals more personal Jacobite links: 'I have a good friend with the King one Doctor Bromfield who has the Kings Eare Every day[;] hee will sollicite the matter' [of the *Diligence*] (12). Bromfield was an English Quaker who served James in Ireland as master of the mint and later was his secretary in France.[49]

Military Perspectives on the Siege and the War

The seven letters sent aboard the *Amity* written by soldiers – most serving in the Jacobite forces, with one French officer – often dwell on different matters from the civilian correspondence, themes peculiar to the military world, including promotion, booty, resupply and recruitment. Two of the five are addressed to Major-General John Wauchope at Saint-Germain-en-Laye, the site of the Jacobite court in exile (26, 27). Wauchope was a professional soldier, the son of a Scottish laird of Niddrie near Edinburgh. Commanding a Scots brigade in the Netherlands at the Glorious Revolution, he returned home to lead a regiment in James II's army. He ended his military career fighting for France. When the Williamite War finally ended in October 1691, following a brief second siege of Limerick, the peace treaty permitted Jacobite troops to depart for France. About 15,000 did so. Louis XIV reconstituted them as regiments under the nominal control of James but integrated under French command. Wauchope commanded one of these units and would die in 1693 at the Battle of Marsaglia in Northern Italy during the War of the League of Augsburg (1688–97).[50]

One of the letters intended for him was penned by Colonel William Dorrington, an English Catholic serving as lieutenant colonel in the Royal Irish Regiment of Foot Guards in 1688, who took command when his superior, the Duke of Ormonde, declared for William. Dorrington fought at Derry and the Boyne and was governor of Limerick in the final year of the war. He was captured at Aughrim, the last major battle of the conflict, but eventually permitted to pass over to France where his regiment had entered French service. He commanded it in Flanders from 1693 until its disbandment in 1697, and then a new one composed of its remnants which served in the War of the Spanish Succession

[49] Dorothy M. Richardson, *The Quakers: Past and Present* (New York, 1914), 54.

[50] Jack Abernethy, 'Wauchope, John [SSNE 8259]', *Scotland, Scandinavia and Northern European Biographical Database*, Institute of Scottish Historical Research, University of St Andrews, at https://www.st-andrews.ac.uk/history/ssne/item.php?id=8259 (accessed 2 December 2022).

(1701–13). Dorrington was promoted to lieutenant general in the French service, retired in 1710, and died in Paris in 1718.[51]

His letter to Wauchope captures the confusion and chaos associated with a night retreat from Birr Castle, which Jacobite forces besieged after the Williamite withdrawal from Limerick. He explained that the pullback was prompted by fear of attack from a Williamite force led by Major General Percy Kirke. It later transpired, he told Wauchope, that Kirke's force itself was pulling back – a rather ignominious finish to what should have been an easy Jacobite victory (26).[52] By his own account, Dorrington had come to Limerick to supervise the rebuilding of its defences but found 'nothing don to ye workes as yet, and our good weather will soon be gon, so y^t^ I feare wee shall never mend' (26).[53] He was pessimistic about the military situation, especially about the recently begun Williamite siege of Cork which it would be impossible to relieve from Limerick.

The second letter to Wauchope is from his brother Francis who would also go on to serve the French (initially as a lieutenant colonel in the Foot Regiment of Dublin).[54] He was still in French service three decades later, as a surviving letter to a Scottish cousin testifies.[55] The Wauchope brothers and Dorrington were part of a small minority of English and Scots in the Jacobite-French forces, which were more than 90 per cent Irish.[56] The Irish military exiles of 1691 built on an established tradition of service in the armies of Spain and France. A first wave of Irish soldiers had left for the Continent after the end of the Desmond rebellion in 1583, a second following the Nine Years War (1594–1603), and a third in the 1650s after the Cromwellian reconquest, when over 30,000 men departed. Seven Irish regiments were recruited for French service starting in 1635, rising to eight in the 1650s.[57] Some of the 'Wild Geese' of 1691, nota-

[51] Nathalie Genet-Rouffiac, *Le Grand exil: Les Jacobites en France 1688–1715* (Paris, 2007), 192, 204.

[52] For the engagement at Birr Castle, see Childs, *Williamite Wars*, 263–6; Wauchope, *Patrick Sarsfield*, 154–63.

[53] Francis Wauchope confirmed this account. 'There has ben nothing doen aes to the fortefeÿing of this toun aes ÿet', he reported, mostly for lack of engineers (27).

[54] Gladys M. Wauchope, *The Ulster Branch of the Family of Wauchope* (London, 1929), 57.

[55] Reproduced in James Paterson, *History and Genealogy of the Family of Wauchope of Niddrie-Merschell* (Edinburgh, 1858), 37–9. See also Genet-Rouffiac, *Grand exil*, 205.

[56] Genet-Rouffiac, *Grand exil*, 163.

[57] Harman Murtagh, 'Irish Soldiers Abroad, 1600–1800', in Thomas Bartlett and Keith Jeffery (eds.), *A Military History of Ireland* (Cambridge, 1996), 295–7; Éamon Ó Ciosáin, 'A Hundred Years of Irish Migration to France, 1590–1688', in Thomas O'Connor (ed.), *The Irish in Europe, 1580–1815* (Dublin, 2001), 99.

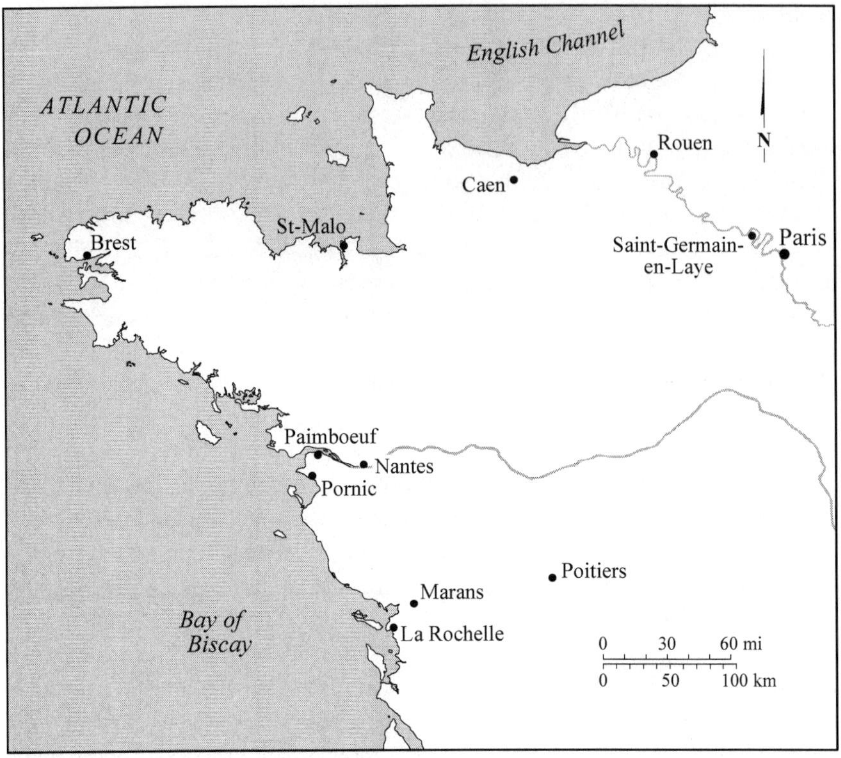

Map 5. Northern and Western France

bly Sarsfield, had already seen military service in France.[58]

Both Dorrington and Francis Wauchope dwelt on a problem presumably commonplace in armies: disputes over the spoils of war. Controversy surrounded sacks of wool claimed by both John Wauchope and Colonel William Barker. Wool sacks requisitioned by the army were used to protect artillery batteries and even parts of Limerick's walls.[59] In the aftermath of the siege they might have some commercial value. There was a market in France for Irish wool, and we know of at least one other Jacobite officer who tried to export wool to France in 1691.[60] Referring to the wool remaining in Limerick, Dorrington told Wauchope that 'neither you nor Barker has any right to it', a view he promised to

[58] Genet-Rouffiac, *Grand exil*, 164.

[59] Lenihan, 'Ballaí Luimnigh', 140.

[60] Guy Rowlands, 'An Army in Exile: Louis XIV and the Irish Forces of James II in France, 1691–1698', *Royal Stuart Papers* 60 (2001), 12.

communicate to Barker as well. In any case, he argued, the quantity in question was not worth fighting over. According to Francis, Barker claimed all the sacks used at the artillery batteries he commanded, even the eight in the church near the Irishtown gate where only a single cannon had been stationed. '[A]t this raet there is not on[e] pack ÿou can pretend to', he warned his brother. Francis hoped to appeal the matter to the Duke of Berwick. Still, it would be no easy matter to realise any profit even if Wauchope's rights were recognised, Francis claimed, for 'I am also told for certentÿ that there wel not be Sufred one pack of wolle to goe out of the Contre' (27).

Another soldier's letter is from Christopher Fleming, 17th Baron Slane (1669–1726), who commanded a regiment at the Boyne and Limerick, to James Rice in Rouen. Slane asks the merchant to procure for his unit a 'careffull s^{r}geant barber' and 'four good hoboyes'. The barber-surgeon was presumably needed to treat the wounded. Hoboyes were musicians often used by armies, so called for the instrument they played, the hautboy or hoeboy (similar to a modern oboe). Slane also wanted 200 firelocks for guns and six bottles of Queen of Hungary water – perfumed wine that was used medicinally (11). These requests have an air of unreality about them given the circumstances of the Jacobites after Limerick, a suspicion confirmed by the covering letter from Francis Rice emphasising that Slane had no money to pay for any of this (10). Just twenty-one years of age in 1690, the baron may have been acquainted with Rice from his days as a student in France, where he had been educated from 1677 to 1683. The tone of the letter is familiar, addressing 'a man that has being extream obliging to me in every thing' (11). Slane's appeal never reached Rice, of course, and one may wonder whether the hoeboys would have been found if it had. Slane was subsequently taken prisoner at Aughrim but permitted into exile in France where he too commanded a regiment. In 1704, he passed back into English service, fighting with English forces in Portugal at the rank of lieutenant general and subsequently in Spain as a brigadier. Queen Anne created him Viscount Longford in 1713, a title that died with him in 1726.[61]

The most atypical of the soldiers' letters was sent by James Missett to his brother Andrew (c.1652–1702), a merchant in La Rochelle (7). James commanded an infantry company in Slane's regiment – and also served his brother as a commercial intermediary in Ireland. While the letter briefly discusses the siege, it is mostly devoted to commercial matters, discussing the difficulties of marketing brandy and wine shipped by Andrew in the face of Jacobite requisitioning and the forced circulation of 'brass money', a wartime coinage. The Missett brothers were born in the parish of Athboy, Co. Meath – James men-

[61] G. E. Cokayne, *The Complete Peerage of England, Scotland, Ireland, Great Britain, and the United Kingdom*, ed. Geoffrey H. White, 13 vols. (London, 1910–59), vol. 12, part 1, 19–21.

tions a family home at Pluckstown. Andrew had settled in La Rochelle about 1673, marrying a local woman, Jeanne Taussiede, in 1685. Another Missett brother, Patrick, is also mentioned in James' letter as serving with the Jacobite forces near Athlone. He subsequently became a grenadier captain in Nugent's regiment and then in the Duke of Berwick's, and also settled in La Rochelle in 1700 when he married the sister of Andrew's wife, Jeanne.[62]

Also unusual is the single letter written by a French soldier, one Ducorail, an infantry major serving under Colonel Guillaume Thutes in Limerick. Little more than a covering note for two, presumably more substantial, other letters, both of which have disappeared, Ducorail's missive says nothing about the siege or conditions in Ireland except that the writer is sick of it all and anxious to get home (62).

Two other letters are from Adam Cusack, a junior officer, the first addressed to Mathew Rooth (a spelling variant of Rothe, a prominent Kilkenny Jacobite family). Cusack told Mathew that his brother, a fellow officer, was in good health and appealed 'when next yow write to him desier him to stand my frind for hee is very great wth Dorrington' (52). At the time, Michael Rothe (1665–1741) was a captain in the regiment Dorrington commanded and would later succeed him as its colonel.[63] Promotion was also on Adam's mind in a second letter, to his brother Patrick, where he relates that a third sibling, Christy, was to be made a cornet (equivalent to a second lieutenant). To Adam himself, Dorrington had urged patience but promised him a company command in time (52). Cusack's letter contains numerous details of the siege, expressed with a military precision often wanting in the civilian letters. He is more optimistic about Jacobite prospects than the letters of the older, more experienced men. He reckoned Jacobite strength in Ireland at above 50,000 men, including a force of volunteers mostly raised in Ulster by Hugh Balldearg O'Donnell, the commander of a regiment in the Spanish army who landed in Ireland after the Boyne.[64]

These hopes were misplaced. In the 1691 campaigning season, Jacobite strategy called for holding a line at the Shannon and wearing down the enemy. However, in June the strategic bridgehead at Athlone fell to the Williamites, and the Irish began to fall back once again on Limerick, intending a protracted siege. Instead, the marquis de St Ruth, the French officer in command of Jacobite forces, chose to make a stand at Aughrim in Co. Galway. Early on, the Irish appeared to have the upper hand until St Ruth was killed in action. In the confusion that followed, the Jacobite army suffered roughly 7,000 dead – 'the

[62] D'Alton, *Army List*, 2:229–30; Gilbert, *Jacobite Narrative*, 231; AMLR, GG 353, view 124; AMLR, GG 354, view 403

[63] Éamonn Ó Ciardha, 'Rothe (Roth, Root), Michael', *DIB* (accessed 15 January 2025). See also Richard Hayes, *Biographical Dictionary of Irishmen in France* (Dublin, 1949), 278–9; Genet-Rouffiac, *Grand exil*, 204.

[64] Simms, *Jacobite Ireland*, 165; Murtagh, 'Irish Soldiers Abroad', 296.

most disastrous battle in Irish history'.[65] The survivors fell back on Limerick. Remaining strongholds such as Galway capitulated. At Limerick the defenders withstood a heavy bombardment for the second time as the two sides negotiated terms of surrender. The treaty, signed on 3 October 1691, brought a formal end to the Williamite War. According to the English Jacobite, John Stevens, Limerick had been 'reduced to a heap of rubbish, the greatest and best part utterly demolished and scarce a house left that sustained not some damage'.[66]

Limerick's Trade with France in 1690: A Tale of Two Networks

The letters carried by the *Amity* were mostly intended for a thriving Irish community settled in France, bound by close ties – often of marriage – from one French port to another. This network maintained tight links with Ireland, where other family members remained, often serving as partners. The spur to this diaspora was partly political and religious, but it was more fundamentally commercial – the opportunity to profit from a growing trade in Irish commodities in the Atlantic economy. Between 1660 and 1688, Ireland emerged as an exporter to Atlantic markets – notably France – of agricultural products including wool, tallow, hides, salt beef, and butter.[67] France in turn supplied Ireland with wine, brandy, salt, linens, fashion goods, and commodities from farther afield reexported through French ports. Taking advantage of this network, Catholic priests and students evaded official religious intolerance in Ireland to be trained in France where some found career opportunities that made them permanent migrants. Yet this was not an exclusively Catholic world. The Quaker merchants of Limerick depended on the same Irish commercial networks in France as their Catholic peers. The letters offer a sense of how, and with what success, Quaker traders collaborated with Catholic compatriots, what the basis was for such collaboration, but how Quaker commercial networks ultimately remained distinct.

At this time, La Rochelle and Saint-Malo were the two most important French ports in the trade to Ireland. La Rochelle may have had an Irish community as large as 200 at its peak. The key links with Limerick were through the Creagh and White families who settled in the French port in the 1630s and 1660s respectively, and were well integrated into French society. Richard Creagh is mentioned in a letter of Robert Hannan's intended for James Power, also based in La Rochelle (56). Born in France, Creagh was the son of John Creagh of Kilmallock, Co. Limerick. He served for a time as a captain in the French

[65] Simms, *Jacobite Ireland*, 223–8.

[66] Murray (ed.), *Journal of John Stevens,* 149.

[67] British Library, Add. MSS. 4759, 'Exports and Imports of Ireland, 1683–1686'; L. M. Cullen, 'Economic Trends, 1660–91', in Moody, Martin, and Byrne (eds.), *Early Modern Ireland*, 387–407.

army before settling down as a merchant in La Rochelle in the 1690s.[68] Three other La Rochelle merchants with Irish connections are mentioned in the letters. Andrew Missett, whom we have already met, was the intended recipient of a letter from his brother James. Andrew traded not only with Ireland, but the French West Indies and Newfoundland.[69] It was to Edmond and John Gould in La Rochelle that the owners of the *Amity* ordered John Mitchell to consign their goods, should he make for that port (20, 21). Hailing from Kinsale, the brothers had settled in La Rochelle in the early 1680s. After the war, Edmond (c.1651–1705) helped at least fifteen family members migrate to France.

As early as the 1660s, more than twenty Irish merchants and their families were settled in Saint-Malo in addition to some Irish seamen. In the late seventeenth century, an average of fifty ships a year sailed between the city and Irish ports.[70] Saint-Malo would eventually be superseded by Nantes in the traffic with Ireland, though Nantes shared with it a deficiency that would make this pre-eminence fleeting. The chief French goods shipped to Ireland – salt, wines, brandies, and vinegar – were staples of the French southwest. The more natural source for these goods was Bordeaux, which emerged by the 1740s as the chief French hub for the trade with Ireland.[71] Even so, more of the *Amity* letters were destined for Nantes than any other city – twenty-eight of the fifty sent to France – testifying to its place in wartime commerce with Limerick.

Well before the Williamite War, various Irish merchant families had established themselves in Nantes.[72] The most prominent were the Lees, the Barnavals, the Geraldins (also spelled Gerraldin, Giraldin, Geraldine), and the Sarsfields – all part of the Cromwellian exodus from Ireland, with the exception of Thomas Barnaval who came to Nantes in 1645. Paul Sarsfield, who had settled in the city after the forfeiture of his father's lands in 1653, came from a branch of that family with holdings in Co. Limerick. Another Limerick name

68 Micheline Walsh, 'O Neills in Exile', *Seanchas Ardmhacha: Journal of the Armagh Diocesan Historical Society*, 8:1 (1975/6), 61.

69 AMLR, GG 353, view 124, and GG 354, view 463; ADC-M, Notaire Teuleron, 3E1367; Notaire Rivière, 3E1811, ff. 53–54v [1694], ff. 21v, 53v–54r, 55 [1695], ff. 171v–172r [1696]; Notaire Rivière, 3E1812,version f. 14 [1697], ff. 28, 46 [1699], f. 130 (1700), f. 68r [1701]; B 5693, ff. 189–90 ; B 5695, ff. 254, 279, 289–90; B 5690, ff. 361, 363). The editors thank Sandrine Tromeur for these references.

70 Mary Ann Lyons, 'The Emergence of an Irish Community in Saint-Malo, 1550–1710', in O'Connor (ed.), *The Irish in Europe*, 107–26.

71 L. M. Cullen, 'The Irish Merchant Communities of Bordeaux, La Rochelle and Cognac in the Eighteenth Century', in P. Butel and L. M. Cullen (eds.), *Négoce et industrie en France et en Irlande aux XVIIIe et XIXe siècles* (Paris, 1980), 51–2. See also L. M. Cullen, John Shovlin, and Thomas M. Truxes (eds.), *The Bordeaux–Dublin Letters, 1757: Correspondence of an Irish Community Abroad* (Oxford, 2013).

72 Cullen, 'Irish Merchant Communities', 51.

with a prominent future in Nantes was McNemara (or MacNemara). The family relocated permanently to the French port in the exodus after 1691. Thomas McNamara is represented in the *Amity* papers ordering his Lisbon correspondents to remit money to Mme Lee and Sons of Nantes (41).[73] With a fortune assessed at 850,000 *livres tournois* in the early 1720s, the McNemaras were the richest merchants in the port.[74] While it is usual, and reasonable in many cases, to think of these families as exiles from political or religious persecution, their success as merchants derived from close family and business ties in Ireland.[75] Nantes' Irish commercial networks extended to Bordeaux, Brest, Caen, La Rochelle, Rouen, and Saint-Malo, to St Sebastian and Bilbao in Spain and Lisbon in Portugal. Such connections explain why, wherever the *Amity* first put in, the writers could expect their letters to be delivered eventually to more than a dozen other continental and British ports.

Of the letters bound for Nantes aboard the *Amity*, five were addressed to Mme Lee and her partners, and she is mentioned in several others. Marie Lee was a daughter of Nicholas Geraldine of Waterford who had settled in Saint-Malo in 1649. She married Nicholas Lee of Nantes, son of another Waterford merchant exiled in 1649 and naturalised in France four years later.[76] At the death of her husband in 1684, Marie established a trading partnership with her son –another Nicholas – and, from 1688, with a second son, John, and a son-in-law Edward Luker (or Lucker, an Irish merchant family hailing from Cork). Having served his apprenticeship under his mother, Nicholas set up on his own as a merchant in Cork that same year. Intended for him aboard the *Amity* was a letter from his wife Ellen imploring him to 'ma^{ke} hast home'. She was in desperate straits: 'my youngest guirl Anstus is verry sick & ye Little boy Thomy is ded', she told him, '[T]hings goes verry hard wth me' (62). All we know of the couple subsequently is that Nicholas had left Cork by 1693, entering a new partnership with his mother in Nantes that lasted until his own death in 1709.[77]

[73] On the Irish families of Nantes before the Williamite War, see Guy Saupin, 'Les réseaux commerciaux des Irlandais de Nantes sous le règne de Louis XIV', in David Dickson, Jan Parmentier, and Jane Ohlmeyer (eds.), *Irish and Scottish Mercantile Networks in Europe and Overseas in the Seventeenth and Eighteenth Centuries* (Ghent, 2007), 128–33. The Irish trading community in Nantes was considerably expanded by new exiles from Ireland after 1691. In addition to the McNamaras, there were the Clarkes, Galweys, MacCurtins, O'Sullivans, Reidys, Shiels, Stapletons, and Walshes, the last named perhaps the most prominent Irish family in eighteenth-century French commerce and the Franco-Irish Jacobite cause. See Richard Hayes, 'Irish Associations with Nantes', *Studies: An Irish Quarterly Review* 28:109 (1939), 115–26, at 122.

[74] Cullen, 'Irish Merchant Communities', 56.

[75] Cullen, 'Irish Merchant Communities', 53.

[76] For Nicholas Lee, see David Hancock (ed.), *The Letters of William Freeman, London Merchant, 1678–1685* (London, 2002), xxviii, 89–92, 107, 112, 115, 157, 170–75.

[77] Saupin, 'Réseaux commerciaux des Irlandais de Nantes', 118–19.

From the letters, we learn the most about another Irish merchant in Nantes, Patrick Rirdan, who played an important role in the trade with Limerick, if not always a satisfactory one for his correspondents. Patrick was in business in France with his brother Robert. Their father – also Robert – and another brother, John, were partners in Limerick (28, 29). A regular correspondent of Samuel Taverner and Thomas Pearce (12, 25), Rirdan was also to handle Zachary Holland's share of the *Amity's* cargo if the ship put into Nantes – a first piece of business which, if it went well, might lead to more (22). Rirdan also handled business for Limerick merchants Robert Hannan and James Cravin (43, 49). Hannan chided Rirdan about the mishandling of a previous shipment (43). Cravin too seems to have been in some dispute with him and hoped Mme Lee might be able to intercede on his behalf (35). Rirdan's cousin in Limerick, Thomas Creagh, complained that Patrick had failed to write for six months, 'wch makes me admire of yor Neglect' (40).

Limerick merchants faced enormous obstacles to continuing the trade with France in the midst of the war. One factor unsettling commerce was the requisitioning of articles meant for export at regulated prices denominated in 'brass money', a wartime currency circulating in areas controlled by Jacobite forces. James' regime in Dublin had begun to mint coinage from base metal in June 1689 as a way to pay his Irish troops. The coins were to be redeemable for silver once the king was restored. They bore a bust of James in profile on one side with a crown and two sceptres on the other. A second mint was established in Limerick, at the Deanery, in March 1690, and the last coins were struck there in October of that year. One of the letter writers, Francis Rice, told his brother that he was still employed there 'makeing ye brass mony wc^{h} is of litle vallew heere' (10). At least £1.1 million, nominal value, was issued, and possibly considerably more (the pre-war national income was perhaps £100,000, and the total pre-war money supply estimated at £450,000). By the spring of 1690 at the latest, confidence in the new money was slipping, in part because French soldiers demanded to be paid in silver. After the Boyne, and James' flight, the prospect that it would ever be redeemed was fast fading.[78]

Not willing to part with goods in exchange for a depreciating and potentially worthless currency, farmers withheld their goods from market, leading to shortages and high prices. Nicholas Skyddy complained of 'The deareness of privision by reason of the little vallue sett uppon Brass monny' (37). Had he been permitted to barter for local provisions, John Rirdan explained to Andrew Gerraldin, he might have bought more readily. But he was compelled to use brass money, 'wch now by the Distraction of the times is brought soe Loe that

[78] Gerard Rice, 'Gunmoney and the Limerick Mint', *OLJ*, 212–14; James Heslip, 'Brass Money', in Maguire (ed.), *Kings in Conflict*, 122–35.

wee Can Gett noe Countery Goods' (31). Merchants also competed with the authorities for supplies, though not all played by the same rules. 'I have severall goods on my hands & have obtained tolleration from the govrnm^{t} to by more,' wrote Robert Hannan, a former mayor of Limerick, 'tho other men heere had their goods seized on' (56).

Government restrictions on the export of certain staples posed another set of problems. Both butter and beef exports were restricted after the siege: '[Y]^{u} maye expect but very litle thrade from this Kingdom now or att any tyme hereafter,' wrote Hannan (43). A small amount of butter remained on hand, but 'litle may y^{u} expect hence', he told his correspondent in La Rochelle (56). Tallow, made from rendered animal fat and used in making candles and soap, was another mainstay of trade to France. But shippers sometimes had to pay stiff bribes to get it past customs. 'I asshure y^{w} them 21 Hogh^{ds} Tallow Cost me neare theire vallue to preserve them from being seas^{d}', John Rirdan told his brother in Nantes (29). The export of salted hides was permitted, but its future was uncertain.

Despite these obstacles, the opportunities for profit in a city suffering shortages of all kinds spurred merchants to pull together cargoes that could be used to purchase French goods. Following the siege, there was strong demand in Limerick for wine, brandy, tobacco, clothing and cloth. From Patrick Rirdan in Nantes, the owners of the *Amity* wanted 'sixteene hogsheads of Anjou wine ... sixteene quarter caskue of Brandie and the rest In Sault' – staple products in Franco-Irish trade (47). In addition to such essentials, Robert Hannan requested a long list of specialised, more luxurious items: 'four dozen of the best black French hatts', 400 pounds of Castile soap;[79] one hundred weight of whalebone; ten pieces of kenting, fine linen made around Saint-Quintin in Picardy; fifty reams of Pantaleon paper; a barrel of molasses; lemons and oranges; a cask of anchovies; sweet meats; and some 'fationable' drugget (a heavy fabric made of wool mixed with silk or linen) (54). Requests for clothing, or fabric to make clothing, were common in the letters, both in the merchant correspondence and in exchanges among family members. This is hardly surprising in a city recently subjected to the privations of war. Interestingly, it is fine and fashionable clothing that is most emphasised. 'Butt deare bro:' Francis Rice wrote, 'if you Cann send mee as muche rateene or drugett as will make mee asute of Close of ye fasionable stufes & as much as will make mee halfe a dusein Churtes of fine Lineing ... wth a good frenche hatt & apaire of mille stockes youl for Eaver oblidge for I am gott none herare for Love or mony' (10).

As noted, Nantes was an assembly point for most of these goods, not their

[79] A white soap made of olive oil and barilla ash and used both for laundry and personal hygiene. See Susan North, *Sweet and Clean? Bodies and Clothes in Early Modern England* (Oxford, 2020), 281.

original source. Striking is the Mediterranean origin of many of the minor luxuries Hannan ordered – the soap, paper, lemons and oranges, capers, and anchovies (43). By contrast, the only Asian commodity mentioned in the letters is a pound of whole nutmegs, also ordered by Hannan (43). Tea is mentioned nowhere in the letters. It would become a major item of consumption in Ireland only in the following century. American commodities had a more familiar place in seventeenth-century Irish life, and this too is reflected in the *Amity* papers. Jacques Mahon wrote to Jacques Souchay, a banker in Nantes, to tell him of his arrival in Limerick 'from Santo Domingo with a thousand odd rolls of tobacco, 10 casks of leaf, and a keg and a quarter of indigo' (72). Robert Hannan ordered similarly large quantities of tobacco from his correspondents in France (43, 54–6, 60, 61).

Tobacco made major inroads among Irish consumers in the seventeenth century, with nearly three million pounds imported yearly in the early 1680s, a consumption of roughly a pound and a half per head of population. Sugar did not surpass tobacco in value among Irish imports until the 1730s.[80] Reflecting this, while tobacco is mentioned in eleven of the letters, sugar appears only twice.[81] Christmas Smith, merchant of Tralee, describes in a petition to Tyrconnell the loss to French warships of a vessel from Antigua bound for Ireland bearing 26,000 lbs of tobacco he had bought in the Caribbean and 14,000 lbs of sugar (4).

As Smith's experience underlines, among the perils of trading in wartime was the loss of ships to enemy navies or privateers – the ultimate fate of the *Amity* and an anxiety widely reflected in the letters. From early in the war, the highest risk of seizure lay in the Celtic Sea and the Bay of Biscay where English warships patrolled in search of vessels supplying enemy forces in Ireland. In May 1689, the capture by an English warship of Thomas McNemara's ship *Speedwell* off the coast of France – and 'bound for Nants' – was typical of wartime hazards.[82] Limerick vessels also ran the risk of seizure by the French if

[80] Louis M. Cullen, 'Colonial and Exotic Products: Their Place and Role in Irish Economy and Society', in *Economy, Trade and Irish Merchants at Home and Abroad, 1600–1988* (Dublin, 2012), 103–17.

[81] The letters mentioning tobacco are 4, 6, 31, 33, 42, 44, 53, 55, and 59. Three centuries ago, it was more often goods, such as tobacco and sugar, rather than travel that connected people to distant places. Yet some writers had been to the other side of the Atlantic, especially the Caribbean – still in 1690 a more important site of English and Irish settlement than the colonies of North America. Christmas Smith expected to return to the Caribbean, though 'how, or when ... heavens only can resolve', he told Abraham Lloyd (17). Other letter writers, if they had not been to America themselves, knew people who had or who might go. Zachary Holland hoped to recover money in London before the debtor absconded to the West Indies (23). Thomas Pearce worried that a renegade business partner, Thomas Flaxon, 'will be gon to ye west indies wth our consm^t^' (33).

[82] Affidavit of Joseph Philcett, Portsmouth, 27 August 1689, in TNA, HCA 32/20 (*Speedwell* of Limerick). In addition to the *Speedwell,* the letters mentioned two other Limerick ships captured by the English Navy: the *Diligence* (2) and the *Providence* (12).

they carried the false documents disguising their true destination necessary to evade English capture.[83] Smith complained that the French captain who seized his vessel had illegally sold the cargo in Galway without a proper legal proceeding to condemn the ship as a prize. He hoped Tyrconnell might intervene to secure him some redress. A second petition to Tyrconnell, from Samuel Taverner, complains that the *Diligence*, on which he owned cargo, had been seized by Williamite forces at Baltimore, Co. Cork, and brought to Minehead in Somerset. On the vessel's release, it was made prize again, this time off the Blasket Islands by a French privateer from Saint-Malo (2).[84]

At the centre of the saga of the *Diligence* was Joseph Reade, master, 'y[t] Monstrous knave', in the words of Taverner, who blamed the captain for straying from his orders, leading to the loss of the ship. Taverner told Patrick Rirdan that Reade had 'run away with my ship, hee did what hee pleased acting all things without my orders but following his owne imeigination' (12). Taverner was no less blunt in his letter to Reade himself. 'I ... am sorry for thy misfortune,' he told the ship captain, who was a prisoner in Nantes, 'but much more for my owne for thy villany has quite ruined mee, thee acteing Every thing after the imagination of thy owne Brayne runing away, with my ship, and Goods' (14). To Mme Lee and Sons, the aggrieved merchant presented a more charitable face. '[P]ray remember mee to the poore Unfortunate master, Joseph Reade,' he told the widow, 'and for my sake doe him what kindnes you Can, In procuring his Liberty or releasement, you may suply him with twenty Crownes on my Acompt and If you can helpe him to An Employ' (13). To Reade though, Taverner claimed that he had asked Lee to 'doe thee what kindnes shee Can, but to Employe thee, I dare not Encorage her'. 'If I had 90 ships', he continued, 'thee shouldst never put thy foot In Any of y[m]' (14).

Lee's nephew, Nicholas Gerraldin Jr, explained to his wife that he planned to turn privateer himself on his voyage home from Ireland 'wherby to meete wth Some pryse y[t] may in Some manner recompence y[e] owners [of the ship]'.[85] Privateers,

[83] Letters 2 and 4.

[84] Petition of Christmas Smith of Tralee (4); petition of Samuel Taverner of Limerick (2). Nor was the *Diligence* Taverner's only such loss. After his ship, the *Providence*, had been taken, he complained that it was 'my hard fate as is Every thing else, I put my hand to' (12).

[85] Letter 65. Nicholas was the son of Nicholas Geraldine (d.1693) who had left Waterford for Saint-Malo in the 1650s. His mother, Anna Fitzgerald, was from another Waterford family that would go on, after the Williamite War, to build a large and successful eighteenth-century merchant network with branches in England, France, Spain and the Caribbean. See Jacob M. Price, *France and the Chesapeake: A History of the French Tobacco Monopoly, 1674–1791, and Its Relationship to the British and American Tobacco Trades*, 2 vols. (Ann Arbor, MI, 1973), 1:557–62, 2:1026 n. 91. On the London branch of the Fitzgeralds and their continental connections, see L. M. Cullen, 'The Two George Fitzgeralds of London, 1718–1759', in Dickson, Parmentier, and Ohlmeyer (eds.), *Irish and Scottish Mercantile Networks in Europe*, 252–65.

or corsairs, were privately owned ships that received a licence from their home states to take enemy ships at sea To engage in private war at sea was typical of the Saint-Malo milieu in which Gerraldin had been raised. The port dominated French privateering from the 1680s to 1715. James II commissioned Nicholas's cousins, Antoine and Raymond Gerraldin, as privateers. For Nicholas, turning privateer was a question of making the best of a bad situation: 'a saveing voyadge in soe unhappie a Conjoughture'. Yet there seems also to have been a certain relish in turning to this option. Likening himself to a Tartar, Nicholas told his wife, 'I have noe mynd to Come whom butt wth Spoyle as ye tartars doe' (65).

Did Nicholas follow through on his intention to seek prizes on this occasion? All we know is that he survived to fit out another privateering ship, the *Soleil*, in 1691. James knighted him in 1700 in reward for his services to the Jacobite cause, principally as a corsair. He would survive to invest in subsequent Malouin privateering ventures in the Pacific during the War of the Spanish Succession (1701–13). Other Irish in Saint-Malo also invested in privateers, as did several in Nantes including Edward Lucker, Mme Lee's son-in-law.[86]

That the Catholic merchants of Limerick depended on these established Irish commercial networks in France to handle their business in 1690 is hardly surprising. That the city's Quaker merchants did so too raises an interesting problem. Historians have shown that, in the absence of formal institutions to enforce contracts efficiently and effectively, early modern merchants – especially those engaged in long-distance commerce – did business predominantly with members of their own family, caste, or religious community, people they had stronger reason to trust than strangers. However, if they wanted to participate in the expanding trade to France, the Quakers of Limerick had little choice but to trade outside faith and family. While there were small communities of Friends in business on the Continent, these were overwhelmingly concentrated in the Dutch Republic.[87] The Quaker merchants who owned the *Amity* intended their cargo to be placed in the hands of an expatriate Irish trading house with ties to Limerick, whichever French port it entered. Holland, Pearce, and Taverner authorised the sale of part of the cargo on credit, relying on their correspondents to discern who was a good credit risk and who might not be. How was the trust

[86] J. S. Bromley, 'The Jacobite Privateers in the Nine Years War', in Anne Whiteman, J. S. Bromley, and P. G. M. Dickson (eds.), *Statesmen, Scholars and Merchants: Essays in Eighteenth-Century History presented to Dame Lucy Sutherland* (Oxford, 1973), 23–4; Henning Hillmann, *The Corsairs of Saint-Malo: Network Organization of a Merchant Elite Under the Ancien Régime* (New York, 2021), 292 n.3; Mary Ann Lyons, 'The Irish in Saint-Malo', unpublished paper delivered at the conference 'Waterford and the Wider World 1500–1800', 8 November 2024.

[87] Sünne Juterczenka, 'Meeting Friends and Doing Business: Quaker Missionary and Commercial Activities in Europe, 1655–1720', in A. Gestrich and M. Schulte-Beerbuhl (eds.), *Cosmopolitan Networks in Commerce and Society, 1660–1914*, Bulletin of the German Historical Institute London, suppl. no. 2 (2011), 187–218.

created for Quaker merchants to do business in this fashion, especially at such a perilous moment?

Scholars have found other instances of long-standing, successful business relationships in the early modern world that transcended communities of identity. In such cases, the ready availability of information about trading partners, conveyed in regular correspondence from others in the same network, could substitute for the reassurance offered by ties of family or religion.[88] This is surely also the case for the Limerick Quakers who did business in France. We have direct evidence in James Craven's letter to the Widow Lee and Sons. Craven did not know Lee, had not done business with her, yet hoped she might help him in a dispute with Patrick Rirdan on the basis of what he had learned from others of her character: 'Tho: unknowne unto you yett [I] am imboldened by the good Carracter I have heard of yor Just and faire corespondency wth frinds and Acquaintance for to desire the favour of you to answer my Expectacion in what you cann in A matter of some Controversie that may happen betwixt Patrick Rirdane & my selfe' (35).

This is not to imply that Quakers and Catholics were, in the full sense, a part of the same networks. They were closely intertwined, to be sure, yet distinct all the same. The principal difference between the Quaker merchants of Limerick and their Catholic counterparts was the central place of London in Quaker commercial networks. This should not surprise us. With perhaps 50,000 Friends scattered across the Atlantic World, London's 5–8,000 Quakers constituted by far the single largest concentration. Moreover, London Friends were prominent in the ranks of overseas merchants, one in six of whom was a Quaker.[89] Limerick Quakers depended on London connections to handle remittances from the Continent, to shelter family members, and even to intercede – where they thought it possible – to recover ships or goods seized at sea. Zachary Holland asked Patrick Rirdan to remit the proceeds of the sale of his goods to Thomas and Joseph Carpenter, Quaker merchants in London. He asked the Carpenters to follow up on debts owed him and to remember him to his friends there.[90] James Craven's son – also James – was a merchant resident

[88] Francesca Trivellato, *The Familiarity of Strangers: The Sephardic Diaspora, Livorno, and Cross-Cultural Trade in the Early Modern Period* (New Haven, CT, 2009).

[89] F. B. Tolles, 'The Trans-Atlantic Quaker Community in the Seventeenth Century', *Huntington Library Quarterly*, 14 (1951), 239–58; Esther Sahle, 'Quakers, Coercion, and Pre-Modern Growth: Why Friends' Formal Institutions for Contract Enforcement Did Not Matter for Early Modern Trade Expansion', *Economic History Review*, 71:2 (2018), 418–36, at 418. On the place of London in Quaker life, see Jordan Landes, *London Quakers in the Trans-Atlantic World: The Creation of an Early Modern Community* (Basingstoke, 2015).

[90] Holland also wrote to a brother, Joseph, in Minehead sharing worries about the failure of a Bristol merchant, Abraham Elton, to remit money from the sale of five tuns of tallow Holland had consigned on him (50). Elton (1654–1728) was not himself a Quaker, but a dissenter who would

in London, where his brother Johny had also been sent, perhaps to keep him out of trouble in Limerick (48, 49). For both Samuel Taverner and Thomas Pearce, the Quaker linen draper Joseph Scriven was a key London connection. He was Pearce's cousin and may have provided refuge to Pearce's wife in London (74). He certainly did so for Taverner's wife, Prudence (who served as her husband's temporary financial agent in London). Should she leave London, Taverner instructed Patrick Rirdan, the latter was to remit the value of goods sold to another London Quaker merchant, Richard Haynes (47). The owners of the *Amity* hoped that Scriven and the Carpenters could free the *Amity* from the clutches of the Prize Court (74). This is not to imply that Catholic merchants had no English connections. Robert Hannan did business with John Degrave, a Huguenot merchant based in London, and asked Degrave to remember him to John Kirwan, a Galway merchant also settled there (19). But London connections were denser and more essential for the Quakers, and more likely to be underpinned by family ties.

Another difference is that while Limerick Quaker interests in France were purely commercial, Catholic merchant networks there facilitated other kinds of opportunities for relatives in Ireland. A few of the *Amity* letters reflect the importance of France as a place for Irish boys and men to study, and for clerics to make a career. Robert Hannan's son, James, studied in Poitiers, about 200 kilometres southeast of Nantes. Robert complained that his son did not write home often enough but counselled the boy above all to 'Mynde well yor stoody' (55). The elder Hannan voiced the same concern to Patrick Rirdan, who was to convey the letter: 'lett me know if he mindes his stoudy well' (43). Whether James Hannan was studying for the priesthood in the Irish College of Poitiers or was a lay student is unclear. Catholic priests could not receive a vocational education in Ireland at this time because of penal legislation, but families who could afford it sent their sons to French seminaries. Catholic boys bound for the professions could also be educated on the Continent.[91]

Two of the Limerick writers addressed their letters to Irish priests living in France. Adam Cusack, a soldier we have already met, intended one of his letters for his brother Dr Patrick Cusack. Robert Hannan tried to contact the reverend John O'Molony (1617–1702), bishop of Killaloe and Limerick. Hannan hoped to recover money he had loaned to Captain Daniel Molony, the bishop's nephew, who had died in the war (58). O'Molony, a prominent cleric,

in time become one of Bristol's richest merchants and an MP for the city.

[91] L. W. B. Brockliss and P. Ferté, 'Irish Clerics in France in the Seventeenth and Eighteenth Centuries: A Statistical Study', *Proceedings of the Royal Irish Academy: Archaeology, Culture, History, Literature*, 87C (1987), 527–72; Liam Swords, 'Collège des Lombards', in Liam Swords (ed.), *The Irish-French Connection, 1578–1978* (Paris, 1978).

was educated in Paris and lived much of his life there, participating in theological disputes over Jansenism, and befriending Vincent de Paul, before being consecrated bishop of Killaloe in 1672. Only such an eminent position would have attracted him back to Ireland from a flourishing career in France. In the following fifteen years he divided his time between Killaloe and Paris, where in 1676 he helped acquire the Collège des Lombards as a seminary for Irish priests. In 1688, James II appointed him bishop of Limerick though he stayed on as administrator at Killaloe.[92] A Catholic merchant such as Hannan clearly had a network and social ties in France much more extensive than any of the Quaker owners of the *Amity*.

The capture of that vessel off Milford Haven and the start of condemnation proceedings against it in the High Court of Admiralty opened our story. What became of the ship and its cargo? Taverner, Pearce, and Holland hoped the *Amity* might escape condemnation. Through their London connections, Joseph Scriven and Thomas and Joseph Carpenter, they made a claim for recovery of the vessel. 'I hope shee will bee gott of,' Thomas Pearce wrote to Scriven (74). This was not entirely unrealistic. The *Amity* conducted trade in a legal grey zone. Under the relevant statutes of the Irish Parliament, the trade with France was clearly legal.[93] By a royal proclamation of 6 June 1689, William of Orange banned trade without prior authorisation between any of his British subjects and Ireland. The same decree prohibited communication with any part of Ireland in Jacobite hands.[94] But this proclamation did not affect Irish trade with France as such. A law passed by the Westminster Parliament, effective August 1689, made illegal the import of French goods into Britain and Ireland. This would have banned the return trade from Nantes, or any other French port, but did not apply to exports. (On the other hand, the court had evidence in depositions taken from passengers that the *Amity* 'had traded from Limbrick to ffrance these last six Months'.[95]) It was apparently not until November 1690, after the *Amity* sailed, that the English Parliament prohibited trade generally between Ireland and France.[96] Still, having sailed from a port in Jacobite hands, carrying a passport from the Duke of Tyrconnell, the *Amity* could readily be viewed as

[92] John Cronin, 'O'Molony, John', *DIB* (accessed 15 January 2025); and Hayes, *Biographical Dictionary*, 245–6. On the history of the Collège des Lombards, see Liam Chambers, 'Rivalry and Reform in the Irish College, Paris, 1676–1775', in Thomas O'Connor and Mary Ann Lyons (eds.), *Irish Communities in Early Modern Europe* (Dublin, 2006), 103–29.

[93] Act for the Advance and Improvement of Trade, and for the Encouragement and Increase of Shipping, and Navigation, 1689 (James II's Irish Parliament, c. 29), reproduced in Appendix III below.

[94] See Appendix I below.

[95] Depositions of Philippe Lepeulire [sic] and James Ronan. See Appendix IV.

[96] Siobhan Talbott, '"Such Unjustifiable Practices": Irish Trade, Settlement, and Society in France, 1688–1715', *Economic History Review*, 67:2 (2014), 556–77, at 560.

an enemy ship in wartime, and thus subject to seizure.

The case for recovery of the vessel appears to have hinged on the owners' claim to be victims of circumstance. Were the vessel and its cargo forfeited, Pearce complained, 'Its a most severe thing, that wee should Loose on Every side, wee canot have Liberty to send else where, and when wee doe send wee are forct to give seccurity to returne goods from franc hither, will not your Governm^t consider, that wee Canot doe what wee would doe, If our goods were safe heare wee would send nothing awaÿ, those perillous times sure I hope they will consider our condition, I am sure in justice they ought to doe it' (74). The sincerity of this appeal cannot be judged.

The Carpenters along with Joseph Scriven appeared at court in the name of the owners, and initially seem to have been successful in arguing their case though, in the end, the ship and its cargo were declared forfeit. The record of proceedings fills no more than a few scant lines in the ledgers of the Admiralty Court, but they state that on 16 January 1691 'The said ship and lading decreed to be delivered to Mr Joseph Scriven and Mr Joseph Carpenter or their assignes for the use of the claimers'. Then, ten days later, 'The said vessel and her lading condemned as perquisites of Adm^ty'.[97] Was an initial decision in favour of the owners subsequently overturned? All that appears certain is that the *Amity* and its cargo were ultimately declared lawful prize. And so it came to be that the ship's papers, strung together on a thong so none could be removed, and rolled in a tight bundle, entered the archives of the Admiralty Court and disappeared – to resurface over 300 year later.[98]

Editorial Conventions

The letters, petitions, and shipping papers collected here have been transcribed in a format that aims to be faithful to original texts. For a modern reader, these editorial conventions are certain to present some challenges. A particular difficulty is the systematic lack of punctuation in letters. To decide where one sentence begins and another ends, it may be necessary to read the text aloud, and even then, ambiguity may persist. Lack of punctuation, and inconsistent

[97] TNA, IND 1/9013/7.

[98] A few letters escaped the clutches of the Admiralty Court and may have reached their addressees. A French passenger on the *Amity*, Philippe Lepeulier, captain in the regiment of la Marche, stated when deposed that he had been carrying a letter from John Rowland, a 'Counselor in Limbrick to be deliverd to his sonn'. Lepeulier claimed to have met the younger Rowland onboard the ship and to have passed the letter onto him. If the recipient was a crew member or a passenger on the ship, he was not deposed by the officials of the Admiralty Court and the letter has disappeared. See deposition of Philippe Lepeulire [sic], Appendix IV. A French infantry major named Ducorail mentions two letters enclosed with his own which have not survived (63). We have no way to know whether Captain Mitchell or any other member of the crew managed to conceal other papers from their captors.

spelling and capitalisation was typical of the period. We find it not only in merchant letters, but in those of more elite writers. It is not necessarily an index of imperfect literacy. That said, we can discern degrees of literacy among the letter writers. Some of the seamen's correspondence, in particular, is brief and formulaic, contrasting sharply with the detail and intimacy of other letters.

1. The documents are presented in the order they were written. Each begins with a heading that includes an identifying number. For letters, the name of the writer and the place from which they wrote appears in a standardised form, then the recipient's name and address as it appears on the envelope, followed by the date of the letter. The five bills of lading (two of them duplicates) are not transcribed and numbered separately but placed below the text of the letters in which they were presumably enclosed. Bills of lading were printed for use by merchants, with spaces left to write in all relevant details of a specific shipment. Italics are used in the transcriptions to set off the handwritten parts of the bills from the printed portion. Each document also carries a number assigned to it in the course of the Prize Court proceedings. While it is unclear what significance the court attached to these numbers, they are reproduced at the end of each heading. (The exceptions are letters 73 and 74, which were written after the *Amity's* capture, and submitted in evidence to the Prize Court. These documents, while archived with the rest, were not assigned a number.) The same information is reproduced in the Calendar of Documents (pp. xvii–xxii).

2. Spelling, capitalisation, and punctuation have been preserved. The sole exception to this rule is that, in cases where it might be difficult for modern readers to distinguish where one sentence ends and a new one begins, a full stop in square brackets has been inserted (such as [.]) and occasionally a comma (such as [,]) to clarify syntax. The spelling of names in the introduction and the notes accord with the spelling in the documents, even in cases where existing scholarship uses a different spelling, or where modern usage strongly suggests an alternate spelling (e.g. Rirdan rather than Riordan; Molley rather than Molloy).

3. Where the original text is damaged or indecipherable, this is indicated in square brackets. In rare instances, missing letters are supplied in square brackets to make a word intelligible. While we have high confidence in the accuracy of the transcriptions, in a handful of cases, due to the difficulty of the handwriting, the editors had to make a best guess as to what the writer intended to say.

4. Monetary symbols and units of measurement, which are usually abbreviated in the letters, presented occasional problems of transcription. We have sought to reproduce, as closely as modern typography will permit, the original symbols used and have not translated them into a standardised form. Fuller discussion of

abbreviations relating to money, measure, and weight will be found in a Note on Weights, Measures, Money, and Corresponding Abbreviations.

5. Because Britain and Ireland used the Julian calendar until 1752, dates in the 1690s, as reckoned in the British Isles, ran 11 days behind the Continent, which used the Gregorian calendar. For instance, in the Julian calendar, the Battle of the Boyne was fought on 1 July, which was 12 July in the Gregorian calendar – the date on which the event is commemorated today. In rare cases, authors indicated that they were using the Julian calendar by appending 'old style' after the date, but usually there is no such indication. It was conventional in the British Isles to date the beginning of the New Year to 25 March, but this does not affect dates in the documents aboard the *Amity*, as they were all written after that date. (It affects the dating of Appendix II, and this is noted.) Many letter writers used the convention that September was the 7th month, October the 8th, and so on. Thus, the abbreviation '3 7ber' is to be understood as 3 September, not 3 July, as it might be in a modern letter. In the document transcriptions, all dates are reproduced as they appear in the originals.

6. Paragraphing (in the rare cases paragraphs are used) conforms to the original texts, but there has been no further attempt to reproduce the format of the original documents. Salutations at the opening of letters and valedictions and complimentary closings at the close have been retained and their placement standardised.

7. The standard p.s. or p.p.s abbreviations for postscripts were not used in the seventeenth century but have been added in square brackets to set off material that appeared below the signature or as additions in the margins of letters.

8. The transcriptions of documents in the appendices conform to the same conventions as the ship's papers.

9. Six of the letters were written in French and two in Dutch. These are transcribed following the same conventions as the letters in English, but immediately following each transcription comes a translation of the original into English. With the translations, we have sought to render the original text comprehensible to readers of modern English while remaining true to the sense of the original. Where a literal translation would have made the meaning ambiguous or incomprehensible, we have opted for clarity rather than exact fidelity to the original wording. No effort has been made to preserve the voice or rhythm of the original, or to reproduce idiosyncrasies of spelling or punctuation. Rather, translations are punctuated and capitalised in accord with modern English usage. The spelling of surnames and place names has been corrected in the translation where such corrections could be made with confidence.

THE
AMITY
PAPERS
1690

The Siege of Limerick and Franco-Irish Mercantile Networks

From the Collection of
The National Archives, Kew

1. **Thomas Burton [address unknown], 'For Mrs Ellen Lee,[1] at Kilrush',[2] 9 April 1690. No. 44a**

April 9th 1690

Nell Lee

This serves to Acquaint you that your husband[3] is at Corke who I here will be wth you assoone as ye ship Discharges[.] [He] likewise has sent you six shillings wch he desired I would convey to you Some time since. wch I would have sent you before but did not meet wth a convenient Oppertunety, now you have them inclosed wch is all at prsent being in hast
from Your Frend to serve you
Tho. Burton

[1] Ellen Lee was the wife of Nicholas Lee, Jr (see note 3 below).

[2] Kilrush was a suburb of seventeenth-century Limerick, as well as a coastal town in West Clare near the mouth of the River Shannon. It is not possible, on the basis of context, to be sure which location is in question here.

[3] Nicholas Lee, Jr (b.1664) was active in trade between Ireland and the French port of Nantes. He was the son of Nicholas Lee, Sr (1636–1684), a native of Waterford, and Marie Lee (née Geraldin) (1639–1707), frequently addressed in these letters as 'Madame Lee' (Joël Rilat, *Ces messieurs de Nantes,* 5 vols. [Morrisville, NC, 2014–19], 4:351).

2. **Petition of Samuel Taverner,[1] Limerick, 'To his Grace the Duke of Tyrconnell Lord Deputy Genll & Genll Governor of Ireland',[2] 2 August 1690. No. 4**

To his Grace the Duke of Tyrconnell Lord
Deputy Genll & Genll Governor of Ireland

The humble Petition of Samuel Taverner one of those called a Quaker
Most humbly

Sheweth unto your Grace that the shipp called diligence burthen one hundred tunns Joseph Reade Master loaden at the port of Lymerick with beeff butter and leather belonging to yor Petr who allways demeaned himself a loyall Subject, and has beene serviceable in this kingdom by importing of Goods necessary for the subsistence of his Maties Army, and who delivered the same for the Kings use at the Kings rates, that the said shipp with the said Goods by contrary winds was driven into Baltimore in the County of Corke where shee was seized by some of the Kings Enemys, and brought into Minehead in the Kingdom of England. That yor Pet^{r} could not gett the said shipp released but by assureing shee should goe for Barbadoes, and after shee came there the Master was forced to take out Cocketts[3] for England, though really the said Master according to the Directions he had from yor Pet^{r} intended to returne for this Citty of Lymerick, but meeting of the Blasquetts[4] within fourteene leagues to land a Privateer from St Malos[5] tooke yor Pet^{rs} said shipp as a prize to his & his familys utter ruine if not releeved by y^{r} Grace

May it therefore please yor Grace yor Pet^{r} having ever demeaned himself a loyall & good Subject to recommende yor Pet^{rs} sad and deplorable Case to his Ma^{ty} whereby the said shipp may not be condemned a prize

And yor Pet^{r} as in duty bound shall pray

[*Below is the Irish government's response that appears at the bottom of the manuscript page.*]

Upon consideracon of the above Petition, and his Grace knowing the Pet^{r} demeaned himselfe allwayes as a loyall & good Subject ought to doe his Grace ordered me to desire you to recomend his Case to his Ma^{ty} whereby the Pet^{r} and his famyly may be releived.

Dated att Lymerick the 2^{d} of August 1690
Riverston[6]

To Sr R^{d} Nagle Kn^{t} his Maties principall Secretary of State[7]

[1] Samuel Taverner (b.1653), a native of Co. Cork, was a prominent figure in Limerick's Quaker merchant community and one of the three owners of the barque *Amity*. He migrated to Limerick sometime before his marriage to Prudence Pearce in August 1680. The brother-in-law of Thomas Pearce (another of the vessel's owners), Taverner was linked by marriage to one of the founding families of Limerick's Quaker Meeting ('Samuel Taverner [1653]', at https://www.wikitree.com/wiki/Taverner-197 [accessed 27 September 2024]; Edward MacLysaght [ed.], 'McLysaght Papers', *Analecta Hibernica*, 15 [Nov. 1944], 368; James O'Shea (ed.), *Irish Maritime Trade in the Restoration Era: The Letterbook of William Hovell, 1683–1687* [Dublin, 2022], 31, 65, 306, 316 [hereafter cited as O'Shea [ed.], *Letterbook of William Hovell*).

[2] Richard Talbot (1630–1691) served as viceroy of Ireland in the government of James II (Piers Wauchope, 'Talbot, Richard, first earl of Tyrconnell and Jacobite duke of Tyrconnell [1630–1691]', *ODNB* [accessed 25 October 2024]).

[3] 'A customs document issued to a merchant which is sealed ... and certifies that the merchant's goods have been entered and the duty on them paid' (*OED*).

[4] Blasket Islands, Co. Kerry, 'an archipelago of six islands off the Dingle peninsula. One of the islands, *An Tiaracht* (in Irish), is the westernmost part of Ireland and of Europe' (Brian Lalor, *The Encyclopedia of Ireland* [New Haven, CT, 2003], 97).

[5] For the privateers of Saint-Malo, see Hillmann, *Corsairs of Saint-Malo*, 91–121.

[6] Thomas Nugent was an Irish Catholic barrister who served as Lord Chief Justice of Ireland under James II (Richard Bagwell, revised by James McGuire, 'Nugent, Thomas, first Baron Nugent of Riverston [d.1715]', *ODNB* [accessed 25 October 2024]).

[7] Sir Richard Nagle served as secretary of state for war and attorney general in the Irish regime of James II. Nagle accompanied James to France where he was prominent in the Jacobite court at Saint-Germaine-en-Laye (Richard Hayes, 'Biographical Dictionary of Irishmen in France, Part XIII', *Studies: An Irish Quarterly Review*, 33:133 [March 1945], 109; James McGuire, 'Nagle, Sir Richard [1635/36–1699]', *ODNB* [accessed 25 October 2024]).

3. Morrish Moore,[1] Henry Trant,[2] Grechus and Ambrose Moore,[3] Tralee,[4] 'To the Hon^rble^ Sr Patricke Trant K^t^ and Barronett,[5] [place unknown], 19 August 1690. No. 69

Trally 19th aug^t^ 1690

May it please yor Hon^r^:

was severall yeares our Neighbour The bearer m^r:^ Christmass Smyth[6] who & a good Dealer att Trally, untill misfortune forced him beyond Sea where being those seaven yeares past was lately returneing home wth a sufficent Cargo to pay us, and Severall others of our friends his Creditors untill unuistly taken by a frinch man of warr, as appeares by severall papers & Certifficatts to that purpose, he desires your ayde and this our Letter in his favour, wee are fully satisfied of his honnest intent hither and earnestly desire your favourable assistance and advice to him where in yo^u^ will accomplish a greate act of Charrity and obliedge many of your Relations & frinds, besides it will be a particullar kindnesse done to Hon^le^ S^r^
yor most aff^tt^ Serv^ts^

Morris Moore Hen: Trant Grechus Ambrose Moore

[1] For Morish Moore, see W. Maziere Brady, *The M^c^Gillycuddy Papers: A Selection from the Family Archives of 'The M^c^Gillycuddys of the Reeks'* (London, 1867), 19, 27.

[2] 'The dweling house of Henry Trant, situated and being in Traly in the said county [Kerry]' was the site of local legal and commercial transactions in years leading up to the Williamite War (Brady, *M^c^Gillycuddy Papers*, 130; For Henry Trant, see Letter 18).

[3] Ambrose Moore, under a commission issued by James II in April 1690, was charged with apportioning a levy of £1,052 per month on the rate-payers of Co. Kerry 'on personal estates and the benefit of trade and traffic, "according to the ancient custom of this Kingdom used in time of danger"'. The king had assessed a monthly £20,000 for the counties, together with the principal towns and cities of the Kingdom of Ireland (D'Alton, *Army List*, 1:33, 36).

[4] Tralee, Co. Kerry, 'is at the head of Tralee Bay, where the River Lee reaches the sea, and from which it derives its name' (Lalor, *Encyclopedia of Ireland*, 1065).

[5] Sir Patrick Trant (1630–1694) was a Catholic with family ties to landowning families in Counties Kerry and Limerick. In the 1680s, he served as the London agent for planters on Barbados and the Leeward Islands, notably Montserrat. Trant's reputation was tarnished by a charge of embezzlement brought against him in the mid-1680s by the estate of Sir William Stapleton, governor of Montserrat. Even so, Patrick Trant was knighted in 1686 (Baronet of Coldwell, Co.

Dublin), appointed Commissioner of Revenue by James II, and chosen to sit as an MP for Queen's County in 1688. Trant died at Saint-Germain-en-Laye in 1694 (S. M., 'The Trant Family', *Kerry Archaeological Magazine*, 2:12 [March 1914], 237–62; Donald Harman Akenson, *If the Irish Ran the World: Montserrat, 1630–1730* [Montreal & Kingston, 1997], 99–100).

[6] For Christmas Smith, see letter 4, note 1.

4. 'To His Grace The Duke of Tyrconnell Ld Lieut Genl and Genl Governor of Ireland. The Humble Petticon of Christmas Smith[1] of Traly in Kierry Merchant', n.d. No. 68

Humbly shoing that yor Petticin^r by severall Losses att Sea^e and manie other Disapointmn^ts about seaven yeares Past was much reduced, and fallen in Debtt wch fforced him to Leave then in this Kingdome his Poore fammilly; and for to retreeve his Losses and pay his Credittors, to travill into Ammerica; where ever since being tradeing betweene his Most Sacred Majes^tie King James^s Collonies, and Islands, About Nyne Moneths past he arived att the islands of Antigua,[2] Where meeting with severall Lettors from som of his said Credittors that Informd him of the Great scarsetie there was in this Kingdom of the Groath of that Island; alsoe that hee may return into any part of the Province of Munstor without any daingor of Troble Either from the Subjectts of King James or his Allyes, And that more Especially because your Sup^t[3] was never undor the cercomstances of Absentees; or disafected Persons, as apeares by severall certiffecats undor the hands of the most considerable of the Goverment, Gentry, and Clergey of said Countie, Where your Sup^t Lived manie Yeares in Good Creditt & reputacion, that yor Sup^t being allwayes desiourous to pay his Creditto^rs, relive his poore ffaumilly, and b^ie Serviciable to his King & Contry, according to his answer to said Lettors, and Advices sent sever^ll of his ffriends about six Months before his return Invested all his Substance in said Island in Tobacc^o; and Sugor; and aftor much care and troble had in Providing a Shipp, did att Last Prevaile with one Cp^tn Roger Whitfield Comd^r of a Waterford Built ship Burd^n Seaventy Tuns to take ffraight for Cork in Ireland;[4] & accordingly yor Sup^t shiped abourd him about Twenty Six Thous^nd pounds of tobacc^o; and ffourteene thousand pounds of Sugor; consignd on Alderman Steephen Gould[5] & Mr Nicholas Hubbortt[6] Merchants in Corke, as apeares by bills of Lodeing & Severall other papors to that Purpos now in the ffrench Admirall on Linerffarons hands, That the said Whitfield was forced to deny his Intent for Ireland and Entor his shipp and Goods for Bristoll or other parts of England; the Goverm^t there (then under the Prince of Orriang) seizeing all shipps Suspected to be designd for Ireland, that said Mast^r obleidg^ing all his ffraightors to keep his said designe secrett, did with much diffecultie Get his Cleareing, butt durst not demand any other pass then the said Princes, wth wch he deemed him selfe very safe secure being certified of the safetie of ffour other shipps that Loded att ye same Island, under ye same Pretensess, & sayled wth ye same pass; as apeares by severall Afedavits, & certiffecats to that purpos; and thogh som of them were mett with, undor som troble, yet on due Examination were all cleered paying his Majest^{ies} duties.

[*The following two paragraphs of Christmas Smith's petition suffer from severe deterioration. Those places where text is missing are indicated in brackets.*]

Butt yet soe it is wth yor Poore unfortunate Sup^{t} that on Tewsday the sixth day of July anno Dom^{e} 1690 about som fifteene Leagus S.Wst of Cape Cleere,[7] as he with said Mastor was Standing Towards said Porte of Cork that to Leword of them thay Esp[missing text] six Sayle of ffrench men of Warr undor Convaye of Seiur Eton Comd^{r} of the ffriggot caled Levielly bound for Lym[missing text] that your Sup^{t} concious of his good Intent & Innocency, knowing they were the Most Sacred King Jamess Allyes did [not] Endeavor to Shunn or avoid them (for wch thay severall times since acused yor Sup^{t} & Said Mastor of ffolly) saying thay never Chased yor Sup^{t} but rather your Sup^{t} them [missing text] the said Shipp & said Goods belonging to your Sup^{t}; att [missing text] & severely Imprisoned the Mastor & men, togther wth [missing text] thousand pounds Tobac^{o} & five thousand pounds Cotton [missing text] & Consignd on Aldorman Steephen Gould & Aldorman [missing text] in all not les worth in this Kingdom then fforty Thou[missing text] Two thards of said Cargoe in one of his ffleete; [missing text] Legall Examination, Tryall, conviction or Condemnation [missing text]

The Premmisses Send [missing text] to dierect your order to the [missing text] other Persons concern'd: the said ship [missing text] Ste^{r} ore at Least your Sup^{t} part thereof, being about Twentie Six Thousand pounds of Tobac^{o} & ffowerteene Thousand pounds of Sugor: Otherwise to command the said Capt Eton Imediatly before his departure to Give yor Sup^{t} a ffayor and Legall tryall for said shipp, and Goods, or Elce Entor in this Towne of Gallway Good reason to abide the said Tryall in any part of Ireland your poore Sup^{t} by this Great Lose being rendored altogether Incapable of ffolloeing it for ffraunce, & More Especially because it is the Marittan Law,[8] and ye Custom in this Kingdom to force all such Tryalls in the fierst or second porte where Prizes are caryed, This Port of Gallwaye being the second Porte, and the place where the said Eton hath most unjustly and Ilegally disposed and Sould most of said Carg^{o} without Tryall, condemnation, or conviction.

[1] For Christmas Smith, see Cornelius McGullicuddy's bond for the delivery of 10,000 hogshead staves (to Christmas Smith, merchant) 'att Lughercannon, in y^{e} p'ish of Traly, w^{th}in y^{e} said County of Kierry, neere y^{e} sea shoare, the Just & full number of tenn thousand good merchantable & pickled Hockshead Staves, of att Least four inches in breath & three foote in Length, for the sum of Sixty pounds $ster^{l}$', dated 20 August 1680 (Brady, *McGullycuddy Papers*, 138).

[2] In January 1689, news reached the Caribbean that William of Orange had invaded England. 'In February ships landing at Antigua and Philadelphia reported James II's flight to France. But in April the information was still unofficial; no orders had come from the new English government. James II's governors behaved with the nervousness of men who feared that they were losing power ... On the Caribbean island of Antigua [on 25 July 1689] the chief planters induced the royal Governor of the Leeward Islands, Sir Nathaniel Johnson – the most outspoken supporter of James II among the American governors – to resign his office to Christopher Codrington and sail away' (Richard S. Dunn, 'The Glorious Revolution and America', in Nicolas Canny [ed.], *The Origins of Empire: British Overseas Enterprise to the Close of the Seventeenth Century* [Oxford, 1998], 445, 455).

[3] Read: 'supplicant'.

[4] This vessel was the *St Martin* [possibly of Dublin], Capt. Roger Whitfield, which had been carried into a French port in 1689. Whitfield was released in 1692 and allowed to return to Dublin (Whitfield, Dublin, to Roger Whitfield, master of the *St Martin*, 22 August 1692, TNA, ADM 106/425/271, fol. 271; ADM 106/417/167).

[5] Stephen Goold, a Catholic, was an alderman of Cork. His family departed Ireland for France about 1690, together with members of the Coppinger and Nagle families (Mrs. Morgan John O'Connell, *The Last Colonel of the Irish Brigade*, 2 vols. [London, 1892], 2:136).

[6] Nicholas Hubbard appears on lists of vestrymen of the church of Saint Mary's Shandon in Cork for 1672 and 1704 ('Records of the Church of St Mary's Shandon, City of Cork', at http://www.corkrecords.com/StMaryShandon.htm [accessed 5 October 2024]).

[7] Cape Clear Island, 'Ireland's southernmost inhabited Gaeltacht island, 3 miles long by 1 mile wide, lies 8 miles off the coast of West Cork' ('Cape Clear Island', at http://www.capeclearisland.ie/index [accessed 5 October 2024]).

[8] Read: 'maritime law'.

5. Passport for the ship *Amity* from the Duke of Tyrconnell, Galway, 8 September 1690. No. 1

By the Ld Leu^{t} Gen^{ll} and Gen^{ll} Governour of Irland
Tyrconnell

Whereas humble Suite hath been made unto us by Samuell Taverner for our licence and Passe for the Shipp called the Amity John Mitchell Master Burden Thirty five tunn or there abouts, now beeing in the harbour of Lymbrick, loaden with Salt, hides, and tallow, and Salmon for Nants or Bourdeaux in ffrance, wee are pleased to grant his request therein, and doe hereby strickly Charge and Command you, and every of you to suffer and permitt the said shipp with her loading and ships Crew being six men & Merchant, ffreely and quietly to saile from the said Port of Lymbrick to the said port of Nants or Bourdeaux or any other Port [or] Creek in the said Kingdome of ffrance and returne from thence to any port or Creek in this $King^{m}$ of Irland, without lett Hinderance or Molestation Whatsoever, as you will answer the contrary at yor perill

Given at Galloway the Eight day of September 1690
By his Graces Comand,

Reverston

To all Admiralls vice Admiralls Commanders of his Mat^{ies} shipps att Sea, Governours of Ports or any other whome itt may Concerne

6. Robert Woulfe,[1] Limerick, 'To m^{r} James Molley Mer^{t} recomended to m^{r} John new porte, Merchant In the recurrance in Brest', 3 September 1690. No. 21

Lymericke 3 7^{ber} 1690

Mr James Molley

S^{r}

I have none of yo^{rs} since my 2 severall^{s} as of ye 13 & 29 July by way Nantes[.] in my later have sint y^{or} acc^{t} ye 47 Caske butter bought for both our acc^{ts} is still halfe also yor 4 Caske tallow & 13 halfe hÿds[.] wee heare of some wheate Comeing aboute from Galway wch wee dread for all the goods in Galway sett for ye french markett are all seased on[.] ye like wee feare heare[.] all our Contrie goods are scarce & deare[.] butter 7^{li} p^{r}[.] ox hyds [£]4[:]6^{s} p^{r} from ye butcher[.] tallow raw £3:4^{s} p^{r} yett I could purchase it for whyte mony[2] at 20^{li} p^{r} tun & was offered it the like abatem^{t} in all other goods for ye same[.] no fair Corn in yett[.] I believe y^{u} heared ere now of ye Rebells removeing their siege from our wales[3] wch was proofe ag^{t} their rebellious army being 30000 in number[.] they shattered our wales & made a beach in it oppositt the place wee Kept our Fayer where made two vigorous assaults & some Came into ye towne yett most Couragiously repulsed by oure owne Irish boys who would distroy theire whole body if they had pushed on theire assault[.] its Certaine y^{t} for 21 dayes they Continued theire siege[.] the like was not in some ages such thundreing of Cannons of 24 a 30^{li} bale from 3 severall batteries ag^{t} y^{t} breach they fired from 4 in ye morning till 8 att night 500 Thimes & that incessantly for 10 days & everie night wthoute intermission throwinge theire fire bales bumbs & Carcasses[4] to ye greate terro^{r} of our woomen & Children yett wee sustained no loss by them but tached houses[.] they lost of theire army dureing ye siege 9 a 10000 men Certaine & since they lost more by Corn^{ll} Sarsfilds[5] frequent Coming on some of theire parties[.] our men are stoute & fine boyes if some Corrup^{t} leaders doe not discourage y^{m} & of such pernicious Vermin I feare wee have some wch is ever fatall to our Contrie from such Lord deliver us — forainge goods verie scarce heare as fine linn^{n} Cloaths & triming for officers of whome some may get whyte mony yett Ide not incourage ani goods to bee sint heare if y^{u} Canot first gett our Kings possitive ord^{s} & Comand^{e} to have libertie of sellinge yor good^{s} for mony or good^{s} also his lisence & ord^{s} for shippinge off

such good^{s} as y^{u} Can gett in the Contrie[.] thus y^{u} may persevr in representinge to his ma^{tie} y^{t} y^{u} designe to furnish ye towne wth provissions of wheate wine salte & of ye first y^{t} woud[.] And some being most materiall in getting y^{r} ord^{rs} away had a Cargo of 400^{li} wherein Ile bee Concerned either a moytie or a quarter wch y^{u} please, if y^{t} had, send some fine linen[,] some new & good Clarett[,] some tobacco either leafe or french role[6] wch gett crenulated[.] leafe is heare from 20 a 24^{s} of our Coyne[.] some harlott[7] & trimming^{s} will yeald white mony[,] also some rideing hatt such as y^{t} they cale shappo sans apre[8] & y^{m} edged & bands to y^{m} also and some pretty silke for Cravatte & handkerchers & bee sure y^{u} send mee an excellent Case pistolls & a fured Capp desird formerly[.] yor fa^{r} is well longes to heare from y^{u} & soe does
y^{r} assured humble serv^{t}

Robert Woulfe

[1] Robert Woulfe was among the Catholic burgesses in Limerick appointed by James II in 1687. He continued to practise as a merchant following his pardon under the articles of Limerick. In 1703, along with John Woulfe, perhaps a son, Robert was among a group of renegade Catholic merchants who converted to Protestantism for competitive advantage over those who remained Catholic. There may be a connection between the Woulfes of Limerick and the expatriate Woulfes of eighteenth-century France, 'the last of the Irish "Jacobite" bankers in Paris' (D'Alton, *Army List*, 2:512; Paul MacCotter, 'The "Original" Limerick Woulfes', at http://woulfefamily.com/the_original_woulfes_of_limerick [accessed 5 October 2024]; Cullen, Shovlin, and Truxes [eds.], *Bordeaux–Dublin Letters*, 55, 116, 174–5, 182–5, 225–86).

[2] A reference to silver money (*OED*).

[3] Read: 'walls'.

[4] A carcass is 'a spherical iron shell, filled with an inflammable composition, and having three holes through which the flame blazes; fired from a mortar or gun to set fire to buildings, wooden defences, etc. Formerly also of other shape and material' (*OED*).

[5] Patrick Sarsfield (c.1655–1693) was a Jacobite military commander whose 'daring raid behind Williamite lines to destroy enemy siege equipment at Ballyneety (11 August 1690) contributed significantly to the failure of the first siege of Limerick and consolidated Sarsfield's reputation as the leading Irish commander on the Jacobite side. Described by a fellow Jacobite as "a man of large stature, without sense, very good natured and very brave", he headed the war party within the Jacobite camp, opposed to surrender and critical of Tyrconnell' (S. J. Connolly [ed.], *The Oxford Companion to Irish History* [Oxford, 2007], 524).

[6] 'A roll of tobacco' (*OED*).

[7] 'hap-harlot' was a type of 'coarse bedcovering or coverlet' (*OED*).

[8] Read: 'chapeau sans apprêt'.

7. **James Missett,[1] Limerick, 'To m^{r} Andrew Missett[2] Merc^{nt} In Rochell', 9 September 1690. No. 59**

Limricke the 9th 7ber 1690

Loveing Bro^{r}

My last unto y^{w} was of the 8th august (by the mas^{ter} of the Catherin m^{r} Daniell) wch gave an acc^{t} that if I had not been here the cargoe y^{t} was a board her conseigned to m^{r} tho m^{c}nemara[3] would not signifie much to y^{w}, for when this towne was beseidged, ye s^{d} macnemara left and would advise the s^{d} ship to returne backe to y^{u} wth the same goods shee brought hither because he would not bee admited to send ye goods y^{w} writt for, being prohibuted & keept for the use of the ffreinch for the wheat they brought hither; but Cossen Christopher Gelagh[4] & I hindered the s^{d} advice, and the one halfe of the wine & brandy brought hither, the other Moyety left att Carickefoyle[5] wth m^{r} Luke Garvey who sould and trucked y^{e} s^{d} goods for butter for cossen Gilaghs use, & y^{rs}, the brandy that came to this towne of y^{rs} the greatest part of it was sould for brass mony[6] for 30^{s}, and 40^{s} p^{r} Galon, the wine for 45$^{£}$ p^{r} hocked; Cossen Gilagh trucked some of the brandy, y^{t} for butter, y^{e} butter att £3 10^{s} p^{r} 100^{lb}, y^{e} brandy att 12^{s} p^{r} gallon, and whatt butter he bought here he had it for 3:10 & 4$^{£}$ p^{r} 100^{Cl} in brass, in all he bought a bout 300^{Cl} casq^{ues} of butter in this towne, but when it was turned out of the cealer to bee sent Downe this rever a board y^{e} Catherine it was ceased upon by our Govournor (Maior-General Busloe)[7] for y^{e} use of this Garisson and severall sentrys placed upon it, but I made such interst wth some of our officers here y^{t} I had liberty to send all the s^{d} butter a board the Catherine, who went from hince to Galway three weecks since, and Cossen Gilagh a long wth her, who stays there for a convoy of the ffrench ffleet wishing her a safe and speedy returne to y^{w}[.] when cossen Gilagh left this towne he left wth mee 8 hockeds of Clarett 16 quar^{ter} casq^{ue} & 8 buts of brandy, wch was ceased by the Govournors orders and what could bee found out of all the wine and brandy in this towne, y^{e} brandy att 10^{s} p^{r} Galon, and the wine att 25$^{£}$ p^{r} hocked of clarett, & white wine att 15$^{£}$ p^{r} hocked[.] butt I gott off y^{e} Ceasure of y^{r} wine & brandy, and left to make y^{e} most of it, Cossen Gilaughs Servan^{t} y^{t} is now here sould the s^{d} wine & brandye, y^{e} wine for 44$^{£}$ p^{r} hockett & the brandy all sould to 2 butts for 9^{s}, and 10^{s} p^{r} quarte, I have now here 1200$^{£}$ of brass mony wch was made of y^{e} s^{d} goods,

Cossen Gilagh ordered m^{r} Garvey, and his servan^{t}, m^{r} James Bove to Disburse y^{e} s^{d} supply in butter, talow and other goods for his use, & I suppose for y^{rs}. Y^{w} are to take notice y^{e} s^{d} m^{r} Garvey stayes, and seatles att Carickefoyle where he is to make up 4: or 500 Casque of butter, & other goods for Gilaghs use, I beleive y^{w} are moyetiely concearned there was more mony made of the affores^{d} cargoe then would loade twice the burthen of the Catherin[.] Cossen Gilagh may give y^{w} a more perticular acc^{t} of this concearne. I have a ffoot company in the lord of slanes Regim^{t},[8] I am to Quarter here wth them this

winter, if y^{w} have any oceasion to make use of mee I would thinke my selfe hapy to serve y^{w}, y^{w} may direcit y^{r} letter to m^{r} tho: McNemara who will order it for mee. I doubt nott but y^{w} have an acc^{t} how bravely our men behaved themselfes before this towne (to ye great looss, & confusion of the Prince of oranges Army w^{ch} (wth gods helpe) will bee a meanes to retrieve both our credritt, the rest of our country, and falsifie those that gave ill acc^{ts} there of our countrymen, the Enemy made a breach wth thire canon, upon our wale y^{t} 20 men of a breast might come in upon it, as many of them as came wthin ye s^{d} breach were cutt off, the rest y^{t} a tacked our paleshades were beaten backe, 2 or 3000 of them Killed wounded, & taken prisonors. I had noe acc^{t} from our ffather, and mother since our rout of Drogheda,[9] but that they stayed att thire owne house att Pluckstowne,[10] and thatt the Enemy proteicted them, and I hope thire goods together wth 3-or, 400 sheep I left wth them and tou years woole, pray send mee a french hate p^{r} first convenency, Bro^{r} Patricke is in good health and is now wth his company towards Athloane,[11] being whatt offers att p^{r}sent onely my Kinde respects to y^{r} mother & sister[.] I hope my litle nephew is in good health, my boy is att our ffathers
I Remayne your loveing Bro^{r} & Sev^{t}
James Missett

[p.s.] I can not have linin here for mony[.] there fore shall depend of y^{w} to send mee p^{r} first convenency tow peeces of Kintine[12] tenn yards of holand[13] 8 ÿards of musline, and a feather sutable for ye hate of what coulour yu thinke fitt, whatt monys y^{w} pay for s^{d} goods, I will pay to y^{r} orders if y^{u} send to this towne[.] y^{w} may direcit y^{r} letter to m^{r} Tho: m^{c}nemara who will order it for mee or if to Galway to cap^{t} Robert ffrench[14]

y^{rs} w^{t} ut supra Ja: M:

[1] James Missett held the rank of lieutenant in the Slane Regiment of the Jacobite army. The Williamite attainders of 1691 include James Missett of Pluckstown, Co. Meath (Gilbert, *Jacobite Narrative*, 231; D'Alton, *Army List*, 2:230).

[2] Andrew Missett (c.1652–1702) was born in Athboy, Co. Meath, and settled in La Rochelle about 1673. Born into a Catholic family owning land in counties Meath and Westmeath, Andrew was atypical among Irishmen who settled in La Rochelle. Most were from mercantile families in Irish coastal towns and cities (such as Waterford, Cork, Limerick, and Galway). Missett integrated quickly into La Rochelle's Irish community and local French society. In 1678, he formed a three-year partnership with Nicholas Lee, son of William Lee of Waterford. Missett's extensive trade included ventures to Ireland, the French West Indies, and Newfoundland (AMLR, GG 353, view 124, and GG 354, view 463; ADC-M, Notaire Teuleron, 3E1367; ADC-M, Notaire Rivière, 3E1811, ff. 53–54v [1694], ff. 21v, 53v–54r, 55 [1695], ff. 171v–172r [1696]; ADC-M, Notaire Rivière, 3E1812, f. 14 [1697], ff. 28, 46 [1699], f. 130 (1700), f. 68r [1701]; ADC-M, B 5693, ff. 189-90; B 5695, ff. 254, 279, 289–90; B 5690, ff. 361, 363). The editors thank Sandrine Tromeur for these references.

[3] For Thomas McNamara, see Letter 42, note 1.

[4] Christopher Gelagh and his wife Mary Williams passed through La Rochelle in November 1691, before settling in Nantes (Alain Le Noac'h and Éamon Ó Cíosáin, *Immigrés irlandais au XVIIe siècle en Bretagne: Nantes, paroisse Saint-Nicolas* [Vannes, 2015], 76–7; AMLR, GG 210, view 19-20). For more on this family in Nantes, see Rilat, *Ces messieurs de Nantes*, 4:147–8.

[5] Carrigafoyle Castle, Co. Kerry, 'is situated at the mouth of the River Shannon, and known as the "Guardian of the Shannon" because of its strategic location overlooking the shipping lanes that supplied the city of Limerick' ('National Monuments Service: Carrigafoyle Castle, Co. Kerry', at https://www.archaeology.ie/monument-of-the-month/archive/carrigafoyle-castle-co-kerry [accessed 5 October 2024]).

[6] Brass money is sometimes (though not in contemporary usage) known as gun money. When issued by James II in 1689–1690, the aggregate value of this copper and copper-alloy coinage stood at roughly £1.5 million. Though widely accepted initially, 'its value was depressed by overproduction, by competition with the silver circulating among French soldiers, and by dwindling confidence in the Jacobite cause' (James Heslip, 'Brass Money', in W. A. Maguire [ed.], *Kings in Conflict: The Revolutionary War in Ireland and Its Aftermath, 1689–1750* [Belfast, 1990], 122–35; Connolly [ed.], *Oxford Companion to Irish History*, 60).

[7] Alexandre de Rainier de Droué, marquis de Boisseleau (1650–1698), was prominent among French soldiers sent to Ireland by Louis XIV to assist James II. Major-General Boisseleau had fought alongside James' Irish army in several actions and was instrumental in the successful defence of Limerick in 1690. When many French and Irish officers abandoned the city that they considered indefensible, Boisseleau – as military governor of Limerick – remained behind, siding with the group led by Patrick Sarsfield who believed the town could be held (Éamonn Ó Ciardha, 'Boisseleau, Alexandre de Rainier de Droué', *DIB* [accessed 25 October 2024]; Childs, *Williamite Wars*, 53–4, 179–80, 244, 246, 255, 258–9).

[8] The regiment of Lord Slane fought in every campaign from Derry in 1689 to the capitulation of Limerick in 1691. Slane's regiment had the distinction of being one of three which, 'with their colours planted before them upon the breach, held Limerick upon that historic occasion when the Williamite stormers were repulsed from its walls' (Diarmuid Murtagh, 'Louth Regiments in the Irish Jacobite Army', *Journal of the County Louth Archaeological Society*, 13:1 [1953], 8). For officers of the 'Régiment de Slane', see Gilbert, *Jacobite Narrative*, 231.

[9] The Battle of the Boyne, 1 July 1690 (12 July 1690, in the reformed calendar).

[10] 'Pluckstown is in the Electoral Division of Grennanstown, in the Civil Parish of Athboy, in the Barony of Lune, in the County of Meath' ('Pluckstown Townland, Co. Meath', at https://www.townlands.ie/meath/lune/athboy/grennanstown/pluckstown/ [accessed 4 October 2024]).

[11] Athlone, Co. Westmeath, is 'a town established on both banks of the River Shannon at a strategic Cross point' (Lalor, *Encyclopedia of Ireland*, 55).

[12] Kentings, a type of fine linen cloth, were not made in Kent, as the name might suggest, but around Saint-Quintin in Picardy (North, *Sweet and Clean?*, 116). Fashionable neckcloths made of 'Kenting thread' (*OED*).

[13] Hollands were linen fabrics 'originally so called, from the province of Holland in the Netherlands' (*OED*).

[14] Captain Robert French, a Catholic merchant-sea captain of modest means, was connected by kinship to a Galway commercial family network with vast international connections. In the mid-1720s, he held public office in Galway, serving as sheriff (L. M. Cullen, 'Galway Merchants in the Outside World, 1650–1800', in Cullen, *Economy, Trade and Irish Merchants*, 165–92; James Hardiman, *History of the Town and County of the Town of Galway, From the Earliest Period to the Present Time* [Galway, 1926], 230, Appendix, xxvii).

8. **John Martin,[1] Limerick, 'To Mr Andrew Gerraldin,[2] Marchantt, In Nantes', 15 September 1690. No. 49**

Limbrik the 15th of september 1690 olde still

Mr Andrew Garaldin and good fferind

Sir

I have by severall fformors written you off my unhappie cuming here to this place by Revolting ways; and how being here imbarqued and affter the time spint to purceed in the voaige designed; did pittition for the salls off the goods here and to Carrie the returns to you[.] affter Long time the Marquiss of Albivill[3] ordered me to sell and tould me I should Carrie the Effects off the goods I did sell; soe I did sell well nigh to the Halfe Lading of the Vessell off greene hids; the seige Comming on hott a guint the Citty and the Marquies being runn out off the Citty; one Captin Christopher pepard off Droahaday[4] the King's store Keper with mr Thomas harald Maior off the Citty[5] came two and thirtye daies since and did ffor warne me to discharge any more goods out of the vessel; and saith the store Keeper that he will take it all att the kings oath and will give goods for it in the kings oath; which I Conceive will not be halfe soo much as I should make off it; how or when hee will Cleare the ship I cannot yett write you[,] but shall by first opertunitie; many a ffierballe have passed over the vessell and some with in six feett off her with small shot in abondance yett it pleased god that non did harme uss; severall of our rops and blocks were taken away ffrom the vessell and I cann have them nevrmore;[6] here is non to be had att any rate[.] god hath bien good unto me in preserving my Life heathere to ffor[.] when I was come to this Land in sight off it[,] 4 of the rogues of the Company had a-greed to take me and the stoure man who is since dead; to have throwne us secreatly in to the sea and to have gonn for the bay of biskie[7] or Galissia[8] and sold the ship & goods but it pleased god that one could not agree thare to[.] soo praised be god am yett preserved having binn much sick and am not well yett; the fevuer and Contrie desease sicness doth take a way many people out off this place; your Kirk is here safe to the Kye her brandy and wine is all taken a shore by mr Rardan;[9] whathar the storkeepr will sease it or no I cannot tell; sr assure your selfe my Indostrie shall not bee wanting to promote your Intrust; I have the thoughts to protest a gainst the Maior and the store keeper; for damages and hindrance[.] Sr I understand by yours to Mr Rearden that my sonn is taken by a Biskine and carried ffor biskie[.] iff it Ly within your Compasse to doe him any favor and supplye[,] I shall god willing bee a Countable with humble thanks to you with my humble service and praiors to god ffor your and ffamilies good health[.] I Crave Leave to Remane;

Sr your much oblaiged Servtt

John Martin

[p.s.] I have written in my formore concerning Insurance; as you see fitt & Convenant

[p.p.s.] Sir[,] The ship not proceeding are now is the 22[d] day of the month since which I alow Must som mischance[.] if this please Reardon what the came against my indoustry for your in trust and I have obtained order and doe stop any greene hids to come out the gate to me I shall in time I trust show you them[.] I have writon to Galaway to ye Marquis[10] for my retourn from this place

[1] By April 1691, John Martin was operating as a merchant in Limerick in partnership with John Rirdan. In July 1691, they sent in the 40-tun *Edmond* of Nantes (John Player, master) to Nantes a cargo of 1373 salt hydes, 96 dry hydes, and '5 Caskes of Tallow' (Limerick customs ledger, April–July 1691, in Archives of the Archbishop of Westminster [London], B6, folder 92, Henry Browne Papers). For the connection of Capt. John Martin and the Rirdans to the *Edmond* of Nantes, see Letter 29.

[2] Following the Restoration of Charles II in 1660, several of the 'banisht merchants of Waterford residing beyond the seas at Nantes, St. Malo, etc. petitioned the Duke of Ormond to be permitted to return to their native country'. Among the petitioners were Lees, Lincolns, Hores, Everards, and Geraldins. During the Williamite War, Andrew Geraldin, merchant of Nantes, faced accusations that he traded with Protestant merchants at Cork (Hayes, 'Irish Associations with Nantes', 119n2; Mulloy, *Franco-Irish Correspondence*, 2:245 #1266). For correspondence between Andrew Geraldin, a merchant in Nantes, and John Aylward of Saint-Malo, see 'Aylward Papers', 4).

[3] The Marquis d'Albeville (Sir Ignatius White) 'was a Limerick man who had been James II's ambassador at the Hague' (Simms, *Jacobite Ireland*, 177n11). He was born at Ballyneety, a village near Limerick where his father, Sir Dominic White, had been mayor in 1636. It was from here that Ignatius White took his title of Albeville (*Baile-an-Fhaoite*, the town of White, in Irish). 'When the Jacobite cause was broken in Ireland, whither d'Albeville had accompanied the king in 1689, he followed his royal master to poverty and exile, forfeiting his estates and dying amid hardships at St Germain-en Laye in 1694' (Richard Hayes, 'Biographical Dictionary of Irishmen in France [Part I]', *Studies: An Irish Quarterly Review*, 31:121 [March 1942], 112).

[4] Drogheda, Co. Louth, a river town on the narrowest tidal point of the River Boyne. The Battle of the Boyne (1 July 1690) was fought a few miles west of Drogheda.

[5] Thomas Harold (or Harrold), mayor of Limerick in 1690, was one of two Limerick City representatives in the Jacobite parliament of 1689 at the time he served as a Limerick alderman. 'After the Jacobite defeats at Aughrim and the Boyne, the Harolds were excluded from civic office because they did not conform to the established church. The Harold family remained Catholic throughout the penal times and extant documents show that they were intermarried and otherwise linked with prominent Catholic and Jacobite families' (Diarmaid Ó Catháin, 'General Baron Edmund Harold (1737–1808): A "Celtic" Writer in Germany', *Studia Hibernica*, 30 [1998/1999], 141).

[6] Damage done to the ship during the bombardment of Limerick.

[7] Read: 'Bay of Biscay'.

[8] Read: 'Galicia [Spain]'.

[9] John Rirdan, merchant in Limerick.

[10] Antonin-Nompar de Caumont (1633–1723), count and duke de Lauzun, also called Marquis de Puyguilhem. Sailing with the French fleet, together with Tyrconnell and the French Brigade

that had served in Ireland, he departed Galway for France on 12 September 1690. For his service in Ireland as commander of French troops in 1690, Lauzun was created duke in 1692 (Childs, *Williamite Wars*, 259; 'Antonin-Nompar de Caumont, count and duke de Lauzun: French military officer', at https://www.britannica.com/biography/Antonin-Nompar-de-Caumont-comte-et-duc-de-Lauzun [accessed 5 October 2024]).

9. Robert Woulfe, Limerick, 'To m^{r} Patrick Rirdan, Merchant In Nantes', 18 September 1690. No. 20

Lymericke 18 7^{ber} 1690

Mr Patrick Rirdan

S^{r}

I had yor two severall advicies & receipt of ye 30 ca^{s} butt^{r} for m^{r} molley's acc^{t}[1][.] I tanke y^{u} for adviseinge of y^{r} markett. ye want of shipps som tymes & stopp on goods att other tymes hinders my sending som thing y^{r} waÿ wch assure to have made of ere ye warr if ever[.] ye enemie after vactinge theire siege from our town marched into ye County of Corcke where they are still[,] the weather being so fayer doe feare they will besiege Corcke[.] pray for ward ye inclosed & tell wee hear p^{r} next ye need full from yor partes[.] all Contrie goods unsur extreamly for brass mony but for silver if a body may Cheaper y^{n} ever, beinge what offers from

S^{r}

yor afectionott friend & hum^{b} Sarv^{t}

Robert Woulfe

[1] James Molley, merchant in Brest (see Letter 6).

10. Francis Rice,[1] Limerick, 'ffor m^{r} James Rice,[2] merchant In Rouen', 20 September 1690. No. 40

Lymericke ye 20th 7^{ber} 1690

S^{r}

I writt you severall tymes since my Comeing for these p^{r}tes & Cann gett noe answer, ye p^{r}sent servies to lett you know y^{t} I am alive after a viholent sidge, though often tymes in danger of my life, butt god bee praised Came of well, I would give you ye partiqulars of ye sidge butt for feare itt may not Come to your hands, & y^{t} I beleive you have itt Eare this, I assure you ye Ireshe behaved them sellves during ye sidge more leike Lyones then men, (wthoutt anny assistant from ye frenche army,) wch I am sure will retrive theire former Crosses if they have Justice don them, for I heere ye Enemy gives them a greate prays, wee are in greatt hopes of retreiveing ye Kingdom next sumer if wee have anny assistance from y^{t} kingdom of amunision wch is muche wanting, wee now begin to fortefie this Cittie againste ye next Campan, as for my owne Conserns

I am lefte nackett[3] for my bookes & all y[t] I had in Dublin are distroyed by y[e] rable soe y[t] I know not whatt to doe[.] I alsoe loste £400[li] in brass mony I had there, as I was leaveing Dublin I tooke a breefe[4] of whatt I owe & whatt is dew to mee w[ch] is all I have of acco[tt][.] in fine I muste have patience seeing it's not my Case alone, y[e] inclos[d] Letter my Lord of slane dessired mee to send you, I supose hee sends to y[u] for some things, I doe not find by him hee send you Effects to by them, nor doe I find hee hasse anny silver to pay y[u] heere, soe accordingly goverin your selfe & keepe this to your selfe, butt deare bro: if you Cann send mee as muche rateene[5] or drugett[6] & as will make mee asute of Close of y[e] fasionable stufes & as much as will make mee halfe a dusein[7] Churtes of fine Lineing of aboutt 24[§] p[r] @ wth a good frenche hatt & apaire of mille stockes youl for Eaver oblidge for I am gott none herare for Love or mony, Vizt[,] therefore I pray deare S[r] doe not disapointe mee for I was neaver in greatter neede of them then now, haveing loste all y[t] I had att Dublin for w[ch] I give god tanks, I doe still Contenew my Employ in y[e] ment in makeing ye brass mony wc[h] is of little vallew heere, my sister Anstase fell sicke of a viholent feavor to y[t] degree y[t] shee was given over by y[e] doctor & y[t] I bespocke her Cofin, & y[t] when y[e] sidge was raised, butt now I thanke god shee is well recoverd & all her Childrin, w[ch] tell her sonn, wth my services to all my frends I remaine

Your hum[ble] Sv[t]

Fran[s] Rice

[p.s.] I heere for sertaine alsoe y[t] m[r] Luke Hores[8] house was Rifeld by ye Enemy in searcheing for a prieste & turind y[e] s[d] hores outt of y[e] house[.] my Lord Desirs mee to writt y[u] to send him a fusille & a Case of pistoles wth a soord for him selfe & y[t] y[e] hoboy[9] & sargent bring wth them all their Instrum[st].

[1] Francis Rice, a merchant and burgess in Dublin, was appointed by James II to serve as a commissioner of the Jacobite mint in Ireland (along with Walter Plunkett and one Mr. Mamby) charged with regulating circulation of brass money (D'Alton, *Army List*, 1:203; Gilbert, *Jacobite Narrative*, 129). For William Bromfield, the man appointed by James II to manage the Irish mint, see Letter 12, note 3.

[2] By the mid-1690s, James Rice (c.1666–1733), trading as a merchant in Rouen during the Williamite War, was established in Lisbon where he corresponded with various Goulds, Creaghs, and others associated with his wartime commerce. Rice was a native of Dingle, Co. Kerry (Giada Pizzoni, *British Catholic Merchants in the Commercial Age, 1670–1714* [Woodbridge, 2020], 133; 'Family Search: James Rice', at https://ancestors.familysearch.org/en/KP4P-KLW/james-rice-1666-1733 [accessed 13 October 2024]).

[3] Read: 'naked'.

[4] 'A short statement or account of something that is, or might be, more fully treated; an abridgement, epitome, abstract, summary' (*OED*).

[5] Rateene (also known as 'ratine' and 'ratteen') was 'a kind of coarse twilled woollen fabric, usually with a (curled) nap' (*OED*).

[6] Druggets are heavy cloths 'of wool, or of a mixture of wool and silk or wool and linen, used chiefly for clothing' (*OED*).

[7] Read: 'dozen'.

[8] Luke Hoare, a Dublin merchant, was the scion of a prominent Waterford trading family. He pursued an extensive commerce in the years following the Restoration and was active in the wine trade to the Canary Islands. Hoare played a role in the restoration of Catholic rights in Ireland during the reign of James II. 'In 1685–6 an association originated in Ireland for the object of obtaining Catholic emancipation; … Gentlemen were appointed and entrusted in every county to collect contributions and pay same to the above Luke Hore, then a merchant in Dublin; and whereas several natives of this kingdom are merchants abroad in foreign parts, their contributions are expected, and requested to be paid to the said Luke, who is to deliver all such moneys as he shall so receive, to agents approved of by the Earl of Tyrconnell. … The Attainders of 1691 name the said Luke as "Lucas Hoare of Wexford"' (D'Alton, *Army List*, 2:574–5).

[9] 'One who plays a hautboy ... a wooden double-reed wind instrument of high pitch, having a compass of about 2½ octaves, forming a treble to the bassoon' (*OED*). In 1685 (and perhaps subsequently) 'Mass was said in the King's Castle Yard and in the Citadel near St. John's Gate, to which the Army marched every Sunday in Order, with Drums and Hautboys' (John Ferrar, *An History of the City of Limerick*, second edition (Limerick, 1767), 40.

11. Slane,[1] Limerick, 'for m^r James Rice merchant In Rouen', 20 September 1690. No. 41

Lymerik September 20th 1690

Mr Rice

I wonder you are so great a stranger, I have not heard from you god knows when. I have no neuse to send you out of these parts[.] things are the same way[.] I am sure you know all the neuse where y^w are[.] as y^w are a man that has being extream obliging to me in every thing I shall desire more favears of y^w[.] at present I doe desire the fav^r of y^w youl be pleased to send me out of france a good honest careffull s^rgeant barber which is a thing I now want much: I alsoe desire the fav^r if y^w youl looke out for four good hoboyes for me to serve my regiment[.] I will give them good sallary half a crowne a day a man — besides five pounds a yeare a man, pray S^r lett me have the choice of them, I am sure y^w can guett them, I shall S^r desire the fav^r if you youl send them to lymerick or gallway by the first conveniency with all hast: — youl be pleased to send the sargeant along with them a good sargeant barber for my use. I desire youl be pleased to give them what y^w thinke will bear their charges hith^r. I shall assoone as y^w please remburse y^w y^r money p^r advice. In doing all this yo^ul very much oblige

S^r

your affectionatt friend and humble serv^t Slane

[p.s.] I herre the best hoboyes are all att Rochelle but youl Leanr bett^r^[.] pray send here ass soone as y^u^ can possible
[p.p.s.] I alsoe S^r^ desire the fav^r^ of you youl send me 2 hundered good fire locks[2] for guns for my regiment and alsoe desire youl be pleased to send me fourteen pound^s^ of sueete pouder[3] and a bottle of essence[4] and half a dozen bottles of queen of hungary watter.[5] all what I send for in this Letter I desire you may direct to y^r^ broth^r^ to Lymerick, I shall be kinder to the hoboyes and sargeant then what I writted to y^w^ off.

[1] Christopher Fleming (1669–1726), 17th Baron Slane, was a Catholic of Irish lineage born and educated in Paris. He sat in the Irish parliament of James II in 1689 and was made a colonel of a Regiment of Foot (1689–91). In July 1691, Slane was taken prisoner at Aughrim and subsequently declared an outlaw, attainted, imprisoned (July–October 1691), and stripped of his title and estates. In February 1691/2, he went abroad to serve as a colonel in the French army and, after 1704, as a major-general in the Portuguese army. About 1706, Fleming returned to England where he conformed to the Church of England. In 1709, his outlawry and attainder were reversed, but he was not restored to his title and estates (Cokayne, *Complete Peerage*, ed. White, vol. 12, part 1, 19–21).

[2] A part of the firearm 'in which sparks are generated to ignite the priming' (*OED*).

[3] 'Perfumed powder used as a cosmetic' (*OED*).

[4] 'A rich sweet wine of an aromatic flavour, made near Tokay in Hungary' (*OED*).

[5] 'A Spirit of Wine fill'd with the more essential part of Rosemary-flowers' (*The New World of Words; or, Universal English Dictionary*, ed. John Kersey, 6th edition (London, 1706), cited in *OED* entry for 'Hungary', noun).

12. **Samuel Taverner, Limerick, 'To Patrick Rirdan, Merchants In Nants', 20 September 1690. No. 3**

Lymericke 7mo 20th 1690

Esteemed ffriend

Since my Last, I have receaved thine of the 10th June and 10th July the first by ye Amity who arived heare In safety, I have Given thee Credit for the one moyety being as p^r^ Invoyce £2245:10:10[.] thy Brother[1] Can informe thee, what markett, ye wine and Brandy Came unto[.] Its in a maner soe much Lost but wee are now soe well acquainted with Losses y^t^ small ones are not to bee Valued, Steephen Harris gave mee Acompt of the 41£ thee suplyed him with wch 98£ to thy Credit and soe shall the 50£ 6^s^ under charged In the peece of mode[.] I noate the hides are Sould wch is to Content[.] I have the Acompt of Sale of the Amitys Cargoe, I observe the providence was taken, wch is my hard fate as is Every thing else, I put my hand to[.] I am sorry thee Ensured Any thing on ye Amity for mee[.] Ensure no thing hearafter without my orders[.] wee shall never See our principall on ye Amitys cargoe, Bowmans[2] mony must Lay at thy doors[.] hee had noe more to doe with it than a stranger and hee knowing soe much was a grand knave, pray write him about it and trye to get it from him[.] I hope I have Credit by this time for Allens mony, pray Let mee know how much It is that I may accordingly setle matters with Dick Allen[.] I am obledged for thy Care about ye dellegence[.] thee knows how Inocent I was in all ye transctions of y^{t} Monstrous knave Reade[.] when the ship Left this place bound for Nants It cost mee about Eightie pound Entrance, hee run away with my ship, hee did what hee pleased acting all things without my orders but following his owne imeigination[.] I have procured the Enclosed from the Secretary of State, If thee finds it will take efect, prosecute it[.] doe for mee as for thy selfe and I will allow of ye charges[.] I have a good friend with the King one Doctor Bromfield[3] who has the Kings Eare Every day[.] hee will sollicite the matter[.] Leave noe stone unturned[.] pay Read noe mony on my Acompt but If thee canst doe him Any kindnes with y^{t} Governm^{t} pray doe it, though hee deserves none[.] my true Love unto thee I Am

Thy very affect fr^{d}

Samuel Taverner

[1] John Rirdan, merchant in Limerick.

[2] For Abraham Bowman, see Letter 33, note 7.

[3] William Bromfield, an English Quaker, 'was a medical man who had followed James II to Ireland because of his goodness to the Quakers, had served him for years in Paris as his secretary, and had suffered imprisonment in the Bastille for conscience' sake' [Dorothy M. Richardson, *The Quakers: Past and Present* [New York, 1914], 54). Bromfield played a leading role in establishing the monetary scheme designed to support James II's war effort in Ireland. 'Some sort of emergency coinage was vitally needed to pay for the army and administration and thus prevent the collapse of the Jacobite war effort'. The recourse to token coinage is attributed to William Bromfield, 'the Man that King James trusted the Management of his Mint to'. On 18 June 1689, the government issued a proclamation 'for remedy of the present scarcity of money, and that our standing forces may be the better paid, and that our subjects of this realm may be the better enabled to pay and discharge the taxes, excise, customs, rents, and other debts and duties, which are or shall be hereafter payable to us'. The scheme called for sixpenny pieces to be minted in copper and brass. Refusal to accept the new coinage was to be 'punished according to the utmost rigour of the law'. (David Stevenson, 'The Irish Emergency Coinages of James II, 1689–1691', *British Numismatic Journal*, XXXVI [1967], 169–70).

13. **Samuel Taverner, Limerick, 'To The Widdow Lee,[1] and Sons Lee[2] and Lucar,[3] Merchants in Nantes', 20 September 1690. No. 43**

Limericke 7^{ber} ye 20th 1690

Esteemed ffriends

Its a Longe time, since I receaved Any of yours, but I Receeved from my Brother Jacob[4] a L^{r} of the 22^{d} June, wherin hee writes mee of your Extraordinary kindnes unto him, wch I acknowldg with all Gratitude, and shall allow of the mony hee writes mee you suplyed him, with on my Acompt, I am sorry for his misfortune as well as my owne, but wee must Expect to bee sometimes Loosers, as well as Gayners[.] trade is a Lotterry: pray remember mee to the poore Unfortunate master, Joseph Reade, and for my sake doe him what kindnes you Can, In procuring his Liberty or releasement, you may suply him with twenty Crownes on my Acompt and If you can helpe him to An Employ: It may bee of mutuall advantage, I never yet had the Acompts of Sales of the Butter In Suggirs or of y[e] other Goods sent you by Harry Cotton, w[ch] pray furnish mee with and remitt y[e] neat ballance of my Acompt unto Richard Haynes,[5] as formerly ordered and send mee my Acompt Currant with my true Love is the needfull at present from

Your Verry Lov friend

Samuel Taverner

[p.s.] about the 18th July Last I drew on you for Eightie Crownes payable at two usance[6] unto francis Poyntz or ord[r] at S[r] Daniel Arthur[7] Value of Coll W[m] Barker[8] unto wch bill pray give due honor, and pass it to my Acompt

[p.p.s.] If you have remitted my efects before y[e] abov bill of ex apeare [document damaged][9] you may draw on franc whyte[10] of S[t] Mallows for s[d] Sum who I have ordred to pay it

[1] Marie Lee [née Geraldin], widow of Nicholas Lee, II (d.1684), was in business with her son, Jean [John] and son-in-law Edouard [Edward] Lucar (Rilat, *Ces messieurs de Nantes*, 4:351–52; Saupin, 'Les réseaux commerciaux des Irlandais de Nantes', 118–26). For Nicholas Lee of Nantes, see also Hancock (ed.), *Letters of William Freeman*, xxviii, 89–92, 107, 112, 115, 157, 170–75.

[2] Jean [John] Lee (b.1667), merchant in Nantes, was the son of Marie Lee [née Geraldin], widow of Nicholas Lee, Sr (d.1684) (Saupin, 'Les réseaux commerciaux des Irlandais de Nantes', 119, 120–21, 124, 127; Rilat, *Ces messieurs de Nantes*, 4:351).

[3] Edouard [Edward] Luker was the son-in-law of Marie Lee [née Geraldin], widow of Nicholas Lee, Sr Luker (d.1725) married Anastase Lee (1674–1741) in September 1688 (Rilat, *Ces messieurs de Nantes*, 4:352, 403; Saupin, 'Les réseaux commerciaux des Irlandais de Nantes', 120–21).

[4] Jacob Taverner (1660–1715) of Limerick was a younger brother of Samuel Taverner, one of the owners of the barque *Amity* ('Jacob Taverner', at https://www.wikitree.com/wiki/Taverner-201 [accessed 12 October 2024]).

[5] Richard Haynes, a Quaker, was among the London merchants who invested in William Penn's American refuge for Quakers, Pennsylvania, at the time of its founding (Mary K. Geiter, 'London Merchants and the Launching of Pennsylvania', *The Pennsylvania Magazine of History and Biography,* 121:1/2 [Jan.–Apr., 1997], 102, 109; Landes, *London Quakers in the Trans-Atlantic World*, 87, 175; O'Shea [ed.], *Letterbook of William Hovell*, 148, 157, 208).

[6] 'A period of time (varying between countries) allowed by commercial custom or law for the payment of short-term foreign bills of exchange'. In the mid-seventeenth century, a month was frequently accepted as the normal usance (*OED*).

[7] Sir Daniel Arthur (c.1620–1705), Irish banker in Paris, was born in Co. Clare or Co. Limerick, the son of a Catholic merchant. 'Arthur was one of a small number of Irish bankers in France' looking 'after

the financial interests of exiled English and Irish Jacobites'. He 'had clients among the Irish merchants settled in Dunkirk, Saint-Malo, Brest, Nantes, and Bordeaux'. Arthur 'maintained links with Ireland, in particular Limerick and Kerry', and recruited his employees in Paris from those parts of Ireland (Priscilla O'Connor, 'Arthur, Sir Daniel', *DIB* [accessed 25 October 2024]). For correspondence between Daniel Arthur in Paris and John Aylward in Saint-Malo, see 'Aylward Papers', 2.

[8] Brigadier Colonel William Mansfield Barker, 'an English gentleman' in the Jacobite army, was killed in July 1691 early in the fighting at Aughrim (Gilbert, *Jacobite Narrative*, 147).

[9] Read: 'bill of exchange appears'.

[10] Francis White, of a family with strong Waterford connections, was well established in the Irish merchant community at Saint-Malo, having married there in 1660 (Richard Hayes, *Old Irish Links with France: Some Echoes of Exiled Ireland* [Dublin, 1940], 194; Martin Murphy, 'Varieties of Irishness in Eighteenth-Century Seville: Wisemans and Whites', in Thomas O'Connor and Mary Ann Lyons [eds.], *Irish Communities in Early Modern Europe* [Dublin, 2006], 312, 314–15).

14. Samuel Taverner, Limerick, 'To Joseph Reade, In Nants', 20 September 1690. No. 50

Limericke 7^{ber} 20th 1690

Cap^{tn} Reade

I have receaved thine of the 16th of June, and am sorry for thy misfortune, but much more for my owne for thy villany has quite ruined mee, thee acteing Every thing after the imagination of thy owne Brayne runing away, with my ship, and Goods, as though I had noe Concerne in Either ye one, or ye other, I wondr what kind of a man didst thee take mee for that woud Endure my ruin and destruction by such a vagabond, as thee art, Is it usual for masters of ships, to breake their owners orders[?] but I was allways An Easy foole wch makes mee now to Smart[.] I have ordred the Widow Lee to Suply thee wth 20 Crownes and doe thee what kindnes shee Can, but to Employe thee, I dare not Encorage her, and for my owne part, If I had 90 ships thee shouldst never put thy foot In Any of y^{m}[.] I have wrote to Patrick Rirdane to see if the ship and goods Can bee regayned, hee will show thee what measures I have taken, bee as assistant as thee Canst, I have desired him to doe y^{u} what kindnes hee Can, I never had a Line from Charles Joanes and know not what thee hast done with my beefe, thee Carryed hence, In short thou hast ruined Thy owld friend

Samuel Taverner

15. Samuel Taverner, Limerick, 'To Francis White, Merchant In St Mallows', 20 September 1690. No. 62

Limericke 7^{ber} ye 20th 1690

Loving friend

my Last was the 7th June Last, Since which I have thine 24th July, advising the arivall of the Prudence Steephen Harris, wch am glad off, the hydes may be

Layd up for an Encoraging market, for wee are In noe hast for their sale, that Comodoty must Considerably advance[.] the owld hydes must bee sould out of hand, for they will not keepe, I doe not question but thee will Consult our Intrest with thy best Endeavours[.] I hope thee hast procured An order for the ship to Come hither, with a Ballast of Sault, Let her come Empty, rather than not at all, for wee much want the ship to Carry of more goods, wee have Another Loading of Sault hydes & tand Leather is not sufferred out of the Kingdome[.] Let noe thing bee sent for my Acompt, but Sault[.] I am oblidged to thee, for thy kindnes to my Brother wch pray continue, and if hee bee there, Suply him as farr as one hundred Crownes on my Acompt, remember mee unto him, to the master, and to Lance Glanvill[1]

with kind respects I remaine Thy assured Lov friend

Samuel Taverner

[p.s.] follow my former orders in remitting the mony[.] if the widow Lee draws on y^u^ for Eightie Crownes suply her therewith on my Acompt, and I will alow it

[1] For Lancellot Glanville, see Letter 16, note 1.

16. **Samuel Taverner, Limerick, 'To Lancellot Glanvill[1] at Franc: Whites,[2] Merchant In St Mallows', 20 September 1690. No. 63**

Limericke 7mo 20th 1690

Lancelot Glanvill

I have receaved thine of the 14th July, by wch I am advised of thy Safe arivall at St Mallows with the Prudence,[3] Steephen Harris ma^r^, wch am glad off[.] I hope franc white hath not sould the hydes[.] they must rise and will bee a great Comodoty, theres noe hast for their sale[.] only the owld ones must bee sould of, for they will not keepe, advise Richard Haynes of Every thing needfull. Bring mee home nothing but Sault bring noe drugs nor Linen, nor Any maner of thing that I gave thee a memoreall of, but ye sault, and if sault will not bee sufferred, Let the ship come away for this port in her ballast[.] Loose noe time but Let her come away with all Expedition, for I Extreamly want her to Carry of more goods, remember my kind Love to Steephen Harris, our family are In health, I Supose the Earle of Lymricke[4] is by this time In france, hee will assist In getting of the shipp If hee bee nere her, I remaine

Thy assured friend

Samuel Taverner

[1] Lancellot Glanville was married into the Blennerhassett family of Co. Kerry, English settlers during

the reign of Queen Elizabeth I. The Blennerhassetts maintained a strong involvement in Irish political life ('The Blennerhassetts of Kerry: Earlier English Stock', *Journal of the Kerry Archaeological and Historical Society*, 5 [1919], 34-39; Mary Agnes Hickson, *Selections from Old Kerry Records, Historical and Genealogical* (London, 1872), 61).

[2] For Francis White, see Letter 13, note 8.

[3] Vessel likely named after Prudence Taverner, Samuel Taverner's wife. See Letters 46 and 48.

[4] William Dongan (1630–1698) 'was closely associated with the attempts of his uncle Richard Talbot, later earl of Tyrconnell, to overturn the acts of settlement and explanation in the later 1660s and early 1670s. Created Viscount Dongan of Clane and 1st earl of Limerick in January 1686, he was appointed to the Irish privy council in May 1686 and became colonel of a regiment of dragoons.' Dongan 'retired to France after the battle of the Boyne and was attainted' in 1691. Following the close of the Williamite War, his estates in Dublin and Carlow, 'amounting to nearly 3,000 acres and consisting of several important houses, rectories, glebes, and tithes', were granted to General Godert de Ginkel, earl of Athlone (Éamonn Ó Ciardha, 'Dongan, William', *DIB* [accessed 25 October 2024]).

17. **Christmas Smith, Limerick, 'To m^r^ Abraham Loyd[1] Merchant In Bristol', 20 September 1690. No. 66**

Lymerik Septem^ber^ ye 20th 1690

S^r^

My Last was from Gallwaye wch wth my ferinds from Traly adviesed my unfortunat captivetie from wch heavens favoring the Importunetie of friends I am redeemed[.] but how, or when to get to ye Indies heavens only can resolve, and here I have not Left one Groat to help mee, Pray hasten over to Bartholemew Nagle[2] att Parrise the three hundred Livers drawn on ye^w^ from Gallwaye and an accp^t^ of what other Effects I have in your hands, pray Loose noe time therein for I beleeve I must buey a Small vessell in ffraunce and therefore pray Get redie for Draft what Effects ye^w^ have belonging to

S^r^[,] Yo: Reale Affecn^t^ ffriend & Servn^t^

Chris Smith

[1] Abraham Lloyd (1655–1726) was a merchant sea captain of Bristol with involvements in Atlantic trade, including the African slave trade. In the early 1680s, he was among the first purchasers of land in the recently established colony of Pennsylvania (Michael D. Bennett, 'Merchant Capital and the Origins of the Barbados Sugar Boom, 1627–1672' [unpublished Ph.D. dissertation, University of Sheffield, 2020], 194; Mary Maples Dunn, et al. [eds.], *The Papers of William Penn* [Philadelphia, 1981–86], 2:661; Charles E. G. Pease, 'Descendants of William Harford', at http://www.pennyghael.org.uk/Harford.pdf [accessed 12 October 2024]).

[2] For Bartholomew Nagle, see Letter 18.

18. **Christmas Smith, Limerick, 'For Mr Bartholomew Nagle,[1] Merchant in Parris In France', 20 September 1690. No. 67**

Lymerick 7bre the 20th 1690

Dr Batt

My Last was from Galloway wth the Copie of the Inclosed and several certifficats and Affidavits to that purpose, all wch by the advice of Sr Pat^{k} Trant and most your friends I sent yo^{u} by Tobe his man that waites on him and Least thay or any of them may miscary shall on your advice send ye^{w} a duplicate of them, I have alsoe p^{r} said Tobe sent ye^{w} in a Second letter wth an Inclosed ord^{r} on my ffriend in Bristoll for 300 Livers wch I now confierm with my second to the same purpose and request If before ye^{w} receip^{t} hereof ye^{w} have not dispatched it, that ye^{w} Imediatly forward Either it or this and with all Expedition return mee his Answer seald under covert of your unkle Harry Trant,[2] for I shall deeme evry week a Munth untill I heare from ye^{w} as well to satisfie mee of my affaires out of Bristoll, as alsoe of what Incoridment[3] your Endeavors with his Majestie may affourd in Goeing to Paris, I know ye^{w} must meet with much diffeculties but fierst consider the Great Wronge, next my one,[4] and many of your one[5] friends Necessetie, Thurdly ye uttor ruine its Lose bring^{s} on mee and my unhapie Credittors. I have alredie communicated the inclosed to the Lord Marques Abyviele,[6] the Lord Rivorston,[7] Sr Patrick Trant[8] and severall of the Nobilletie and thay all adviesed mee to Petticion his Maj^{tie} King James and the King of ffrance and Sr Patrik hath Promised mee to Give ye^{w} both his advice and his Asistance wch aded to your care Gives mee Great hopes of succes and If ye^{w} think a tenth is not sufficient take a fifth wch in Justic can not be les worth then ffive hundred pounds Ster[.] in fine Dr Batt spare noe Importunneitie and I beleeve the Duke Tierconnell and Sr William Ellise[9] may both Give ye^{w} thier helping hand thay haveing heare (as I am credebly Informed) all redie Pitied my abuse and adviesed mee to this methwhood and beleeve shall procure Letters to them and others in my behalfe, I know the adverse argum^{t} wilbe the Princes Pase, and som English Lettors and Counterfitt bills of Lodeing, both wch ye^{w} may Easely answer fierst that there is noe other pase given in those American ports,[10] that there is noe coming to sea wthout one, elce^{e} were as a Pirat to any shipp, in the Sea and soe Endainger Life as well as Estate, that my Condition is noe other then a Loyale Subjects that may now be in Dublin whoo desiering to remoove his shipp from Dublin to ffraunce & Pretends for England and makes Lettors and bills of Lodeing accordingly and by y^{t} means Gets off to Sea and on his voyadges is taken and made Prizes off, but indeed my Perticulor condition is much bettor for my bills of Lodeing and all other Papers wth a Lettor from Mr Gerrett Powell to his Brother Col^{l} Edmond Powell[11] Late Capt of his Majesties Gard and once Governor of Antigua (thogh the times there forst it a dubious one) yet said Lettor and bills of Lodeing sufficiently demonstrat my designe, and Mannefest my Absolute designe, and as to other p[r]sons concerned thogh I know Innocent yet shall Wave thier buisnese (If ye[w] see fitt)[.] I have noe more but with my kind Love and respects once more desier yo[r] care[l] and speedie answer whether my Companie may be needfull for untill I heare from ye[w] noe designe can be undertaken by yo[rs] Whilst

Chris Smith

D[r] Batt

[p.s.] My bills of Lodeing & Coll[e] Powells Letter I saw delivered Admirall ffouraings Purssor by said Admirall.

[1] For the connection between Bartholomew Nagle and Co. Kerry, see Brady, *M[c]Gillycuddy Papers*, 130.

[2] For Henry Trant, see Letter 3, n. 2.

[3] Read: 'Encouragement'.

[4] Read: 'own'.

[5] Read: 'own'.

[6] For the Marquis d'Albeville (Sir Ignatius White), see Letter 8, note 3.

[7] For Baron Nugent of Riverston (Thomas Nugent), see Letter 2, note 6.

[8] For Sir Patrick Trant, see Letter 3, note 5.

[9] Sir William Ellis served as a secretary to the Earl of Tyrconnell, and in December 1690 was appointed a commissioner of the treasury. Following Tyrconnell's departure for France in 1690, Ellis was absorbed into the Jacobite household entourage at Saint-Germain-en-Laye (Childs, *Williamite Wars*, 9; J. G. Simms, *The Jacobite Parliament of 1689* [Dublin, 1974], 6; Eoin Kinsella, *Survival in Protestant Ireland, 1660–1711: Colonel John Browne, Landownership and the Articles of Limerick* [Woodbridge, 2018], 38n103; Edwin and Marion Sharp Grew, *The English Court in Exile: James II at Saint-Germain* [London, 1911], 269).

[10] In 1689, there was considerable uncertainty in the English ports of North America and the West Indies as to the legitimacy of Jacobite or Williamite authority extended across the Atlantic (Richard S. Dunn, *Sugar and Slaves: The Rise of the Planter Class in the English West Indies, 1624–1713* [Chapel Hill, NC, 1972], 134–35, 232–37).

[11] Col. Edward Powell served as lieutenant-governor of Antigua under James II (1683–1688). At the outbreak of the 'Glorious Revolution', his plantations on Antigua were seized following a coup by supporters of William III. A document dated 'Whitehall 14 May 1691' declared Powell to be 'now a rebel in Ireland in 1691' (Vere Langford Oliver, *The History of the Island of Antigua, One of the Leeward Islands in the West Indies, from the First Settlement in 1635 to the Present Time*, 3 vols. [London, 1896], 1:111–112; 2:5, 125, 229; 3:33, 303, 320, 356, 401).

19. Robert Hannan,[1] Limerick, 'To mr John Degrave,[2] Merchant In London', 23 September 1690. No. 39

Lymerick, 23 September 1690

Sr

I have none of yors to answer, I hope this will finde you as well as I really wish — pray lett me know where the Hopewell arived & if youl consent to what mr James Rice or I writt you in order to loade her, please to advise how Tallow, English hops, madr[3], allom[4] & Coperas[5] accts wth you at. Irish peace & quietness every where, wee were besidged here for 21d by the Prince of orange & his army who raised ye seidge to loss of abundance of their lives I am

Your most humble sert

Robert Hannan

[p.s.] we have heare plenty of all things I thank God[.] my humble service to mr John Carwyn[6] telling him that his friends here are all well — pray lett me know how he doth in his health — write to mr Lefebve to Dublin & He'l forward it me if yu be pleased that ye Hopewell should remaine att Lixbone[7] on my actt[.] I shall rest contented so as she be — tis found beggarly mr James Rice Fras of Rouen goeing thither.

[1] Robert Hannan, a prominent Limerick merchant and ardent Catholic, served as mayor of Limerick in 1687 and 1688. In June 1688, on the occasion of the birth of the son of James II (James Francis Edward Stuart), Mayor Hannan 'made great rejoicings, and let three hogsheads of wine run among the populace' (John Ferrar, *An History of the City of Limerick* [Limerick, 1767], 138; Lenihan, *Limerick*, 211).

[2] John Degrave, an exiled French Huguenot, set up as a merchant in Pancras Lane, London, and held a minor office regulating activity in the port. During the War of the Spanish Succession, Degrave invested in at least six privateers licensed to seize trading vessels of 'France and other Enemies' (David C. A. Agnew, *Protestant Exiles from France in the Reign of Louis XIV*, 2nd edition (Edinburgh, 1871), 43; London Metropolitan Archives, City of London, MS. A/CSC/635; TNA, HCA 26/17/46, HCA 26/14/45, HCA 26/17/115, HCA 26/3/140, HCA 26/3/134, HCA 26/13/7; 'Jean de Coninck's Last Will and Testament, dated London, 8 May 1690' at 'http://www.crommelin.org/history/Biographies/Frederic/JeanDeConinck/JeanDeConinckWill.htm [accessed 5 October 2024]).

[3] Read: 'madder', a plant 'formerly much cultivated, esp. in France and the Netherlands, for the reddish-purple dye obtained from the root' (*OED*).

[4] Read: 'alum'. 'An astringent mineral salt, typically occurring as colourless or whitish crystals, that is used as a mordant for dyeing, in tanning, for sizing paper and fireproofing materials, in water purification, and in medicine' (*OED*).

[5] Read: 'copperas'. 'A name given from early times to the protosulphates of copper, iron, and zinc (distinguished as *blue*, *green*, and *white* copperas respectively) ... used in dyeing, tanning, and making ink' (*OED*).

[6] For John Kirwan, see Letter 59, note 4.

[7] In the late 17th century, there was a small but vibrant enclave of Irish merchants in Lisbon who enjoyed special privileges based on a shared sectarian identity. There were, wrote one observer,

'several Irish Merchants & Factors, Roman Catholicks, who live here & enjoy his Majesty's protection & the samc privileges wth his other subjects'. Contacts between Ireland and Portugal had a long history, 'facilitated by the ease of maritime access' (Godfrey Fisher, 'A Short History of the British Factory House in Lisbon', in *Annual Report of the British Historical Society of Portugal*, 10 [1946], 11; Andrew Shepherd, 'The O'Neills of Portugal', *British Historical Society of Portugal Newsletter*, 9 [December 2020], 2).

20. Samuel Taverner, Thomas Pearce,[1] & Zachary Holland,[2] Limerick, orders to Capt. John Mitchell,[3] present, 24 September 1690. No. 2

Limbrick 7[ber] y[e] 24th 1690

John Michell

We order thee to goe on board the Amity and take charge of her as Master and with y[e] ffirst faire wind make y[e] best of thy way for Nants or Rachell, if to Nants deliver our Goods unto Patrick Ryrdane, and at Rochell to John and Edmond Gould[4] and receive into the shipp such goods as hee, or they will load on her, and make the best of thy way for this place, urge them to all imaginable dispatch that thee may be here by the very first opportunity[.] keep thy men in order[.] wishing thee a safe voyage and returne wee remaine

Thy Assured ffreinds

Samuel Tavernir
Tho[s]. Pearce
Zachary Holland

[p.s.] When thee arrives att ffrance forward all the letters as directed[.] if thee gets to Nants thee needs not send my letter to Gould of Rochell, and if thee gets to Rochell, thee needs not send my letter thats unsealed to Ryrdane, but the sealed letter send him

Samuel Tavernir

[p.p.s.] sell my mothers[5] caske of butter for the most it will yeeld and lay out the Produce in Kentings one peece very fine, and the rest more ordenary, and some Pinns

[1] Thomas Pearce, a merchant and apothecary, was prominent in the leadership of Limerick's Quaker community. During the siege, when soldiers occupied Limerick's Quaker Meeting House, Friends met at the home of Thomas Pearce and his father, Richard Pearce, a physician and apothecary (Olive C. Goodbody [ed.], *Guide to Irish Quaker Records, 1654–1860* [Dublin, 1967], 46, 147; Emily E. Moore, *Traveling with Thomas Story: The Life and Travels of an Eighteenth-Century Quaker* [Letchworth, 1947], 48–9; Thomas Wight and John Rutty, *A History of the Rise and Progress of the People Called Quakers in Ireland, From the Year 1653 to 1700 ... Now Revised and Enlarged. To Which is Added, a Continuation ... to ... 1751* [Dublin, 1751], 97; Richard L. Greaves, *Dublin's Merchant Quaker: Anthony Sharp and the Community of Friends, 1643–1707* [Stanford, CA, 1998], 125).

[2] Zachary Holland, merchant, was a burgess of Limerick in 1688 (Lenihan, *Limerick*, 272).

[3] By his own deposition, John Mitchell was born in Kinsale but resided in Galway, and was a Protestant (TNA, HCA 32/1851/19).

[4] For John and Edmund Gould, see Letter 32, note 1.

[5] Susanna (Chadwick) Taverner (b. c. 1629), the mother of Samuel Taverner, was born in Tattershall, Lincolnshire. She and her husband, Edward Taverner (1623–1685), a native of Folkingham, Lincolnshire, were the parents of 12 children. Dedicated members of the Society of Friends, the couple arrived in Ireland in May 1653, living in Counties Cork and Tipperary before settling in Limerick ('Susanna (Chadwick) Taverner [abt. 1629]', at https://www.wikitree.com/wiki/Chadwick-3202; 'Edward Taverner [1623–1685]', at https://www.wikitree.com/wiki/Taverner-196 [accessed 22 November 2024]).

21. Samuel Taverner, Thomas Pearce, & Zachary Holland, Limerick, to Capt. John Mitchell, present, 24 September 1690. No. 76[1]

Lymericke 7ber ye 24th 1690

John Mitchell

wee order thee to Goe on board the Amity and take charge of her, as master and with the first fayre wind make the best of thy way for Nants, or Rochell[.] If tis Nants deliver our Goods unto Patricke Ryrdane, and at Rochell to John & Edmond Gould and Receave Into the Ship Such goods as, hee or they will Load on her, and make the best of thy way for this place[.] urge them to all imaginable dispatch, that thee may bee heare by the verry first opertunity[.] keepe thy men In order[.] wishing thee a safe voyage, and returne[,] wee remaine

Thy assured friends

Samuel Taverner
Tho: Pearce
Zachary Holland

[p.s.] when thee arrives at france forward all the Letters as directed[.] If thee getts to Nants thee needs not Send my Letter to Gould of Rochell, and if thee gets to Rochell, thee needs not send my Letter thats Unsealed to Ryrdane, but ye Sealed Letter Send him

Samuel Taverner

[p.p.s.] Sell my mothers caskue of Butter for ye most it will yeeld, and Lay out ye produce In Kentings one peece verry fine, and ye rest more ordenarie and some pinns

[1] This document is a near-exact copy of No. 20.

22. **Zachary Holland, Limerick, 'To Mr Patricke Rirdan, Merchant In Nants', 24 September 1690. No. 5; bill of lading, 25 September 1690. No. 8**

Limericke the 24th Sep^tr^ 1690

Mr Patrick Rirdan

S^r^

This goes by the Amity John Michell Master[.] in s^d^ ship I am concernd a forth[.] one board here I have shiped 198 hyds in Companie wth Ald Sam: Taverner and Tho Pearse, 246 salt hyds in Companie wth Tho Parse, and the 9 of 20 kask^s^ of tallow in Companie wth Samuel Taverner 42 terces of salmon in Companie wth s^d^ Taverner and Parse, thay are choyse goods, I doe not question but thay will come to a good market, my Ord^r^ is that when you disposse of them that it be for redy monie, If it be C^r^ shall to give^s^ 9 months[,] give the same man allowance to pay redy monie, for I am not willing to deale otherwise[.][1] when you have soe done after you have shiped my forth of s^d^ ship wth shuch goods as Mr Tavernor Ord^s^ my desire is that you will remit the produce or give Liberty to drawe one you to my ffrenids Mr Tho & Jos Carpenter[2] in Ald Buris[3] London, this is the first that I have trobled you w^th^ & hope it will Incouradge our farther corypondencis, I doe not doubt y^r^ Interest therefore I will not press you, pray be shure if you remit tacke care the bills be good, As the Or^s^ of Tho Parse and my selfe that twelve hundr^d^ Linen be Inshured here and Back to Bordex Nants or Rochel, as sonne as possible lett me have ye amon^t^ of the saile of this, If one anny occation I can sarve you freely disposse of him who is
y^or^ Moste Humble Ser^t^

Zach Holland

[p.s.] the goods I have on Board is ye 3 of 20 hh^ds^ of tallow[,] 12 barels of Salmon[,] 189 salt hyds

BILL OF LADING

Shipped by the Grace of God in good order and well conditioned, by *Samuel Taverner Zacharie Holland, and Thomas Pearce* in and upon the good Ship called the *Amitie of Limericke* whereof is Master under God for this present Voyage *John Michell* and now riding at Anchor in the *Pool of Lym^r^*, and by Gods grace bound for *Nants, or Rochell, or Bordeaux* to say *four hundred fifty six sault hydes*[,] *fiftie one dry hydes*[,] *fourtie two teirses of salmon fish, and twentie hogsheads of tallow* being marked and numbered as in the margin, and are to be delivered in the like good order and well conditioned, at the Port of *Nants, Rochel, of Bordaux* (the danger of the seas only excepted) unto *Patrick Rirdan of Nants or John & Edmond Gould of Rochell* or to *their* Assigns, he or they paying freight for the said Goods *nothing* with Primage and Avarage accustomed. And witness where of the master or purser of the said ship have affirmed to *three* Bills of Lading all of this tenor and date; the one of which *three* Bills being accomplished, the other *two* to stand void. And so God send the good Ship to her desired port and safety Amen. Dated in *Lym^r^ September ye 25th 1690.* [signed] *John Mitchell*

1 Ordinary commercial credit took the form of book debt, the usance of a bill of exchange (that is, the period of time, usually stated as a number of days, allowed for payment), and promissory notes. These covered most xports sold on credit. The largest share was recorded as book debt. Interest charges – capped at 6 per cent until 1714 – were included in invoiced prices. If the buyer paid prior to shipment, he obtained a rebate for early payment. If he made payment after the goods had been shipped, but before the expiration of 12 months, the rebate was proportional. In case of late payment, the importer agreed to pay interest on the unpaid balance. Such arrangements, of course, worked best when the two parties had a relationship based on trust (Julian Hoppit, 'Attitudes to Credit in Britain, 1680–1790', *Historical Journal*, 33:2 [June 1990], 312; T. S. Ashton, *Economic Fluctuations in England, 1700–1800* [Oxford, 1959], 86–8; John Smail, 'Credit, Risk, and Honor in Eighteenth-Century Commerce', *Journal of British Studies*, 44:3 [July 2005], 439–56. For 'usance', see Letter 13, note 6.

2 Thomas and Joseph Carpenter were Quaker merchants doing business at Blackamore's Head, Aldermanbury, London.

3 Read: 'Aldermanbury, London'.

23. **Zachary Holland 'To Mr Tho & Joseph Carpentter, at the Blackamores head In Alderman burr^e^, London', [?] September 1690. No. 71**

Limericke y^e^ [left blank]^th^ Sep^t^ 1690

Mr Tho & Jos Carpenter

I have not herd from you since yo^rs^ of the 21th Feby wth Copia[1] of two of the 9th & 30th Jan^y^, I had not had that, I presume but that it related to m^r^ Bodkins afaires, I wrote you by severall wayes, but had not the hapyness of a line before, it was very welcome to me, to here of y^r^ affaires[.] m^r^ James Langly had no Ord^s^ to pay me, & I hope my debt of £50 from m^r^ Rawlinsen will not depend one[2] Langly, I presume when times are settled, I shall have the monie of him, if not of others, in the meane time I desire no ordrs to receive monie here, you gave me some hopes of the Recovery of the Butter one[3] Board the Jamie[4] I should gladly here the cartinty, had it gone safe it had bene a considerable sume, by what I can here W^m^ ffaxson prevented it, I hope to live to see him and know the cartinty thereof, I was much concerned to know that m^r^ Abra^m^ Elton[5] had not remited y^r^ £100 & hope before now he has, I admire he should write you he could not, he being not in cash, I sent him before the trobles began five tones of tallow[.] my Ord^s^ was that he should not disposse of it under 40 p^r tn^ redy monie[.] by severall hands I understand it was at 45 p^r tn^. If it should soe hapin that its now unsold & not worth that rate, I leave it to you to doe as you think good, when this comes to y[r] hands, if you have not receved the £100 from him, let him know that you have occation to disposse of s[d] sume for me, I would willingly, what litle I have [unintelligible word] shoud be in your hands, these times has proved advantagus to shop keepers and others butt the contrary to me, Tho Perse and I bult a small barke of 15 tones and lade[d] in Companie wth him 442 salt Hyds for Ostend[6] concined[7] to one Motloe[8] march[t], the Produce to b[e] dispossed by Tho Hanson[9] who gave great assurance that he would retorne backe here, w[ch] if he had it would have bene of considerable advantage to us and him, and by w[ch] wee might had the liberty of landing more goods, he was but in a meane condition but very Ingenious, by what he caried, one[10] his retorne he might have bene a considerable gainor, pray one receipt hereof Inquire ernestly for th[os] sparke[.] I here he is in England and his wife is gone to him, by w[ch] I finde he has some ill desine to goe to the west Indies, pray if you can find him secure him until you can get the produce of 442 hyds and his Barke[.] m[r] scrivin[11] I belive will asist you in this[.] I know I need not press you to be ernest where my Interst is, the chifest Ocation is to aquaint you that I have shiped one board the Amity of Limerik Burdon 36 tone John Michel master for Nants to m[r] Patricke Rirdan[.] if to anny other port, to who the master thinks fit, 198 hyds 12 terces of Samon and some other goods the produce thereof, I have or[d] to be remitted to you, I have or[d] that if you can draw on him, better then he can remit, to Except your bills wth ord for the best [indecipherable], god be praised I am in helth soe is moste of y[r] quaintance here, I should gladly here from you p[r] s[d] Ship[.] the master will write to you one his Arrival[.] forward the Inclossed to my Bro:[12][.] Rember me to my ffrinds Esspecially to m[r] Damier[.] let him know I have not anny of his efects[.] It was p[d] as he knowes I belive it ord[s] him longe since I like to forget my true freind m[r] Tho Mrygrane who with the rest I Longe to see, at present I will not Inlarge but tacke leave and rest for once yo[r] most Humble Serv[t]

Zach Holland

[p.s.] I could be very well satisfied if W[m] fflaxson had come or could yett tho it were but wth the produce of halfe his cargo in smocke would produce more 1000 pounds of our gaine there I will mention yet[.] I am not for Incoradgeing anny other desine

[1] Read: 'Copies'.

[2] Read: 'on'.

[3] Read: 'on'.

[4] Vessel mentioned in Letter 73.

[5] Abraham Elton (1654–1728) was an English merchant, entrepreneur, and politician. 'A Dissenter of humble origin, … Elton became one of the great commercial magnates of Bristol, "a pioneer of its brass foundries and iron foundries, and ... owner of its principal weaving industry, as well

as of its glass and pottery works, besides largely contributing to the shipping of the port."' Elton 'was created a baronet in 1717 in reward for his services in the rebellion of 1715. He sat as a Whig [MP] for his native city from 1722 to 1727'. At his death, Elton left 'a fortune estimated at £100,000' (Shirley Matthews, 'Elton, Sir Abraham, 1st Bt. [1654–1728]', *History of Parliament* online edition [2011], at http://www.histparl.ac.uk/volume/1715-1754/member/elton-sir-abraham-1654-1728 [accessed 5 October 2024]).

6 For the Irish trading community at Ostend, see Jan Parmentier, 'The Irish Connection: The Irish Merchant Community in Ostend and Bruges during the Late Seventeenth and Eighteenth Centuries', *Eighteenth-Century Ireland / Iris an dá chultúr*, 20 (2005), 31–54.

7 Read: 'consigned'.

8 In the early 1680s, Robert Mutloe, a Londoner, became heavily involved with William Goold and other Irish merchants in Ostend prosecuting their trade with Ireland in 'wet' hides to tanners in Antwerp and Brussels. By 1684, Mutloe was resident in Ostend where he traded on his own account and as a partner in the firm Galwey & Mutloe. In 1722, Mutloe was appointed British consul at Ostend (Parmentier, 'Irish Connection', 35; O'Shea [ed.], *Letterbook of William Hovell*, 136, 139–40, 165, 181, 192–3, 203, 228, 262, 265, 268; *The Historical Register, Containing an Impartial Relation of All Transactions, Foreign and Domestick. ... For the Year 1722* [London, 1723], 31).

9 Capt. Thomas Hanson was a London shipmaster in the 1690s (TNA, ADM 106/482/47).

10 Read: 'on'.

11 Joseph Scriven, a linen draper in Watling Street, London, was a kinsman of Thomas Pearce.

12 For Joseph Holland, merchant in Minehead, see Letter 50.

24. **Zachary Holland, Limerick, to unknown, n.d. [Damaged document]. No. 79**

Sir

By the Recomondacion of Severall frenids [reminder of line damaged]
wth 246 hyds in Companie wth m^r^ Tho [damaged]
in Compani^e^ wth Al^d^ Samuel Tavernor, Tho [Pearce] [damaged]
benig 188 thay are choyse allsoe [damaged]
of 20 caske of tallow in Compani^e^ [damaged]
not but will come to a good market [damaged]
to be farther concerned, I doubt not [damaged]
will not press farther only that its [damaged]
it may be for redy monie, If to be [damaged]
to the same parson you deale wth for [damaged]
of debts, my desire alsoe is after [damaged]
p^d^ the charge and lade my part of [damaged]
my frends in London m^rs^ Thos & Jos [damaged]
Perse and Al^d^ Tavernor will give you [damaged]
the mester is one John Michel I think [damaged]
some as you can, If you find that [damaged]
one you, then you can remit [damaged]
pray be careful to get good bills [damaged]

in those parts pray freely [damaged]
At the Ord of Tho Perse & my self [damaged]
to Inshure hither and Backe [damaged]
Rochel or Bordox [word scratched out] twelve [damaged]
Linens

Za Holland

25. **Thomas Pearce, Limerick, 'To Patrick Rirdan, Marchant In Nants', 24 September 1690. No. 6**

Limerick ye 24th 7^{ber} 1690

Lo: ffriends

This goes per ye Amity John Mitchell m^{r} who brought in here a parcell of excelent wine & brandy[1] but in such an ill time as will n^{t} be much to our advantage[.] I feare great part being seazed on by ye Army dureing ye siege for bras mony & at a low rate[.] how ever we venterd a point & are in good hopes upon ye whole we shall n^{t} be loosers how much gainers is hard to guess at presant ye barrer can somew^{t} inlarge on this point therefore I shall forbare – in thine of ye 10th July thee desires my advise w^{t} to do wth Depareer Gouet[2] about ye mony due from him wch is hard for me to do at this distance & truely I cannot but blame thee after my advise not to sell but for ready mony or if y^{t} could n^{t} be for to allow discount y^{t} it might be ready n^{t} y^{t} I would allow discount & hazard to, y^{t} his [sic] hard, my minde was then n^{t} for trusting as it is now, & if I allow discount it should be to ye person y^{t} owed ye mony for presant pay or at least to such an one as would take ye debt to himselfe for payment, this I think is just & plain[.] however I will n^{t} be obstinate in my own cause untill thy answer be given[.] in ye mean time I question n^{t} but thee will do ye needfull to secure y^{t} debt to ye least loss & I shall be very well satisfyed wth what is reasonable — herewith now I send on my propper acc^{o} eighteen teirces of salmon fish, fifty one large dry hydes, ye third part of 198 salt hydes in company wth Sa. Taverner & Zachary Holland, & ye halfe of 246 salt hydes in company wth Zach Holland ye m^{r} will distinguish them a sunder[.] they are very good & large wherefore I hope will sell well — pray trust n^{t} this conscerne but invest it into mony & ye same after receaving as much as will load my fourth part of ship as Samuel Taverner orders & discharging my proportion of expences remite unto my kinsman Joseph Scrivner linnen draper in Watling street London or otherwise advise him how much he may draw on thee for wch is as well, if thee remits [word obscured] take care y^{t} ye bills be good for y^{t} I have lost these times trusting some y^{t} have much wronged themselves as well as me — if any letter from Robt Mutloe or Tho: ffloxon comes to thy hands for me open them & if necessary let thy servant coppy them y^{t} if ye originall should miscary ye coppy might come safe[.] Zach Holland & my selfe sent s^{d} ffloxon for Ostend in Aprill last wth a smale barke of about 15 tuns wth salt hydes &c^{t} but no acc^{o} of him since only we heare he is where he should n^{t} be wch is our loss y^{t} men will not be true to their own interests; I desire y^{t} 100^{li} sterling be insured on Zach Hollands & my part of ye ship hither & back to Nants Rochell or Burdoaux ~~its his desire~~ placeing one halfe of ye insurance to his acc^{o} the other mine[.] its his desire it should be so as well as ye request of thy Lo: ffriend

Tho: Pearce

[p.s.] pray send a breviat[3] w^{t} is remitted Joseph Scriven & how acc^{o} stands, I hope ye beefe & skins are sold y^{t} I may know w^{t} I am to make good to Br^{o} Taverner for my part of Amity, will give me great content to have short acc^{os} y^{t} we may begin anew ye quicker ye better whether proffit or loss, my father allso would know how his acc^{o} is T.P.

[1] The *Amity* arrived at Limerick from Nantes in early July 1690. See Letter 49.

[2] Depareer Gouet, a French artillery officer, was aboard the transport *La Badine* that departed Galway for France in August 1690 (Mulloy, *Franco-Irish Correspondence*, 2:120 #1059).

[3] A breviat or breviate is 'a short account, brief statement; a summary, abridgement, compendium' (*OED*).

26. **William Dorrington,[1] Limerick, to 'Monsieur Wauchope,[2] Brigadier des Armie du Roy de D'anglete A St Jarmin en Laye', 24 September 1690. No. 10**

Lymericke 7^{ber} the 24th 1690

Deare Wacoppe,

A litle vessell being to set sayle tomorrow from heare for france, I could not omitte sending you these fewe lynes to let you know, hae wee are after the old vale,[3] as to order, and generalls: ten days agoe it was thought fitt to passe the revere Shannon to take ye Castle of Bur[4] wch Castle would certainely have surender'd if two hundred dragoones had gon a weeke before to it[.] but our horse foot and Dragoones haveing layne by ye Reversyde for ten days before wch had Alarmm'd them to y^{t}, they were reinforced & a counsiderable body wth Kirke[5] gott to rosgrea[6] but seven miles of them movd towards theire releife, wch movement incouridged them to hould out tho wee had four pices of Cannon playeing against a papper house y^{t} a two pounder would pierce the house, yet wee had two twelve pounders wth us, but our gunners could not hitte the house as is sayd and being a frayd of Kirke, wee raysd our seige at twelve a Clocke at night, and at the same time Kirke was so a frayd y^{t} he did the same retyreing backe in all the confussion Imaginable, as a party of ours Informed us wch had met thirty dragoons of the enemys and kild most of them bringing ye Lui^{t} prisnor wth four dragoons; upon wch account our people had thoughts of advanceing towards Kirke, but y[e] night before the design'd march, he came towards us; and as wee were informd Douglas[7] joy'nd wth him, so y[t] they were reported to be 8 or 9000 men, upon w[ch] wee return'd a this syd of y[e] Rever. I had yester-day an expresse from Corke of 8000 English being landed neare Corke, and Mons[r] Gentlea[8] is march'd wth all the forces he could possibly w[ch] is all y[e] strangers to Joyne them; so Its Impossible for us to hould out long, for in the world there can scarcely be a worse place, and I doe not find wee shall, or indeed can well releive them; for tho its of y[e] greatest consiquence in the world to us; it will be very difficult; for as to the foot you know they have neither armes, shewes, stockins, tents, or can have bread &c., as to yo[r] wooll I beleive it will turn to litle account; for as yo[r] Brother[9] tells mee w[t] was on the Batterrys Barker[10] pretends to it; and the rest is very litle; and as to mine tho my Lord tryconill confirm'd it to mee; I know not y[t] I shall make any thing of it, besydes w[ch], it is so litle y[t] its hardly worth the while; but I hope I shall get some wine and linen for it: now to tell you the truth my opinion is y[t] neither you nor Barker has any right to it y[t] is to saye by waye of right, for if you had as governour, or he as Comanding the ordinance you mought on y[t] pretence have braught betwixt you all the wooll, hempe, flax, towe, or Blanketts in the towne; w[ch] was not the same in mee; now when all this is don I wish both of you had twinty times as much on y[t] condition I had not an ounce; and upon my soul I never sayd to any one any thing of w[t] I saye to you now, tho I will to morrow to Barker[.] I came hither y[e] day before yester-day where I find nothing don to y[e] workes as yet, and our good weather will soon be gon, so y[t] I feare wee shall never mend: my most hum[ble] serveis to my Lord Mount-Cashell[11] I pray and y[e] rest of my friends as Stafford,[12] Beddolph,[13] and my L[d] Chancelor[14] &c.

I am wth greate truth
Yo[r] most ffaithfull & hum[ble] Servant

W. Dorrington

[1] In 1688, the Royal Irish Foot Guards under William Dorrington (d. 1719), an Englishman, remained loyal to James II. Dorrington fought on the Jacobite side in the Williamite War, distinguishing himself at the Boyne. On 6 September 1690, he was appointed governor of Limerick and promoted to major-general following Boisseleau's departure for France. Dorrington was taken prisoner at Aughrim and subsequently incarcerated at Chester, in Dublin Castle, and in the Tower of London. Following the 1691 Treaty of Limerick, he entered French service as a colonel in an Irish regiment, the Royal Irish Foot Guards. After the 1697 Peace of Ryswick and the disestablishment of James' army in exile, the Foot Guards were reconstituted in French service as Dorrington's Regiment (D'Alton, *Army List,* 1:39, 2:11, 784; Childs, *Williamite Wars*, 258–9; Éamonn Ó Ciardha, *Ireland and the Jacobite Cause, 1685–1766: A Fatal Attachment* [Dublin, 2002], 251; Gilbert, *Jacobite Narrative*, 113, 117; Wauchope, *Patrick Sarsfield*, 166, 194–5n, 301; John Cornelius O'Callaghan, *History of the Irish Brigades in the Service of France* [Glasgow, 1885], 75, 88–90).

[2] Major-General John Wauchope (d.1694) was a Scottish Catholic and a prominent figure in the Jacobite army in Ireland. Foll owing the defeat at the Boyne, Wauchope may have been instrumental in ordering the scattered and depleted Jacobite forces to gather at Limerick. He was a staunch

supporter of Patrick Sarsfield, and strongly resisted capitulation to the Williamites at the second siege of Limerick in 1691 before, along with Sarsfield, accepting the inevitable in early October (Simms, *Jacobite Ireland*, 155; Childs, *Williamite Wars*, 380, 383–4, 388; Paterson, *History and Genealogy*, 36–7).

[3] 'old vale' – 'a place of trouble, sorrow, misery, or weeping' (*OED*).

[4] After the lifting of the first siege of Limerick, the Jacobites re-crossed the Shannon and attempted to capture Birr Castle, a potential strong point in a campaign to recover ground lost after the Battle of the Boyne. '[On 15 September 1690], major-general Sarsfield, being desirous to get some quarters in Leinster, went with a party [of 5,000 to 7,000 men and three guns under the Duke of Berwick], over the bridge at Banagher, to besiege the castle of Birr in the King's county [present-day Co. Offaly], garrisoned by a company of Colonel Tiffin's regiment; but major-general Kirke, coming with a greater force to relieve the place, [Berwick and Sarsfield were] obliged to march off' (Gilbert, *Jacobite Narrative,* 118; Childs, *Williamite Wars*, 263).

[5] Major-General Percy Kirke (d. 1691), a high-ranking officer in the army of William III, took part in the unsuccessful siege of Limerick in August 1690 in which he directed fighting that led to the outlying forts being captured by Williamite troops. In the action at Birr Castle a few weeks later in mid-September 1690, 'news that Kirke and [Colonel Sir John] Lanier were approaching with a large force, plus the unexpectedly fierce resistance of the garrison, caused Berwick [on 17 September] to order Sarsfield to suspend the attack and withdraw to a campsite 5 km west of Birr, covering the line of retreat to Banagher Bridge' (Piers Wauchope, 'Kirke, Percy [d.1691]', *ODNB* [accessed 25 October 2024]; Childs, *Williamite Wars*, 264).

[6] Roscrea (Co. Tipperary). Fearing that he commanded an insufficient force to defeat the retreating Jacobite troops after their failure to seize Birr Castle under Berwick and Sarsfield, Williamite Major-General Kirke called for reinforcements to strengthen Roscrea. But caution and delays allowed Berwick and Sarsfield to re-cross the Shannon on 19 September (Childs, *Williamite Wars*, 264).

[7] General James Douglas (1645–1691) was the first Scottish officer to abandon James II in favor of William III in 1688. Douglas commanded the Williamites' unsuccessful assault on the breach in the walls of Limerick on 27 August 1690. In mid-September, Douglas assisted in the relief of Birr Castle. On 16 September, Major-General Percy Kirke 'received information that the castle was under attack and Barwick's detachment very numerous'. Kirke, considering his army too weak, asked Douglas to send reinforcements. On the morning of 17 September, bolstered by Douglas' cavalry, Kirke advanced and camped 2 km south of Birr. By the time his force reached Birr Castle, Berwick and Sarsfield had withdrawn, re-crossing the Shannon on 19 September without interference (George Story, 'A True and Impartial History', *OLJ*, 92, 97–98; Childs, *Williamite Wars*, 255–56, 263–64).

[8] A reference to the Williamite general, Godert de Ginkel.

[9] For Francis Wauchope, see Letter 27, note 1.

[10] Possibly Brigadier Colonel William Mansfield Barker, an English Jacobite commander of Irish infantry, killed at Aughrim (Gilbert, *Jacobite Narrative*, xv, 147).

[11] Justin MacCarthy (c.1643–1694), Viscount Mountcashel and Baron Castleinch, was the 'youngest of three sons of Donough MacCarthy, Viscount Muskerry and Earl Clancarty, and his wife Eleanor, sister of James Butler, marquess of Ormond and lord lieutenant.' An ambitious but non-inheriting son, Justin chose a military career. Following the accession of James II, he supported 'Richard Talbot, earl of Tyrconnell, and took a leading part in catholicising the [Irish] army.' MacCarthy held the rank of general and was appointed to the Irish privy council. Active in the early stages of the Williamite War, he was severely wounded and captured at Newtownbutler in August 1689. After his escape, he sailed to France in April 1690 as commander of the 5,000 to 6,000 Irish soldiers exchanged for French troops supplied to James II in Ireland (John A. Murphy,

'MacCarthy, Justin', *DIB* [accessed 25 October 2024]; Connolly [ed.], *Oxford Companion to Irish History*, 349–50).

[12] An unidentified Stafford, a groom of the bedchamber, and Francis Stafford (possibly a relation) served on James II's staff at Saint-Germain-en-Laye (Grews, *English Court in Exile*, 268–9).

[13] John Biddulph was a gentleman of the bedchamber at Saint-Germain-en-Laye. He had been with James II at the time of his escape from England seeking refuge in France (Grews, *English Court in Exile*, 42, 267, 271; Demetrius Charles Boulger, *The Battle of the Boyne* (London, 1911), 28–9; Charles O'Kelly, *Secret History of the War of the Revolution in Ireland, 1688–1691* [Dublin, 1850], 205; John Burke, *A Genealogical and Heraldic History of the Commoners of Great Britain and Ireland*, 4 vols., [London, 1886], 3:285).

[14] Sir Edward Herbert (1645–1698), judge and politician, served James II as his lord chancellor at Saint-Germain-en-Laye. At the conclusion of the Williamite War, Herbert spent the remainder of his life in France at James' exiled court (Jeffrey R. Collins, 'Herbert, Edward [styled Sir Edward Herbert], Jacobite earl of Portland', *ODNB* [accessed 25 October 2024]).

27. Francis Wauchop[1] [place unknown] to 'Monsieur [John] Wauchope,[2] Bregadier des Arme du Roy Dangletere att St Germin en Lay', 24 September 1690. No. 11

Brother

I have setled ÿour horses neer to Claer[3] at a protesten Gentelmans hous Caled Mes: Burton,[4] and ÿour graes horses, at Claer where ther is vere good grese theÿ are along with Col. Sarbes[5] hors whoe has aguard upon them[.] theÿ shal want for nothing that can be had for them, the laest of the two horses ÿow got from Cap: Berto is a mier jaed[6] he is foundert[7] and weynd brocken[.][8] I intend to send for the horses that are with Seÿmon Luttrel,[9] and put them to graes with the rest: the Leu: of Surlobes Regement ÿow deseÿered me to ask for and give him 16 Crouns is Dead. I am sheur it is not for want of Caer, the excheng betwex mes Brouns[10] Son and Mes: Opton[11] Could not be doen, the Duck of Barwick[12] haveing befoer proposed to have hem Cheanged For Major Routhes[13] Brother whoe has ben a prisoner thes twelve monthes in Dere.[14] There has ben nothing doen aes to the fortefeÿing of this toun aes ÿet, bot Colonelle Darington[15] bieng com to toun two daÿes agoen had viseted what is most naecesere to be doen and is Setting all hands to warck, we want vere mutch ingenieurs[16] hier, when the Duck of Baerwick is com to Towne whoe is expected thes weck theÿ wel condeshend upon the best, and shortest waey of fortifieng it, there is two expreses com from Corck giveng aen acount that there has a fliet landed à graet maene men in the big Eÿland and that theÿ were alredÿ surounded on the other Seÿd, there is 5 regements in gaereson there[.] Mackele[17] got compleans of wanteng amoniton and of the regements being vere waeck, there is 4 regem: in Kensele[18] which is the Saeme[.] I spock to Col: Barcker concerning the wolle[.] he saeys that he has nothing a doe weth ane that was upon the wael, bot aes for what was upon the battres[19] belongst to hem whech he has Secured into hes stoers[.] I asked Col:

Roberts[20] for for [sic] the wole ÿow deseÿered hem to Secure[.] he told me that Col: Barker had Secured all upon the batres and where there was onlÿ on[21] pice of canen, aes in the Church nier Erish toun gaet[22] wher there was 8 packs which he also pretends to becaus of one pice of canen bieng there at this raet there is not on pack ÿow can pretend to, Col: darington gives ÿow has opinion of it in has letter, however I shal Speack of it so Soun aes the Duck of baerwick comes hier and the rest of the Comishoners, I am also told for certentÿ that there wel not be Sufred one pack of wolle to goe out of the Contre, soo [word obscured] would not have ÿow to trust to it[.] theres nieus from the enemie that the King, and Me Lord Melford[23] are at Dunkerk Sheping of men for Scotlend, if Soo, I hope ÿow wel not laeve me hier[.] praeÿ Let me hier from ÿow with the first ocasion, and when ÿow Com over bring wÿen along with ÿow for I intend to drinck ÿour helthe in this with Col: Darington and Saevrael other of ÿour friends whoe deÿnes with me this daeÿ, theÿ have all there Servise keÿndlÿ remembred to ÿow, bring also good Servents along with ÿow if ÿow can leÿght upon them, for I Lock upon it to be the greatest treasure one can have[.] if Mÿ Lord Melford be in france, and Mÿ Laede I praeÿ present mÿ respects to them, and to Mÿ Lord Drumend[24] Franc[s] Staford[25] and all other friends, I shal not fael one ocasion to let ÿow know what nieus hier and what pases
your obedient brother

Fr: Wauchop

[p.s.] My humble Respects to the Count and Countes of Overenge and the yong prences

[1] Lieutenant-Colonel Francis Wauchope was the brother of Major-General John Wauchope. Following the war in Ireland, Francis Wauchope rose to high command in the French and Spanish armies. In March 1708, He was among those captured aboard a French vessel in the Firth of Forth in a failed attempt to land James 'the Old Pretender' on the East coast of Scotland (D'Alton, *Army List*, 1:392, 2:733; Paterson, *History and Genealogy of the Family of Wauchope of Niddrie-Merschell*, 36–7; TNA, SP 35/68/128, part 2, fols. 26–7).

[2] For Major-General John Wauchope, see Letter 26, note 2.

[3] Co. Clare.

[4] Thomas Burton served as a lieutenant in Colonel Robert Clifford's Regiment of Dragoons in the Jacobite army (D'Alton, *Army List*, 1:402, 428).

[5] Possibly Col. Patrick Sarsfield.

[6] '[A] Horse (which tho' he appear fair to the Eye, he is notwithstanding a meer Jade)' (William Burdon, *Capt. Burdon's Gentleman's Pocket-farrier, Shewing How to Use Your Horse on a Journey* [London, 1742], 23).

[7] 'Of a horse: Affected with founder; lamed' (*OED*).

[8] 'In horses: difficulty in breathing, typically with cough, increasing expiratory effort, and reduced capacity for exercise' (*OED*).

[9] Colonel Simon Luttrell (1643–1698), of Luttrellstown, Co. Dublin, was an officer in the French army when war broke out in Ireland in 1689. Returning home, he was governor of Dublin at the time of King James' entry into the city and was a member of the parliament of 1689. Luttrell's troops covered the retreat of James II to Dublin following the Battle of the Boyne. In 1690, he was a member 'of the Irish delegation which went to Saint-Germain[-en-Laye] after the lifting of the first siege of Limerick to call for the removal of Tyrconnell from the viceroyalty'. Luttrell did not return to Ireland until late October 1691, three weeks after the conclusion of negotiations that led to the Treaty of Limerick. Attainted and dispossessed of his property in Ireland, Luttrell returned to France where he continued in military service (J. T. Gilbert, revised by Piers Wauchope, 'Luttrell, Simon [c.1643–1698], army officer', *ODNB* [accessed 25 October 2024]; Éamonn Ó Ciardha, 'Luttrell, Simon', *DIB* [accessed 25 October 2024]; Richard Hayes, 'Biographical Dictionary of Irishmen in France, Part IX', *Studies: An Irish Quarterly Review*, 33:129 [March 1944], 79; Grews, *English Court in Exile*, 181; Childs, *Williamite Wars*, 187–8, 277–8).

[10] Among prisoners taken at the siege of Derry in May 1689 was a 'Captain John Brown, of the Neal, in the county of Mayo' (Gilbert, *A Jacobite Narrative*, 76).

[11] Captain Clotworthy Upton (1660–1725), of Castle Upton, an officer in the army of William III, was taken prisoner at the first siege of Limerick, 'after entering the breach sword in hand, and almost alone, his followers, nearly to a man, being cut to pieces' (Timothy Williams Ferres, 'Lord Belmont in Northern Ireland', at http://lordbelmontinnorthernireland.blogspot.com/2014/12/1st-viscount-templetown.html [accessed 19 October 2024]). In 1691, Upton appealed to the English Crown for compensation: 'Being taken prisoner at Limerick, it cost him above £30 in eight weeks, besides the loss of his best horses. That he is much in debt for their Majesty's service, of whom he never received any consideration. Prays to have £200 allowed him, or what their Majesties shall think fit' (William John Hardy [ed.], *Calendar of State Papers: May 1691–October 1691* [London, 1898], 451; Childs, *Williamite Wars,* 57).

[12] James Fitzjames, duke of Berwick upon Tweed (1670–1734), was an army officer in the French service. He was the natural son of James, Duke of York, later King James II. In March 1689, Berwick joined his father's expedition to Ireland, 'entering Dublin on 24 March. He was made a major-general and saw action at Coleraine, Derry (where he was wounded), and Newry, and commanded the cavalry on the right at the battle of the Boyne'. In August 1690, when Tyrconnell sailed to France seeking additional aid, he placed the youthful Berwick in command of Jacobite forces 'with a council of officers to advise him'. Upon Tyrconnell's return in January 1691, Berwick departed for France (Stuart Handley, 'Fitzjames, James, duke of Berwick upon Tweed [1670–1734]', *ODNB* [accessed 25 October 2024]).

[13] The Major Routhe referred to here may be Michael Rothe (or Rooth, 1665–1741) an officer in the regiment Dorrington commanded, and later its colonel. Letter 52 is addressed to Mathew Rooth, another member of this prominent Kilkenny Jacobite family.

[14] Read: 'Derry'.

[15] For Major-General William Dorrington, see Letter 26, note 1.

[16] Read: 'engineers'.

[17] Possibly John Mackewy of Colonel Robert Clifford's Regiment of Dragoons (D'Alton, *Army List*, 1:402).

[18] Read: 'Kinsale' (Co. Cork).

[19] Read: 'batteries'.

[20] Lieutenant-Colonel Roberts, a Jacobite officer, was severely wounded and taken prisoner at Aughrim, 12 July 1691 (D'Alton, *Army List*, 2:784).

[21] Read: 'one'.

[22] Saint John's Church, Limerick, located in Irishtown near Saint John's Gate.

[23] John Drummond (1649–1715), a Scot and a convert to Catholicism, was earl and titular duke of Melfort. When William of Orange invaded England, Drummond 'fled London on 13 December 1688 and made his way to the French royal court, where he became James's principal secretary of state'. In March 1689, he landed in Ireland with James II where, as part of the king's inner circle, he was appointed secretary of state for Ireland and made a member of the privy council. However, 'As a military organiser he was regarded as incompetent', and, in September 1689, he returned to France. The following month, Melfort departed for Rome as Stuart ambassador to Pope Alexander VIII' (Patrick A. Walsh and John Cronin, 'Drummond, John', *DIB* [accessed 25 October 2024]).

[24] James Drummond (1674–1720), styled fifth earl of Perth, was a convert to Catholicism and supporter of the Jacobite cause. In 1689, he entered the Scots College in Paris, but soon departed for Ireland to join his uncle, John Drummond, Lord Melfort. James 'was present at all the engagements of the campaign', after which he returned to France and his studies in Paris (J. G. Alger, revised by John Sibbald Gibson, 'Drummond, James, styled fifth earl of Perth and Jacobite second duke of Perth [1674–1720]', *ODNB* [accessed 25 October 2024]).

[25] Francis Stafford was part of the palace entourage of James II at Saint-Germain-en-Laye, serving as a 'Gentleman of the Bed Chamber' (Grews, *English Court in Exile*, 268–9).

28. Robert Rirdan,[1] Limerick, 'To Robert Rirdan and Pat: Rirdan, merc^{t} In nantes', 24 September 1690. No. 22

Lymrike 24th 7^{ber} 1690

Son Pat: and Son Robert

S^{r}[,] I Consimed upon you both 20 Caske tallow abourd same tarvera wea[2] grose 85^{Cl}–00–20^{l} tar at be the margaret 9^{Cl}–00–12^{l} net 76^{Cl}–0–8^{l}[.] sell when price offers, and kipe the net prownew[3] for me use, mr keth // In ye margaerut wth R[illegible], use Robert white kindly[.] I am trubled wth a plasie, God quire its ye net price after after [sic] payinge all Charge[.] Kipe upon you hands afored you fundes // my Bleasinge to you all[.] it would doe my goode to here for yo^{u} both I remayn yor Etc &se

Robert Rirdan

[p.s.] Courell Ronance[4] his San Goe in ye shipe, his father desires me to use him kindly In those strange places[.] ~~in~~ doe soe it wont lose of Purs Nothinge be it

[1] Robert Rirdan – father of Robert (Jr) and Patrick Rirdan in Nantes and John Rirdan in Limerick – served as a burgess of the City of Limerick in 1687 and 1688 (Lenihan, *Limerick*, 272).

[2] Read: 'tare weight'.

[3] Read: 'produce'.

[4] The son, James Ronan, travelled as a passenger bound for France aboard the *Amity*. His name appears among those in Limerick whose property was confiscated in 1691 (Examination of James Ronan, 12 December 1690, TNA, HCA 232/33 [part 2]; Lenihan, *Limerick*, 297).

29. **John Rirdan, Limerick, 'To m^{r} Patrick Rirdan, Merchant In Nantes, france', 24 September 1690, No. 15; bill of lading, 23 September 1690, No. 17; duplicate bill of lading, 23 September 1690. No. 77**

Lymerick the 24th Sep^{t} 1690

Bro Pat Rirdan

S^{r}

I have yo^{rs} 10th July p^{r} the Edmond[1] Keach In s^{d} was all Copy of y^{rs} 10th June both wch Doe observe[.] this Goeth p^{r} the Amity whoe unfortunately arrived at this Harber som Dayes before wee weare beseidged[.] the Condition of the times made me Conclude Leaveing my share with the wast under one sale and was all putt Into one seller[.] we sould twenty or thirty Hogh^{ds} Wine for time & brass monny[.] the remainder was forced from us at the Kings rate by officiers[.] som paid otthers are still In Debt som of wch are gon out of the Countery[.] In fine I Cannot give Y^{w} anny sattisfactory acc^{tt} & though I Doe my Indevers to serve yow or anny otther yett I Cannot expect but y^{r} Displeasure[.] I promise yow that I have not above 16 salted Hydes & four hundred wg^{t} tallow on acc^{tt} of the produces of that Cargoe[.] the master will tell y^{w} w^{t} Wee suffer[.] y^{w} Inclos^{d} have a Bill of Lodeing of 41 Casks Tallow wch waies Gross 175^{Cl} 20 of wch belongs to my father whose nett we^{tt} he sends y^{w} with his orders[.] The 21 are my one[2] wch I Doe Lode[.] y^{w} will admire that I Lode none for your acc^{tt} but In fine I Doe Refer y^{w} and the Cause till som other time[.] oure Condition is I say as to trade is soe as Cannot be well repressented[.] if wee Have forraigne Goods wee must sell at a regulated prisce for brass monny[.] If wee Imploy that Brass monny In Countery Commoditys they are seaz^{d} and taken up for the Kings use to pay for wheat and otthere nessessarys[.] I asshure y^{w} them 21 Hogh^{ds} Tallow Cost me neare theire vallue to preserve them from being seas^{d} on and had them hid in Divers plasces[.] I have the Greates throuble Imaginable to get goods for m^{r} Gerraldin[3] In retourne[.] His vessell will be ready In 10 Days[.] If oure Governors doe not Hinder I expect He will have twenty tuns of Goods on His one acc^{tt}. I shall [torn, missing word] som betwixt me & tho. Arthur[4] and shall give father som Coplement[.] pray Inshure a hundred & fifty pounds fer my acc^{tt} on s^{d} vessell[.] If possible I shall p^{r}chase som Goods fer y^{w} & Lode them on s^{d}[.] yow Inclos^{d} Have y^{r} father Leatter wch I feare will be the Last[.] He is Lately taken with a palsy soe as He Cannot speake to be understood[.] He is very peevis & Cross[.] wee are sadly opprest with Soldiers & officiers whoe scarsly allow our Sealves an ordinary bed to ly on somtimes In the Garrat & atther times In the shope & Celler wch uneasynes our Dyet being In proportion has tyred us soe wee Could wish our Sealves out of the Countery[.] noething Hinders me to take my passadge for freance but my fathers Condition[.] I write y^{w} p^{r} the Edmund as alsoe by ould Martin[5] whoe will be ready soone if Can gett Cleare[.] my father Has som Tallow and I shall gett som if possible now In the season fer retourne of y^r^ wine whearefore y^w^ should Doe well to fraight a vessell to Com heare with som salt som wheate wine & brandy to Carry of w^tt^ goods wee Can [torn: two words missing] y^w^ theare Can better Judge of the state of this Countery then wee heare; the Ennemy is Every wheare amongst us and are very Numerous[.] not one protestant In the Countery but are In armes with them[.] yow have the p^r^ticuler acc^tt^ of all that past Heare this Last summer & of our seidge[.] the Ennemy had a very great Defeate heare and quitted theire seeidge with ye Loss of at Least Eight or Nine thousand men. wee Lost not above 200 Kil^d^ and Like number wounded[,] som Housses ruined and a Lardge breach Made on ye walls eastward of the Cittadell. wee are scarsce of Bread[;] all the Corne of the Countery burned[.] wee Depend of y^r^ supply for our Subsistance as alsoe on y^r^ assistance of forces ottherwise wee shall be overun by the ussurpers Dannis and Hollish army[6] who spares neither adge nor sex but ruines all from whose power Good Lord Deliver us. I have noe more to In lardge butt thatt full of Griefe I am y^r^ Loveing Bro and most Humble Servt

John Rirdan

[p.s.] My service to Bro Robt whoe has not leasure to write us.

[p.p.s.] I say bussnes this way the tan^d^ Leather I got In truck fer his Rice wch Could not send him fer the prohibition is now forced from me[.] I gave him Intrest in those goods I sent and am beforehand with him[.] wee have noething shure Heare[.] wee must all Depend on y^w^ for maintaynance[.] i feare me Sister nell is very Ill soe are manny frindes[.] sustenance for sick people scarsce milke 4^s^ p^r^ pottle[,] 18^d^ for an eg as soe in portion. Judge oure Condition.

BILL OF LADING

Shipped by the grace of God, in good order and well conditioned, by me *John Rirdan of Lymericke* in and upon the good Ship called the *Amity of Lymericke* whereof is Master under God for this present voyage *John Mitchell* and now ridinh [sic] at Anchor in the *Kay of Lymericke*, and by God's grace bound for *Nantes,* to say *forty one Caskes of Tallow computed to be [in two batches: 20 hogsheads and 21 hogsheads]* being marked and numbered as in the margent: And are to be delivered in the like good order and well conditioned, at the aforesaid Port of *Nantes* (the danger of the seas only excepted) unto *Mr Patrick Rirdan of Nantes* or to *his* Assigns, he or they paying freight for the said Goods according to agreement with Primage and avarige accustomed: In witness where of the Master or Purser of the said Ship have affirmed to *three* Bills of Lading all of this tenor and date; the one of which Bills being accomplished, the other *two* to stand void. And so God send the good Ship to her desired Port in safety. Amen. Dated in *Lymericke this 23 Day of 7^ber^ 1690.* [signed] *John Mitchell*

[1] John Rirdan and John Martin of Limerick, together with Patrick Rirdan of Nantes, held ownership shares in the *Edmond* of Nantes, a 40-tun vessel that sailed between the two ports through the summer of 1691 (Limerick customs ledger, April–July 1691, in Archives of the Archbishop of Westminster [London], B6, folder 92, Henry Browne Papers).

[2] Read: 'own'.

[3] Andrew Geraldin, a merchant in Nantes with roots in Waterford (Saupin, 'Les réseaux commerciaux des Irlandais de Nantes', 129–30; Richard Hayes, 'Irish Associations with Nantes', *Studies: An Irish Quarterly Review*, 28:109 [March 1939], 119n2).

[4] Thomas Arthur was a prominent Limerick merchant. The Arthurs were a wealthy Old English merchant family deeply involved in civic life. Thomas Arthur served as a burgess for the City of Limerick in 1687 and 1688 (Lenihan, *Limerick*, 272; Mary Ann Lyons, 'The Role of Graduate Physicians in Professionalising Medical Practice in Ireland, c. 1619–54', in James Kelly and Fiona Clark [eds.], *Ireland and Medicine in the Seventeenth and Eighteenth Centuries* [Farnham, 1988], 18).

[5] John Martin, merchant ship captain of Limerick, see Letter 8, note 1.

[6] For Danish and Dutch troops in the Williamite army at Limerick, see Kevin Danaher and J. G. Simms, 'The Danish Force at Limerick, 1690', *OLJ*, 111–25, and Peter Tesch, 'The Dutch in Limerick', Ibid., 135–43.

30. **John Rirdan to Pat Rirdan [Nantes] [n.d., but probably enclosure in above letter]. No. 16**

Bro Patrick

mr John Ronan[1] his son[2] goeth by this vessell[.] pray serve in wtt yw Can wch is the request of yr humble Servt John Rirdan[.] it is very Iill that yw Doe not write frindes Heare of rect theire goods adrest to yw pr severall vessells. I am asshamed of it. pray if anny heare sends anny vessells Hitther Lett them order none to my Consignement for at this time I will not anny way be Conscerned in buissnes

[1] John Ronan served as a burgess for the City of Limerick in 1687 and 1688 (Lenihan, *Limerick*, 272).

[2] For the son, James Ronan, see Letter 28, note 4.

31. **John Rirdan, Limerick, 'To mr Andrew Gerraldin, Merchant, In Nantes, france', 24 September 1690. No. 48**

Limericke the 24 Sept 1690

Sr

My Last to yw was by way of galloway[.] I have now to advise that yr Keach[1] will be ready in 10 Dayes if Can Gett prmittance[.] I have the Greatest throuble Imaginable to gett goods for yr Returne[.] If I weare at free Liberty to Barter one Commodity for annotther I Could Doe for yw to som sattisfaction butt I am Compelled by the officers to sell them Goods at a prisce Currt Limited and wth our Coyne wch now by the Distraction of the times is brought soe Loe that wee Can Gett noe Countery Goods & w^{tt} wis to be had are at such excesive rates that its admirable[.] I underfoote write the rates now p^{d} for Hydes & tallow wch are the onely goods to be admitted out. Butter & tan^{d} Hydes not to be exported, noe Salmon fish to be had. I have about 12 or 14 tuns of salted Hydes and about 5 tuns of tallow wch is w^{tt} I expect to make upe[.] I say I have soe much bought If Can gett them in from the undertakers I Delivered Brandy to r^{cd} the vallue In butter wch is not admitted out soe must keepe it for y^{r} acc^{tt}[.] y^{r} Kentings I proffered at 3^{s} p^{r} ane[2] to r^{cd} the vallue In tallow at 30^{s} p^{r} C^{l} wch Cannot obtayne[.] I have thought of sending them backe as the best Commodity and of most vallue[.] they are worth 12^{s} p^{r} ane In brass If one may Depend on it[.] I asshure y^{w} w^{tt} wee have of it[,] wee Intend to lay it In the threassary[3] and wth assurances on ye Croune rentes for its paym^{t} with the Interest and soe pin our fortune on the Kings wch we hope will make all Good. In time this wee p^{r}fer rather then pay soe excessively for goods wch though bought soe Deare and paid for wee Cannot say are oure one,[4] wee Lost great pieces of wooll & tallow seas^{d} on[.] Mr James Galloway[5] being In that Countery will I hope give you The Sattisfacton in y^{r} vessells Last voyadge wch y^{w} Desire[.] I had noe hand In selling s^{d} Cargoe though I in my Consience am sattisfied that He did for y^{w} as if it weare his one p^{r}per Conscerns and wheare y^{w} Imagin those that bought it made Great advantage of it I asshure y^{w} the Contray[.] they Could p^{r}chase more Brass monny by the one half for theire butter then they Did for the salt & brandy or tobaco, y^{w} r^{cd} a Letter from m^{r} Martin[6] p^{r} this convenience[.] he will be ready In 10 or 12 Days. he has Imployed the produce of his Salt & brandy In Hydes[.] he has taken Great paines about the Concerns[.] its vaine tradeing for this Countery till better setled wch is w^{tt} offers at p^{r}sent from S^{r} y^{r} asshured Humble Servt

Jno Rirdan

[p.s.]
Salt p^{r} barrell now Limited to 40
Brandy was sould for 40^{s} p^{r} gallon as is now limited to 20^{s}
Tallow 8$^{£}$ P^{r}C^{I}
Salted Hydes 4$^{£}$ pr^{CI} scarsce to be had[.] wee must sell our forraigne Commoditys on paine of Death at those rates wch is now soe narrowly loocked to that noe pretense Can serve

[1] A ketch is 'a two-masted sailing vessel, ... with the mizzen-mast shorter than the mainmast and stepped forward of the rudder post' (*OED*).

[2] Aune, a French measure of cloth.

[3] Read: 'treasury'.

[4] Read: 'own'.

[5] Sir James Galway, Bart., a Catholic merchant, served as alderman for the City of Limerick in 1687 and 1688. Doing business in La Rochelle following the war, he was accused of trading with Protestant merchants in Cork (Lenihan, *Limerick*, 272; Mulloy, *Franco-Irish Correspondence*, 2:245 #1266).

[6] For John Martin, merchant-sea captain of Limerick, see Letter 8, note 1.

32. Thomas Pearce, Limerick, 'To John & Edmund Gold, Marchants In Rochelle,'[1] 24 September 1690. No. 58

Lymerick ye 24th 7^{ber} 1690

Esteemed ffriends

This goes per ye Amity John Mitchell m^{r} wth three tuns of salmon fish in 18 teirses the third of 198 salt hydes in company wth Sa. Taverner & Zach Holland & ye halfe of 248 salt hydes more in Company wth Zachary Holland[.] ye m^{r} will distinguish them so y^{t} after sales ⅓ of one parcell & ye halfe of ye other is to my acc^{o} wth ye fish & 51 dry hydes[.] ye hydes are good & doubt n^{t} but will sell well for ready pay for I am averse to give time at presant so y^{t} if my part will n^{t} sell without allowing discount do it rather then trust & ye produce (after deducting out as much as will load my fourth part according as Sa. Taverner shall order) remite to Joseph Scriven linnen draper in Walting street London or observe his draft on thee wch is as well[.] pray allsoe get 100^{li} sterling insured on ye ship hither & back upon ye acc^{o} of Zachary Holland and my selfe for our halfe placeing one halfe of ye insurance to his acc^{o}[.] its his desire it should be so as well as ye request of thy Lo: friend

Tho: Pearce

[p.s.] let insurance be hither & back to Nants Rochell or Burdeaux

[1] Edmond (c.1651–1705) and John Gould were brothers who migrated from Kinsale to La Rochelle in the early 1680s. Although the brothers entered into a six-year trading partnership in 1684, Edmond likewise traded on his own account and provided financial services, such as discounting bills of exchange, in cooperation with Daniel Arthur, one of a small group of powerful Irish Catholic bankers in Paris. After 1690, Edmond Gould facilitated the migration of at least fifteen members of his extended family to La Rochelle (Saupin, 'Les réseaux commerciaux des Irlandais de Nantes', 118; Siobhan Talbott, *Conflict, Commerce and Franco-Scottish Relations, 1560–1713* [London, 2014], 125; AMLR, GG 208, view 17, and GG 354 [1704–1711], view 28; ADM-C, B5689, f. 173, B5691, f. 1695; ADC-M, B5687, ff. 76, 162–3; ADC-M, Notaire Rivière, 3E1808, f. 36r; ADC-M, Notaire Bagard, 3E400, ff. 53, 67, 74, 84, 102, 105, 123, 167, 186).

33. **Thomas Pearce, Limerick, 'To Joseph Scriven, linnen draper in watling street, London', 24 September 1690. No. 74a**

Lymerick ye 24th 7^{ber} 1690

Lo: Cosine

I wrote thee by way of Dublin ye last weeke about Tho: fflexen[1] by whom Zach Holland my father & selfe sent in ye John of Lym^{k} Peter Clement m^{r} in Aprill last consigned to Robert Mutloe[2] of Ostend 442 salt hydes a tun of butter & about 100 dosen of rabet skins[3] a smale firkin of sperma Caety[4][.] ye barke was our own allso[.] ye s^{d} fflexen had orders to lay out ye produce in tobaccoe there &c^{t} since wch we here nothing from him but my sisters letter[.] we understand she reced ours by him wch makes us judge he got safe to his port, where he should be now we know n^{t} unless in London or some part of England[.] if so I pray on thy endevour to call him to acc^{o} for barke & produce of cargoe[.] w^{t} thee do, do it to purpose least he be to cunning, I am n^{t} willing to further venter him though if he were on his way it would do well, my sister knows him & may from his Br^{o} learne where he is[.] his wife being out of ye gates of this place went of wth Kits party & as we hear designs for England[.] if so I feare they will be gon to ye west indies wth our consm^{t} so y^{t} Cosin pray do w^{t} thee can in this matter, Tho: & Joseph Carpenter will assist in this on Zach Holland acc^{o}[.] thee may write to Robert Mutloe about him & w^{t} mony ye goods came to[.] ye bills of loading writ for ye propper acc^{o} & risque of Tho: Cooke[5] consigned on Mutloe for sales[.] it may be y^{t} may do some good for us; I know it is n^{t} pleasing to thee thus to be troubled, nor y^{t} we should so much stir in ye world[,] but its incident to all to endevour rather to be before hand & to have to spare then otherwise[.] indeed we would be willing to part wth much to be hence[,] so troublesome it is & our substance daily goeing a way[,] but how to goe unless hazarding y^{t} wch is nearer then all we know n^{t}[,] though some have gon of well[,] others have endured much hardships n^{t} to be exprest[.] to write how we fared in ye Seige is to large[.] many fell on both sides but as I remember but one or two of ye English inhabitants lost, though ye bullets, red hot balls, Karkasses bums & smale shot came in ye towne in an exceeding manner both day & night for ye last two weekes[.] ye next house to my fathers was fired twise of one hand & on ye other a bum broake down to ye Cellar[.] ye towne & walls esspessially one part is so battered & wth out ye Gates so ruinated & alltered as is n^{t} to be imagined, severall I think were wounded & lost their lives at ye breach y^{t} adventerd to p^{r}serve them from ye Cruielty of ye foriners y^{t} as its s^{d} intended to put all to ye sword for ye plunder sake of wch Number was Ed Taverner, if it should be beseiged again we will I think if it be possible leave it[.] severall of our English have lately died & its a very sickly time w^{t} wth ye alteration of food & drinking water to gether with disquietness of minds I feare have shortned some mens days, if my sister sees Ab^{r} Bowman[6] let him know y^{t} his father,

Mother, John Hart, & wife are dead[.] his Br^{o} Daniel come out of ye Cuntry where he was hanged allmost to death but is now well[.] Alb^{t} War, Richd Abell, Nicholas Starkey,[7] Cap^{tn} Lucas, Martha Marten, Ed Wight wife, Betty Marten, Mary Bonnet, Joan Cooke & severall others are dead[.] many more sick so y^{t} she will[,] if[,] please God[,] we see back other [sic][,] want many [of] our old acquaintance, & Irland looks as if it would be a new plantation such is ye great ruen here aways, — this gos by ye Amity y^{t} James Craven[8] was taken in by whom I send three tuns of salmon fish in 18 tersses, five tuns of salt hydes & 57 dry hydes consigned if she goes to Nants on Pat. Rirdan, if to Rochell on Jno & Ed^{m} Gold, at Burdeaux on Power & Agnes[9] to whom I have wrote to remite ye produce except a smale matter to thee or to accept thy bills on them wch is better[.] so y^{t} as soon as this comes to thy hands write them to know how much thee may draw for, as I judge if she arrives safe will p^{r}duce cleere 250^{li} sterl. I could wish I had a line or two from Theophilus Downs of ye paymen of ye 60^{li} to ye Lord of Kerry[10] sonn to satisfy ye Lord here who is so hard of faith in y^{t} point & a line or two of your well fare will be very acceptable[.] all our loves here to my Cosin & sister & we would have my sister write a full letter on all sides of our frends well fare as Tho: Cooke & wife any thing else &c. to thy very Lo: Kinsman

Tho: Pearce

[1] For Thomas Flaxon, see Letter 34, note 1.

[2] For Robert Mutloe of Ostend, see Letter 23, note 6.

[3] Read: 'rabbit skins'.

[4] Read: 'spermaceti'.

[5] Possibly Thomas Cooke (1648–1709), a prominent London merchant-banker and director of the East India Company (Mark Knights, 'Cooke, Sir Thomas [? c.1648–1709]', *History of Parliament* online edition [2011], at http://www.histparl.ac.uk/volume/1690-1715/member/cooke-sir-thomas-c1648-1709 [accessed 5 October 2024]).

[6] Abraham Bowman, having agreed to the Test Act of 1692 required of all mayors and sheriffs of corporate towns and cities in Ireland, served as sheriff of the City of Limerick in 1693 (Lenihan, *Limerick*, 292, 704).

[7] Nicholas Starkey was an Irish Quaker activist, organising meetings in Athlone, Ballykilroe, and elsewhere in Ireland. He had been listed among property owners in Limerick City in 1655 (Wight and Rutty, *History of the Rise and Progress of the People Called Quakers*, 112, 117; Alan O'Driscoll and Brian Hodkinson [eds.], 'Who Was Who in Early Modern Limerick', at https://www.limerick.ie/sites/default/files/atoms/files/who_was_who_in_early_modern_limerick_1.pdf [accessed 18 October 2024]).

[8] In 1687, Alderman James Craven, Sr, was a member of the Common Council of Limerick and had served as sheriff in 1681. He was among the founders of Limerick Quaker Meeting. Between 1661 and 1674, he experienced periodic imprisonment for practicing his faith (Goodbody, [ed.], *Guide to Irish Quaker Records*, 147; Lenihan, *Limerick*, 272; 'Limerick and Quakerism', at https://ourancestorsandtheirtimes.wordpress.com/limerick-and-quakerism-1650-to-1770/ [accessed 19 October 2024]).

[9] For commercial correspondence between Power & Agness of Bordeaux and John Aylward at Saint-Malo, see 'Aylward Papers', 12.

[10] Captain William FitzMaurice, 20th Baron of Kerry and Lixnaw (1633–1697). Earlier Barons of Kerry had taken Irish wives, but William took an English wife and fought on the English side at the Battle of the Boyne and subsequent engagements (Childs, *Williamite Wars*, 373; 'William Fitz-Maurice, 20th Lord of Kerry and Lixnaw', at (https://www.geni.com/people/William-FitzMaurice-20th-Lord-of-Kerry-and-Lixnaw/6000000010695070740 [accessed 19 October 2024]).

34. **Thomas Pearce, Limerick, to Capt. Thomas Flaxon,[1] [place unknown], 24 September 1690. No. 74b**

Lymerick ye 24th 7ber 1690

fflexen

ffriend

I have not had one line from thee since thy departure but by my sister receaving our letters sent by thee[.] I question not but thee got well to thy port & I hope for a good market but what to say or think I know not[.] I thought thee would not have don as others have[.] if any hazard was it was on our part not on thine who might a gon of againe & thee had performed thy promise[.] I am satisfyed thee would not a reported thy comeing both as to thy Credite & profitt as well as ours, & feare ye season of ye year is to late for such a smale barke all things else would answer better than before, but I judge what I may write thee will nt regard as to yt part, therefore I shall forbare & only by this give thee my my [sic] minde yt is yt thee give my kinsman Joseph Scriven a full acco of barke & cargoe & wt it produced after charges pay it him & let ye barke be to his disposall — thy wife went to Rakeel[2] a few days before ye seige & when yt party went hence she as well as severall others went wth them[.] many of ye old English Standards are gon of ye stage of this world[.] severall more sick of ye Cuntry disease & feavour, thy father Buck, & brother well but I think thy Bro wife is sick[.] Wm Willoughby in thy shop where he have a far greater trade then ever old Garrut had to receave 100li a day for Mangulum is comon wth him[.] Wm Davis[3] takes up yt trade as well as severall others[.] just now I heare of a Dogger[4] from Ostend or Dunkirk to be come into ye river[.] what her loading or to whom come I know not[.] she have been but eight days a comeing as they say — I am wth kinde love to thy selfe & all our friends as thee meets them[.] thy Lo: ffriend

Tho: Pearce

[1] Thomas Flaxon and John Higgins served as high sheriffs of Limerick in 1697 (Lenihan, *Limerick*, 704).

[2] Rathkeale, Co. Limerick.

[3] William Davis, having agreed to the Test Act of 1692 required of all mayors and sheriffs of corporate towns and cities in Ireland, served as sheriff of the City of Limerick in 1693 (Lenihan, *Limerick*, 292).

[4] A dogger is 'a sturdy two-masted fishing vessel with bluff bows, resembling a ketch, formerly used for deep sea fishing in the North Sea. Now *historical*' (*OED*).

35. **James Craven, Limerick, 'For the Widdow Lee and sonns John Lee & Luckar March^{ts}, In Nantes', 24 September 1690. No. 23; bill of lading, 24 September 1690. No. 24**

Lymerick 24th September 1690

Widdow Lee & Sonns

Tho: unknowne unto you yett am imboldened by the good Carracter I have heard of yor Just and faire corespondency wth frinds and Acquaintance for to desire the favour of you to answer my Expectacion in what you cann in A matter of some Controversie that may happen betwixt Patrick Rirdane & my selfe in Relation to the fourth Part of a smale vessell caled the Amitty of Lymerick wch my sonn was Concerned in: the Mast^{r} John Mitchell cann informe you the whole Matter: I have sent you by him a Letter of Procuration to act & doe the needfull as you shall thinke fitt on that subject & desire you will pursue the same as to Justice shall be thought fitt Nott Questioning but that Patrick Rirdane will adhere to the same and send to me that wch is reasonable for ye fraight of one Quarter p^{t} of said ship hither and tither[.] I had Loaded on Board her two hogsheads of tallow as p^{r} Bill of Ladeing sent yo^{u} ne^{t} weight as under written: wch have Consign^{d} on you: wch dispose of as you cann: & that wth what you receiv^{d} from Patrick Rirdane dispose of as I have orderd by his Letter of Atturney[.] I have noe more to Add: But referr myself to yor care & kindness in this matter & remaine

Yo^{r} Afectionate frend

James Craven

	Cl	li
No 1:	7: 2: 5	tare 55
2:	6: 0 :27	tr^{e} 57
	13 3: 4	
	1	
	12: 3 4	net[1]

BILL OF LADING

Shiped by the grace of God in good order, and well conditioned, by *James Craven of Limerick merchant* in and upon the good Ship, called the *Amitty of Lym*^rk^ whereof is Master under God for this present voyage *John Mitchell* and now riding at Anker in the *River of Lymerick*, and by Gods grace bound for *Nantes in France,* to say *two hogsheads of Tallow containing thirteen hundred three quarters & four pounds* being marked and numbered as in the margent, and are to be delivered in the like good order and well conditioned, at the aforesaid Port of *Nantes* (the danger of the seas only excepted) unto *Widow Lee* or to *her* assigns, *she* or they paying freight for the said goods *at the rate of [undecipherable] pounds* [undecipherable] with primage and average accustomed. In witness where of the Master or purser of the said Ship have affirmed to three Bills of Lading all of this tenor and date; the one of which Bills being accomplished, the other two to stand void. And so God send the good Ship to her desired Port in safety. Dated in *Lym*^rk^ *24 September Anno. 1690.* [signed] *John Mitchell*

[1] As the bill of lading indicates, the units are hundredweight (112lbs), quarter hundredweight (28lbs), and pounds. Tare refers to the weight of the empty hogshead in pounds. The calculation shows a net weight of tallow of twelve hundredweight, three quarters, and four pounds.

36. Nicholas Skyddy,[1] Limerick, 'To Mr Pat^rk^ Riordane, In Nants', 25 September 1690 [damaged document]. No. 9

Lymer^k^ 7^ber^ ye 25th 1690

Mr Patr^k^ Riordane

S^r^

I have had none of yo^rs^ these manny monneths[.] I pray lett me heare from yo^w^ p^r^ bearer wth an acc^t^ of my smale concernes of the beefe in yor hands how it stands & what is comeing due to me. I thinke my last unto yo^w^ was by m^r^ Andrew Creagh[2] [2–3 words missing] giveing yo^w^ prices to the beefe [3–4 words missing] yo^w^ p^r^posed The [4–5 words missing] yo^w^ wth The one being for my br^o^ Cap^tn^ Skiddys daughter att the Convent of the Ellisabeths[3] wch I shall desire yo^w^ to deliver on Receipt here of it being of greate concernmt to me to be speedily deliverd & the other can yor man to putt into the poste to Paris wherein yo^w^ will very much oblidge Yo^r^ aff^tt^ hum^ble^ Ser^t^

Nicholas Skiddy

[p.s.] pray let [1 word missing] heare from yo^w^ p^r^ bearer.

[1] Nicholas Skyddy, a Catholic, served as Collector of Limerick and as an officer in the Jacobite army. Having departed for France with Lord Mountcashel at the conclusion of the Williamite War,

he was attainted for high treason and his property confiscated in 1696 (Lenihan, *Limerick*, 297–8; D'Alton, *Army List*, 204; S.M., 'The Trant Family [Continued]', *Kerry Archaeological Magazine*, 3:13 [October 1914], 24).

[2] This may be the Andrew Creagh, a Limerick merchant, who was the beneficiary of a bequest of £7,000 by a kinsman, Jean Creagh, likewise a Limerick merchant, in 1663 (J. F. Bosher, ed., *Négociants et navires du commerce avec le Canada de 1660 à 1760: Dictionnaire biographique* [Ottawa, 1992], 58).

[3] See Letter 37, note 1.

37. Nicholas Skyddy, Limerick, 'To m^r^ Christian Skiddy[1] att the Convent of the Ellizabeths[2] In Nantes', 25 September 1690. No. 12

Lymr^{k} 25th 7^{ber} 1690

My deare Niece

This Serves to Cover both the incloseds the one from me to yor father & the other from yor Sister Connell to her husband[3] as yo^{w} will finde by theire adresses on the side where the Seales are, they are lefft for yo^{w} to write an address uppon according as yo^{w} knowe where my bro: is[.] faile not to be very carefull in forwarding them wth all expedition & [torn: word missing] me have by the very next ship bounde hither or to Galway or to both an acc^{t} of yor father & of yor selfe & my sonn Andie[4] where he is, yor Aunt my wife deyed in this Citty on the 21st of July[.] god be Mercifull to her Soule[.] pray deare Childe write to me att large & m^{r} Riordane or Some of [torn: word missing] Irish Merch^{ts} of Nantes will forward me yor letter[.] direct it to Nicholas Skyddy Esqr Collector of Lymerick[.] I am in haste

yor afff^{tt} Uncle to Com^{d}

Nicholas Skyddy

[p.s.] Yo^{r} mo: & all yor friends here & in Kerry are well

[1] Evidence in Letter 38 suggests that Mother Christian Skiddy, a native of Dingle, Co. Kerry, was the sister of Capt. George Skiddy, an officer in Clare's Irish Regiment serving in France. For her likely Kerry ancestral roots, see 'Christian Skiddy (widow)' among the 'Forfeiting Proprietors in Ireland under the Cromwellian Settlement [commencing in 1657]', in John O'Hart, *The Irish and Anglo-Irish Landed Gentry When Cromwell Came to Ireland* (Dublin, 1892), 351.

[2] By 1650, eight Irish nuns of 'l'ordre de Saint-François de Sainte-Elisabeth' had established a community in Nantes, with Sister Marie-Baptiste as superior and Catherine des Roches, a native of Ireland, as interpreter. They lived on charity and told French officials that they 'did not want to get used to the community in Nantes or stay there', and that their dearest wish was to return to Ireland when it was safe to do so. In 1690, the flow of Irish refugees into Brittany grew dramatically, and it is likely that the convent of the Order of Saint-François de Sainte-Elizabeth in Nantes grew as well (Jules Mathorez, 'Notes sur les prêtres irlandais réfugiés à Nantes aux XVIIe et XVIIIe siècles' *Revue d'histoire de l'Église de France*, 3:1 [1912], 165–7; Hayes, 'Irish Associations with Nantes', 122n1).

[3] See Letter 39.

[4] Andrew Skiddy was mustered as a lieutenant in Clare's Regiment of the Irish Brigade in France (O'Callaghan, *History of the Irish Brigades*, 291).

38. Nicholas Skyddy, Limerick, 'For Captn Skiddy,[1] [Nantes]', 25 September 1690. No. 14

Lymer^{k} 7^{ber} the 25th 1690

Dr Bro:

My last unto you was from Scatterie Roade aboute 10 days agon by a Squadron of the ffrench ffleete wch were then att Anchor there[.][2] I tould yo^{w} then that I have mett wth m^{r} Pierce[3] Leff^{tt} Coll^{e} F^{z} Maurice[4] his gen^{ln} on boarde of the Admerall of that Squadron who gave me an acc^{t} of yor being in health & of the reducem^{ts} made in the Irish Brigade by reduceing the whole to 3 Regim^{ts}[.][5] he alsoe told me that a new Lff^{tt} Coll^{e} to witt Leff^{tt} Coll^{e} Lee[6] was the man prefferd in the roome of Coll^{e} F^{z} Maurice[.] if it bee fformer Cap^{tn} Lee of Hamiltons Regim[,][7] he is yor acquaintance & by that meanes may prove more yor friend then to anny other of the Regim^{t}[.] besides that I am sensible yo^{w} cann manage affaires soe as to gaine his favo^{r}[.] I understand that yo^{w} have noe granadairs in anny of ye Regim^{ts} & that Cap^{tn} Ned F^{z} Gerrald[8] is Command^{r}[.] m^{r} Pierce tells me that Andie was Musterd one of yor Leff^{ts}[.] I hope in time yo^{w} will prevaile to see him prefferd better, pray lett me Knowe how yo^{w} finde him & how he emprovd his time in Paris, m^{r} Pierce tould me that he brought a letter from yo^{w} to m^{r} James Trant[9] wch he left att Lixnawe[10] haveing not mett wth anny convenience whereby to Send it to the lland of Kierry,[11] I am afraide it will miscarry in his hands[.] Itts the commen Reporte here that yor Brigade were att the Engadgemt wth the Duke of Savoy's troops where yo^{w} have all donn brave service, this makes me longe the more to heare from yo^{w} least anny miscarriage might come to either of yo^{w}, this I enclose to my Niece Kittie[12] to Nantes to be forwarded to yo^{w} my last being directed to yo^{w} att the Irish brigade in ffrance wch m^{r} Pierce tould me would serve to convey my letter to yor hands, pray in your next lett me Know how to address my letters to yo^{w} for most commonly we have a convenience offering for Brest when p^{r}haps none may offer for Nantes or Rochell, this is the acc^{ts} given me by m^{r} Pierce of yor affaires in ffrance & I will as briefly as I cann give yo^{w} the State of oures here. I presume as ill newes are wont to ffley soe yo^{w} must have had an acc^{t} of the unfortunate defeate of oure Armeÿ att Droheda by that of the Prince of Orranges th^{e} first daÿ of July last And of theire randevouseing here in some dayes after where they were by degrees pursued by the Ennemy takeing all places in theire waÿ from Dublin hether Even Waterford & DunCannon wth oute fireing a shot & soe continued theire conquest untill the Prince in Person wth the whole boddy of his Armie Consisting of att leaste 45000 men lay downe before this towne the 9th of August where they fell (by theire entrenchm^{ts} to make theire approatches) & wth theire batteries most violently made soe greate a breatch in the Easte corner of the Irish towne wale that 50 men may well in a breast affend it, wch they lost no time resolutely & viguorousily to putt in Ex^{on} for the 27th of August theÿ made theire attack wth att least aboute 8000 of the choice men of theire Armie who came on wth such resolution & currage & in such greate numbers that they beate oure men oute of theire pallisades on the side of the breatch wch they presently mounted, nay some of them enterd it but oure men being att first surprized att the attack wch they little Expected that day & were therefore the more careless & negligent of theire postes, haveing recoverd them Selves from the consternation they were in did soe bravlÿ & manfully sett appon them both in the breatch & pallisades that they were forcd to give way wth the loss of att leaste 2000 men, oure loss that day being not above 150 men. the next day as wee are enformed the Prince offerd himself in p^{r}son to head an other attack butt could finde butt feow to followe him such was theire entertainment the day before wch he findeing did imediatly scoure[13] away for Waterford in order to goe for Eng^{d} haveing left orders to raise the seige wch accordingly was donn the 30th of August that 3 weekes that they lay downe before the towne haveing by theire owne Confession dureing the Siege lost both by sicknesss & bale uppwards of 8000 men of the flower of all the armie, besides the greate Number of sick they carried off, & besides aboute 300 that were soe desperatt ill in theire hospitall as they thought them irrecoverable & therefore to save carriage burnt them alive moste barbarousely[.][14] wee had a garrison of att leaste 12000 men such as feow could be parralleld unto for vallour & endureing of greate fatigues[.] I have seene them come from the trenches after being th^{r} 48 houres wth oute tasteing abitt & yett when it happend as Severall times it did that they were allarmd just as they were beginning to feede in theire q^{rs} they would quitt theire vittles & runn to theire Armes as free & as willing as anny fresh men in the world, this is what hastie discription I cann give yo^{u} of Oure Siege. The ennemie are now in the Countie of Corck where tis said that they had wth in two day a recruite of 8000 foote come to them to Barrys Iland from Eng^{d}[.] if soe the weather being now as faire as anny summ^{r} will encurrage them to besiege Corck wch is Governd by Coll^{l} m^{c}Elligot[.][15] if this vessell wch onely waites for a winde stays for 24 houre longer I shall be able to give yo^{w} the certaintie thereof[.] I almoste forgott to tell yo^{w} that the Prince of Orange (who thought that Lymer^{k} would as Easily surrender as other places have donn) left his best Batterie gunns att Dublin & findeing them wanting to him sent for them to come hether, wch Coll^{l} Sarsfield (that Brave Heroe) haveing notice of march^{t} night & day wth such Expedition & soe very secrett that att 2 a Clock in a morneing two miles beyonde Cullen,[16] he did Surprize those that guarded the traine of Artillerie the fairest of the biggness that was in Christendom, & after haveing putt 500 horse & Dragoones to the sworde bursted 7 pieces of the gunns wth manny a thousand bumbs & a very greate quantitie of Powder[.] these were the success of oure partie since the route att Drogheda, besides the raiseing of a Siege by Sarsfield wch the Ennemie layd to Athone to theire loss. Oure ffrench succo^{rs} come over last Spring have quitted uss some daÿes before the Siege & wch was worse carried away all theire gunns & amonution & are since gone for ffrance, wee have dunn oure work I thanke god wth oute the assistance of anny of them I neede not tell yo^{w} the designes that were lay^{d} to betray the whole Kingdom[.] yo^{w} will have it att large there this much as to the affaires of the poore Nation, & now I will give yo^{w} a relation of my owne Condition.

Aboute a fortnight before the siege shiping presenting hence for ffrance severall went on them of the Natives of this Cittie & m^{r} John Rice[17] in particular, by his absence the coll^{rs} place[18] became vacant & I was orderd by the Goverm^{t} to manage it wch oblidged my continuance here dureing the Siege & now it is Confirmed uppon me but to noe advantage more then the bare sallarie wch the deareness of privision by reason of the little vallue sett uppon Brass monny Exhausts from me in a large measure, aboute 5 dayes after the route of Droheda my bro, W^{m} ffagan,[19] fa Barth: & John came hether, they all have theire qrs[20] wth me onely that Jo^{n} is onn into Kierry & two nights agonn Cap^{tn} Patr^{k} & his wife came from Dublin & are now of the ffamellie, I must now lett yo^{w} knowe deare Bro: wth a bleedeing heart that god was pleasd to deprive me of my onely comfort in the world[,] my dearest wife who deyed the 21th day of July haveing beene 16 weekes sick after childebearing & after her in 2 daÿes followed her faire boy who was the Occation of her sickness, yo^{w} knoweing how deare that woman was to me, may imagen in what measure I grieve for her loss[.] Kittie, Billie, & Sukie are all in health[,] I thanke god[,] & soe are oure frds in Kierry onely yor sonn James Trant who I am toulde is taken ill in a feaver, if the Ennemie prevailes in this countrie as they are like to doe unless Considerable supplyes are sent uss from ffrance, I must wth my child^{r} goe for ffrance for here wil be no liveing for anny man that was in anny employm^{t} civill or millitarie[.] I advised yor sonn James Trant to make a tender to Sr Patr^{k} Trant[21] of the Mortgage of Logh but it seemes he thought it sufficient to make it to Ambrose Moore,[22] wch Connell[23] tould him was not sufficient whyle the Principall person were in the countrie, Step: Rice[24] has enterd into the possession of Ballym^{c}doyle[25] & sayes he will make voyde yor lease butt my bro: Will is aboute driveing his stock which is on the land for the arr^{s}[26] of rent due thereunto[.] if wee finde anny quietness they shalbe driven to Kilarney[27] & slaughterd forthwth & soe give m^{r} Rice a yarde of his owne illegall p^{r}ceedeings[.] att least my bro: will threaten soe to doe I believe when oure Lord Com^{rs}[28] comes to towne that he will gett an order from them to disposses Rice[.] yor sheepe as yor sonn Trant toulde me aboute 3 monneth agon that he was here, have beene driven from Logh by Walt^r^ Trant & Blinde Gari^tt^ Pretend some bargaine made wth them by my sister Ellen were they now to be tould she would have yealded 30^£^ apeece[.] I presume m^r^ Trant has given yo^w^ an acc^t^ here of and of all yor affaires in Kierry ere now att leaste he toulde me he woulde, my Lady Slane[29] & my Lady Rice[30] are in Kierry the later wth Dom: Rice[31] & his ffamelly were lately in Galwaÿ to Embarque for ffrance butt have alterd theire resolutions, if I cann prevaile wth the people of Kierry to take brass monny as I am a fraide I cannot I wilbe soone unto of theire debt[.] yo^w^ must have a speciall care of Andie and Keepe a straight Eye over him yo^w^ knowe his faileings, my poore wife has left him entirely to yor managemt[.] I have donn the same likewise, my Co^n^ Connell[32] writes to her husband by this ship[.] I enclose her letter to my niece Kittie as I doe this to be forwarded to yo^w^[.] pray lett me have the satisfaction to heare from yo^w^ wth all speede, wee have an acc^t^ here that a peace is Concluded twixt the Emp^r^[33] & King of ffrance[.] its such good newes that I am a very doubtffull thereof, sure I am that something we want to be donn abroade that may preserve uss att home[.] the Ennemie are Rosolv'd (& I am a fraide if no succors come to uss that it will happen soe) to pein uss upp in the Countie of Clare and Province of Connaught wch will cause a greate ffamen amongst uss through scarsitie of bread, they are very powerfull & numerouse in horse & now in foote if they have the recruites come oute of Eng^d^ as wee are Enform'd[.] wee are Just now confirmed in the Newes that Corcke is surrounded wth the ennemie[.] I am in haste the vessel being Just on her departure. My blessing to Andie

Yo^r^ aff^tt^ Bro

Nicholas Skyddy

[1] Captain George Skiddy served in Clare's Regiment of the Irish Brigade in France. Having 'acquired a good estate in France', he rose to the rank of lieutenant-colonel and was made a 'Knight of the Military Order of St Louis' (O'Callaghan, *History of the Irish Brigades*, 290).

[2] 'The French navy kept the Jacobite resistance in western Ireland alive by frequent running of supplies to Galway and our western ports' (John de Courcy Ireland, 'The French Navy at the Time of the Williamite War', *OLJ*, 28).

[3] Thomas Pearce, a Quaker merchant in Limerick and one of the owners of the *Amity*.

[4] For Lieutenant-Colonel FitzMaurice, see O'Callaghan, *History of the Irish Brigades*, 38.

[5] In 1689, Lord Mountcashel brought a contingent of 5,000 Irish troops to France to replace the regiments that Louis XIV had sent to Ireland. These troops were initially formed into five regiments (Mountcashel's, Butler's, Fielding's, O'Brien's, and Dillon's) but in 1690 were consolidated into an Irish Brigade of three regiments (Mountcashel's, O'Brien's, and Dillon's), collectively known as Mountcashel's Irish Brigade (David Murphy, *The Irish Brigades, 1685–2006: A Gazetteer of Irish Military Service, Past and Present* [Dublin, 2007], 10–11).

[6] Lieutenant-Colonel Andrew Lee (b.1650) of O'Brien's Irish Regiment in France (later Dillon's). He rose to the rank of lieutenant-general and was honored as a Commander of the Order of Saint Louis (O'Callaghan, *History of the Irish Brigades*, 33–5, 38, 39, 646).

[7] In 1671, 'an infantry regiment of 1500 men, besides officers, [was] permitted by King Charles II to be levied in Ireland for service in France by Sir and Count George Hamilton, from whom, as its Colonel, it was called the "regiment d'Hamilton"' (O'Callaghan, *History of the Irish Brigades*, 33).

[8] Captain Edward Fitzgerald received his commission in the Irish army after Tyrconnell became Lord Deputy of Ireland under James II but before the outbreak of war. He served as an officer in Thomas Butler's regiment of infantry (D'Alton, *Army List*, 1:10; 2:242).

[9] James Trant, the son of Sir Patrick Trant and a lieutenant in the infantry company of Major-General Boisseleau, was killed at the siege of Cork in September 1690 (S. M., 'The Trant Family', *Kerry Archaeological Magazine*, 2:12 (March 1914), 240; D'Alton, *Army List*, 2:489).

[10] Lixnaw, Co. Kerry, was the principal seat of the FitzMaurice family (T. J. Barrington, *Kerry: Its History, Heritage & Topography* [Dublin, 1976], 257). For William FitzMaurice, see Letter 33, note 10.

[11] 'The island of Kerry' (Castleisland, Co. Kerry). The village got its name, 'Castle of the Island of Kerry', from a castle built in 1226 by Geoffrey Maurice, Lord Justice of Ireland during the reign of Henry III ('Castleisland', at http://homepage.eircom.net/~dinglemaps/genuki/KER/Castleisland/index.html [accessed 10 October 2024]).

[12] For Mother Christian Skiddy, see Letter 37.

[13] Scoure: 'to move about hastily or energetically (*OED*).

[14] Before departing Limerick, 'the Williamites set fire to their camp, burning everything that they could not take away, and the fire, having taken hold of the hospital, many of the sick perished in the conflagration' (Lenihan, 'Ballaí Luimnigh', 147).

[15] Roger MacElligott served as governor of Cork at the time of the siege of the city by Williamite forces in September 1690 (Childs, *Williamite Wars*, 268).

[16] Cullen, Co. Tipperary.

[17] John Rice was a Limerick merchant who served as collector in the weeks before the siege. He was among those attainted in 1691 (Lenihan, *Limerick*, 297; D'Alton, *Army List*, 1:204).

[18] Collector for the port of Limerick.

[19] For Fagans of Feltrim, see Hickson, *Selections from Old Kerry*, 233; D'Alton, *Army List*, 1:186, 2:17–18.

[20] Read: 'quarters'.

[21] For Patrick Trant, see Letter 3, note 5.

[22] For Ambrose Moore, see Letter 3, note 3.

[23] Several 'Connell' families in Co. Kerry were listed among the 'forfeiting proprietors in Ireland under the Cromwellian settlement, 1657' (John O'Hart, *Irish Landed Gentry* [Dublin, 1884], 247, 350–51).

[24] Sir Stephen Rice (c.1637–1715) – a native of Dingle, Co. Kerry – was a lawyer and chief baron of the Irish exchequer. 'After the battle of the Boyne (1 July 1690), Rice accompanied the king to France,' returning with Tyrconnell and Sir Richard Nagle the following January. In the aftermath of the Jacobite defeat in 1691, Rice 'retained his property and resumed his career at the bar' (Hazel Maynard, 'Rice, Sir Stephen', *DIB* [accessed 25 October 2024]).

[25] Ballymacdoyle (*Baile Mhic an Daill*), Dingle Civil Parish, Barony of Corkaguiny, Co. Kerry (Barrington, *Kerry: Its History, Heritage & Topography*, 242; 'Ballymacdoyle Townland, Co. Kerry', at https://www.townlands.ie/kerry/corkaguiny/dingle/glin/ballymacdoyle/ [accessed 19 October 2024).

[26] Read: 'arrears of rent'.

[27] Killarney, Co. Kerry.

[28] Richard Talbot, Duke of Tyrconnell.

[29] Anne Fleming (née Trant), Lady Slane, wife of Christopher Fleming, 17th Baron Slane (C. Clark and W. Finnelly [eds.], 'The Slane Peerage [1830–35]', in *The English Reports: House of Lords [1677–1865]*, vol. 7, ed. Alexander Wood Renton [London, 1901], 317).

[30] Mary Rice (née Fitzgerald) was the daughter of Thomas Fitzgerald of Ballylaghan, Co. Limerick (Hazel Maynard, 'Rice, Sir Stephen', *DIB* [accessed 25 October 2024]).

[31] For Dominick Rice, see D'Alton, *Army List*, 1:204.

[32] For E. Connell, see Letter 39.

[33] Holy Roman Emperor Leopold I (1640–1705). No peace was concluded in 1690, and the war continued until 1697. But the French had won a major victory on 1 July 1690 at the Battle of Fleurus in Flanders, which may have sparked optimism about an end to the War of the League of Augsburg on the Continent.

39. E. Connell,[1] Limerick, to Capt Connell[2] [place unknown], 25 September 1690. No. 13

Lymerick ye 25th of 7ber (1690)

My Dr Life

I recived a Letter from yu this day dated ye 2 of july from Burginberree; & two more out of nants one of ym this day 12 weekes in ye very weeke that ye Irish army broake in Drohydahy & a nother since & speedyly after began our distrucktion; in short all ye kings forceses drew highther hors & foote & destroyed all ye corn every where within 8 mile of ye town; nay all ye County of Clare & galway so as we are Like to have famine in this Country; I had ye timelyest & best harvest in ye county for somuch & sow all ye land yt wauld yeild a grain of corn; it was just reaping & all ye meddowes in ye whole farm was kept som mode[3] some not but ye kings hors capn came & did not Leave me one hand full of one nor ye other; & yn ye enemy Came at theire heels & I sent what cattell I had left to ye mountains & had neyther hors sheep nor cow Left but two milsh Cowes & 3 dry Cows; no friend had I to take care of me but every one minded his own concerns[.] I did not see Cosn Connell not of month [sic] before ye siege nor did not send to Look what was be com of me since; bro Robbin went to Sr William Kings[4] where he stayd dureing ye siege which helde 3 weeks & were at hot work for 30 days; at Johns gate[5] where they made a greate breach but Lost their arme & presently went of; & bro Robbin went up to dublin along with som of ym & there he is & cannot heare from hime nor se him; bro Stephen came for me to goe to dingle[6] but I being not in a readyness to goe with him staid in my own house till the Enemy Came; for they were at Cullin when my bro Came for me[.] he was ye only friend I had but he was forc'd to take to his heels towards dingle & Leave me to ye wide world; in short the enemy did not so much prejudice me as ye kings party before &

after btwixt them ass they left me nothing. ye prince of orrang came to knock[7] to take possession for I held it in spight of all till y^n & doe still though to no purpose[.] ye Enemy stript Nick Rice[8] & som Einglish gentle women that were with him in hospitall stark naked[.] Mrs holdanby was with me dureing ye siege & was stript 3 times[.] providence orderd it so as ye Enemy neyther striypt me nor any of my children nor famyly; & did use severall others most barbarous espesially in ye County of Lymerick both porestants [sic] & Catholiques; they were all a Like to ye forrainers that were in that army[.] they were with me severall times before they pluderd me till som of our neybours came to shew y^m ye way one fi^z Garrald he that Collected ye hearth money in ye County of Clare; then they tooke what they met in ye house which I did not much value[.] I had all last years wheat & malt in ye house som of my wheat thrashed som unthasht & about fiufty barrall of maltt all seasd on for ye king but not sent to ye stores till ye Enymy Came; of all this ye Enemy did not take above two barell of wheat from me & halef a barrell of malt not any oats though I had som thrast & unthast; but when ye sieg was raisd ye kings souldiers geting out of Lymerick plunderd ye whole country within sixe mile of ye town; I preservd all my gardens till y^n but now I have not a speads Length un-dugg of y^m; in fine I have just as much Left as will maintain us this winter if it be Left us now y^e Enemy is gon to take Cork haveing all y^e Kingdom but Gallayway & Lymerick; which will falle of Course if they have not aide of men & provision out of France; as for my part I know not what to doe till I heare from y^u for I have not money to $carr^y$ me over; & if y^u had staid with me I had don well enough for they did not mollest any body that did not beare arms since y^e 10 of july last; if our people makes good theire winter quarters & that y^u see they have aide out of france your best way is to Come to your charge; I shall (by y^e help of god) indeavour to hold till y^n if I live; I am bigg with child among ye rest of my misfortunes & expect to lyin before Xmass[.] tell David barry[9] his wife & children are well & were in this town durein ye sieg only ye Little who is in ye County of Corck with his friends; they want only their father as yet[.] m^r holdanby & his wife who is my very deare friends disires to be kindl [sic] remembred to you[.] I had one bedd Left me by ye Enemy & ye kings men tooke it away till my friend Jo sent me a bedd to Ly on[.] my chilldren & I lay on ye ground for a weeke so y^t wee are very well a quainted with y^e ruins of war[.] I writt to y^u be fore y^e siege[.] I never yet had a Letter from Rierdane nor I doe not belive his son ever sent any inclosed to him[.] this Last Letter came to key [tear: one missing word] gallayway[.] I got it axsidentally in this [tear: two missing words] where I have an $accomp^t$ of my Childes sickness which [tear: one missing word] me with admyration & aifflicktion when I consider all tis tru as times have hapned[.] I am glad to thinck you are in y^t plentifull Country; but at y^e sam time nothing can afflict me more y^n y^r absince & my Childes nor no Earthly thing can Comfort but that of your presence & his; I pray god direct you what to doe; y^u may well guese how it is with me & like to be with me haveing six smale Children to finde for & nothing to begin ye world with[.] nay if I had ever so much in this troublesom Country as it stands now I could Convert it to noe good use for neyther town nor Country is saffe & all people are impoversht of a sudden; I am glad y^{u} sent nothing by y^{m} officers[,] though I heare they are now landed in gallayway[,] for I finde so much falshood in ye world now that I know not who to trust; my Cou^{n} skeydys wife is dead. I meane Nick[.][10] your mother & all your Children & friends are well; my blesing to my dear Childe[.] my Love to bro^{r} Thady & ye rest of our friends my sister & father skeydy & tell him his old woman is still well; my dear I am still in so much Confuion & trouble that I know not what I write nor what I have writt but I suppose you have by this time had a full accomp^{t} of ye state of this country

Deare Joy I am yours whilest I live

E:C

[1] 'E. Connell' was the sister-in-law of Mother Christian Skiddy, a Catholic nun in 'l'ordre de Saint-François de Sainte-Elisabeth' in Nantes and the cousin of Nicholas Skyddy in Limerick. See Letter 37.

[2] 'Capt. Connell' was an officer in one of the Irish regiments in France, possibly Lord Clare's Regiment of Dragoons. See note 9 below.

[3] Read: 'mowed'.

[4] Sir William King (d.1706) owned land in six Irish counties. King served as mayor of Limerick in 1656. During the Williamite War, his sympathy lay with the Prince of Orange. 'Imprisoned during the second siege of Limerick, on 18 August 1691 he escaped, providing information to the Williamite army as it advanced on the city'. King was constable of Limerick castle in 1692 and MP for Co. Limerick in the Williamite parliaments of 1692–3 and 1695–9 (John Gibney, 'King, Sir William', *DIB* [accessed 25 October 2024]; Lenihan, *Limerick*, 704, 742).

[5] St John's Gate was the point in the fortifications defending Limerick's Irishtown where Williamite forces attempted to enter the city.

[6] The town of Dingle, Co. Kerry, is located on the northernmost of the five peninsulas on the south-west coast of Ireland.

[7] Read: 'came to call'.

[8] Nicholas Rice (b. c.1652) was a native of Dingle (Rice Family Newsletter, 4:3 [March 2011], at http://archive.constantcontact.com/fs051/1101861701430/archive/1104693840643.html [accessed 19 October 2024]).

[9] David Barry served as a lieutenant in Lord Clare's Regiment of Dragoons (D'Alton, *Army List*, 1:351).

[10] For the death of Nicholas Skyddy's wife, see Letter 38.

40. **Thomas Creagh,[1] Limerick, 'To M[r] Patrick Rirdane In Nantes', 25 September 1690. No. 18**

Lymerick y[e] 25th 7[ber] 1690

Cos Pat

S[r][,] I have not Reced any of yo[s] this six or seven month w[ch] makes me admire of yo[r] Neglect, this is to advise yo[w] that I desir[e] yo[w] will send me the acco[tt] curran[t] of the sales of y[e] 19 terces of salmon and allsoe the acco[tt] of the 214 Casques of butter left in yo[r] hands by frances Roch[2] if sould and and [sic] the like for the 80 Casques of butter sent yo[w] last w[ch] was included in Jo[n] Rirdanes bill of loading w[ch] I hope yo[w] have sould before this time[.] if not I desire yo[w] dispose of them wh[n] yo[w] think fitt to y[e] best of my advantadge, att the receipt hereof I desire yo[w] will be payer to madam Lee and Cleare the acco[tt] of the 20 Casques of butter shee Reced of mine w[ch] was Consined on James power of Rochell[.][3] but the master did put in to y[e] next port which was Nantes and there did dischardge and left my 20 Casques of butter to dispose of wth madam Lee[.] this acco[t] I have of M[r] James power of Rochell[.] pay[4] be carefull of my consernes and alsoe of y[e] consernes wth y[e] Insurance and frances Roch labor and paines not forgettting y[e] butt[r] that was lost there[.] I am yo[r] faithfull Kinsman after a blody sidge yo[r]

Tho Creagh

[p.s.] my love to Cos Rob[tt]

[1] Thomas Creagh, a Limerick merchant, was active in civic life, servings as a burgess of the City of Limerick in 1687 and 1688 and high sheriff in 1689 (Lenihan, *Limerick*, 272, 704).

[2] Francis Roch, a Limerick merchant, was pardoned 3 June 1699 by William III for adherence to the cause of James II (Jim Roache, 'Roache/Roach/Roche/Roch: Cambro-Irish Timeline', at https://rochelineages.wordpress.com/wp-content/uploads/2011/07/cambro-irish-timeline.pdf [accessed 7 October 2024]).

[3] James Power, a merchant in Limerick, had close associations with La Rochelle and was an occasional short-term resident of the French city. John Power, possibly a kinsman, served as mayor of Limerick in 1690 (ADC-M, Notaire Rivière, 3E1810, ff. 53v–54r; AMLR, GG 210, view 19; Lenihan, *Limerick*, 704).

[4] Read: 'pray'.

41. **Thomas Creagh, Limerick, 'To Madam Lee and sonn Jo[h] and Lucor, Merc[ht] In Nantes', 25 September 1690. No. 19**

Lymerik the 25th 7[ber] 1690

Madam Lee

I have Reced advice from Mr James Power[1] of Rochell that yo[u] have Reced twantie Casque of butter of mine Loaden on board the Virgin of Waterfoard whereof was master Luke figgins bound for Rochell but did a Rive in nantes and there did dischardge and left in yor hands for me 20 Casques of butter wch I doe not doubt but is sould before now[.] I desire yo^{u} will deliver ye acco^{tt} Cur^{tt} of s^{d} butter to my friende m^{r} patrick Rirdane who will forward it wth others acco^{tts} to me and therein yo^{u} will oblidge yor most humble ser^{tt}

Tho Creagh

[p.s.] I pray my harty love to my dear friende Mrs Leonard in telling her wee are all in good helth after the blody siege

[In left margin] 20 Casques butt^{r} marked [brand shows a capital 'C' imposed over a capital 'T']

[1] For James Power, see Letter 40, note 3.

42. **Thomas McNemara,[1] Limerick, 'for Messieurs Clerke and Quinn,[2] Merc^{ts}, In Lisborne', 25 September 1690. No. 32**

Lymericke 25th 7^{ber} 1690

Messrs Clerke and Quinn

I have none of y^{rs}[.] I long since desired y^{u} to Remit the nett proceeds of the Spedewels[3] Cargo, and doe hope y^{w} have Effected my s^{d} orders, if n^{t} please in receipt hereof, to make good one quarter part thereof unto the order of Alderman Robert Hannan of this towne, I say after all deductions he being concerned soe much too and from Lisborne, I am Gen^{t}

Y^{r} assured humble S^{t}

Tho: Macnemara

[p.s.] two of this tenner to date

[p.p.s.] Pay ye Contents of the within to Madam Lee & Company of Nantes for Robert Hannan

[1] Thomas McNemara was a prominent overseas merchant and ship owner in Limerick where he served on the board of burgesses in 1687 and 1688. By 1713, he and a kinsman, Daniel McNemara, were trading as 'Irish merchants in Nantes' (Lenihan, *Limerick*, 272; Saupin, 'Les réseaux commerciaux des Irlandais de Nantes', 132–6; Talbott, *Conflict, Commerce and Franco-Scottish Relations*, 136; Rilat, *Ces messieurs de Nantes*, 5:429).

[2] The Quinns were well established in Lisbon's mercantile life. Elsewhere in Portugal, Alexander Quin, an Irish merchant in Setúbal, was a powerful figure in the Portuguese salt trade. According to one authority, 'No merchant bought salt without his permission' (Ángel Alloza Aparicio, 'Portuguese Contraband and the Closure of the Iberian Markets, 1621–1640: The Economic Roots

of an Anti-Habsburg Feeling', *e-Journal of Portuguese History*, 7:2 (Winter 2009), at https://www.brown.edu/Departments/Portuguese_Brazilian_Studies/ejph/html/issue14/html/aaparicio.html [accessed 7 October 2024]).

[3] The *Speedwell* of Limerick, John Creagh, master, was bound for Nantes when it was captured by an English warship in May 1689. According to the deposition of a mariner on board, 'ye sd shippe Did belong to Thomas Mackmaroe, Ald. [Thomas] Creagh, one Mr White, and others, all being Reputed Roman-catholicks' (Deposition of Joseph Phitcett, 8 June 1689, TNA, HCA 32/1932/1 [*Speedwell* of Limerick]).

43. Robert Hannan, Limerick, 'To mr Patrick Rirdan, Merchant In Nantes', 25 September 1690. No. 33

Lymerick 25th Septbe^{r} 1690

m^{r} Patrick Rirdan

S^{r}

My last was 16th Cur^{t} since have none of y^{rs}[.] alderman Thos Harrold[1] our Mayor & I writt ye 22^{d} Cur^{t} to fraight a vessel of 100: or 150^{tts} writing on both our acc^{tts} hither & back to y^{e} & theron or on a vessell more or lesse to loade ten tun^{s} brandy ½ in pipes & ½ in q^{r} Casques 15 a 20^{tts} wheate to be baged up in ye ships sterne 3^{tts} best angy[2] or canery wine[3] & 6:^{tts} best Burd^{x} Clarrett want thereof 6^{tts} of ye best Clarett yo^{u} can find & one Tun vinigar in q^{r} Casques, 60 @ lining[4] of 24 to 26 § pr @ for shurting, one dozen of fasionable freunch hatts & the rest of y^{e} vessels loadeing to be in the whitest coarse salt[,] y^{r} insureing all to & froe on our acc^{tt}[.] It seemes by yr le[tter] on 18th ult to him that y^{u} concerned him $^{1}/_{9}$ in 204: Roules tobacco, he writt y^{u} in several letters that he consented I should have amoity[5] thereof & y^{r} to loade it on the vessell y^{u} are to freight it for him & I if y^{u} did not allredy loade it, I formerly writt y^{u} that if you loade the $^{1}/_{3}$ of y^{e} s^{d} 204 Rouls (yo^{u} say aldn Harrold refused) on this desired vessell on my acc^{tt} that I will accept of it & yo^{u} to loade it mainely level ald^{n} Harrold & I placeing ½ its cost to his acc^{tt} & ½ to myne which be all he writt 22° wth his consent to y^{u}, yor insuering it all – pray be nemble in this afraightm^{t} for that I have goods on my hands & am buying more wth full ad^{rs} not to be seazed on as som of neighbors was

Yo^{u} writ me the Hopewell went from London to Lixbone[.] its but fayre and just either to arrest & serve her by the forme & send her hither from thence att my risque wth salt 10: boxes of lemons & ten of oranges & one thousand pound of St Domingo tobacco[6] & if m^{r} Degrave be bound to indemnify y^{u} as y^{u} say he is yo^{u} can ye better effect it[.] I pray lett me have her & gett the rest of y^{r} s^{d} goods insured & 4000^{lt} tur on y^{r} vessell hither if this youl doe; on the word of a Christain[.] I am [deleted word] a very great looser by yor not sending her to me according my ord^{ers} when you sent her contrary thereto for London — pray send me ten p^{s} fine kintin of 26 § p^{r} @ & ten p^{s} d^{o} of 18 § p^{r} @ p^{r} m^{r} John Mitchell m^{r} of the Recovery[7] of this Island & 12 @ of fationable striped silck mixed wth severall cullers of 40: to 50 § p^{r} @ & six fationable black french hatts of 4lt prs & 15 @ of lining of 26 § pr @ to make new shurts advise please of ans & yr goods & write me often via Brest, Rochell, & St Mallo — I am Sr Yr most Humble Servt

Robert Hannan

[p.s.] better for yr governmt will be in great esteem wth yu for that yu maye expect but very litle thrade from this Kingdom now or att any tyme hereafter[.] however sell myne & my lords tallow as yu thinck fitt but haysten not wth ye butter till weere Quit — pray send Aldn Harrold & I the vessel wth all speede — if not allwed[8] then pay mr James Rice Francis twelve hundred livres to be given mr Wm Creagh[.] Writ a woord about this in yr next & pray write me often[.] pray send 10: a 12:lt worth of sweete meates of severall sortes send me 20 @ of sad cullerd fationable drugett pr the Recovery mixed also a little silck — Send me also one pound of fine white led, & a pound do finer pr sd Recovery & a few Capers if any & a few limons and oranges — send me one pound of nutmegs — faward my son James ye inclosed & write to him to send me his answer pr this vessell & to write yur owne in 20 ds enclose a lettr for me therein, lett me know if he mindes his stoudy well

[1] Thomas Harrold, a Catholic, served as sheriff of Limerick in 1687 and mayor in 1689 (Lenihan, *Limerick*, 704).

[2] Anjou wine, i.e. white wine from the Loire Valley, upriver from Nantes.

[3] Wine from the Canary Islands.

[4] Read: 'linen'.

[5] Read: 'a moiety'.

[6] Tobacco from Spanish Santo Domingo on the island of Hispaniola transshipped through Lisbon, Portugal.

[7] The vessel on which John Mitchell served as master was the *Amity* of Limerick, not the *Recovery* of Limerick. Hannan was mistaken or unforeseen circumstances altered this plan.

[8] Read: 'allowed'.

44. **John D'herbe, Limerick, to 'Monsr Jean Stalpaert,[1] Marcht a Nantes', 25 September 1690. No. 51[2]**

Lymeryk 25 Septemb 1690

Monsieur John Stalpaert

Monsr Ick bevinde my vereert met UE aengenamen dato 31 maij Lastleden met incloss brief van d'heer Phillipe van Tours van Brugghe, aen de welcke aen hem onder couverte van UE synne antwoorde gaet, versoeken UE deselve aen hem, ditto voort te steuren. Wat aengaet van de negotie alhier is schaers niet te doen, geen persoon is bequaem om satisfactie te geven soo well in t' regard vande negotie als met 't incorrageren der selver, ter cause van t' copergelt dewelcke alhier niet gerespecteert en wort, maer ofte imant een scheepie van 35 a 50 vatt mett saut, wyn die goet is & brandewijn hadde, daer soude een moye cause aen te becommen wesen dewyll wy alhier goederen wtlantsch voor dese connen becommen Andersits isser niets tedoen, & alles ter cause van t' coper gelt alhier regeert.

Van deser stadt isser geen scheepen te becommen omme te bevrachten, dat UE een schepie van ontrent 40 vatt conde becommen onder sauf conduit geladen met sout brandewijn & wyn ten beste prijs alhier soudemen sulcken prijs in trocq van goederen maeken dat het ongeloovelck is behalve alle soorten van mersenerije die hier manqueren tot spellen toe die hier inde wijnkells 1 stuyver stucq vercocht worden, de prijs der waech is: dat geen vleys encan vercocht worden, boter is niet af te schepen, roet moet vercocht worden beneffens de gesoute huyden in trocken omme redens dat sout hier gelt 8£ coper de brystoll barrill Des volghens moet de negotie van nu voortaen met geen ghelt alhier maer bij trocquen gedaen worden agannerno

Soo UE eenig voordeel voor goederen voor goederen te senden naer dese quartieren soo UE t' geradyg vint k' will myn ¼ met UE adventuren @ daer in sall UE groot voordeel bevinden met t'senden ofte afschepen van dese inlantse goederen.

In trocke van de [wyn] brandewyn, saut, lynen, canthen, garen, moden, etc. versoeke UE tselve te considereren, eenigh voordeel te vinden elc ende waerin ik UE dienst can doen command[t] te gelick aen die blyft in de qualiteit van [obscure word]

Mons[r]

John d'herbe

Translation

Limerick 25 September 1690

Monsieur John Stalpaert[1]

Mons[r] I am honoured by your welcome [letter] of 31 May last, with the enclosed letter of my lord Phillip van Tours of Bruges, to which I send his reply under cover of your honour's, requesting your honour to send the same on to him. As regards the trade here, it is barely possible. No person is able to give satisfaction, both regarding the trade and in encouraging it, because of the copper money, which is not respected here. But if one shipped 35 to 50 tuns of salt, good wine, and brandy, that would provide a fine opportunity because we can obtain foreign goods for them here. Otherwise there is nothing to be done, and all because of the copper money here.

From this town no ships can be found to take freight. If your honour could obtain shipping of around 40 tuns, under safe conduct, loaded with salt, brandy, and wine at the best prices, they would fetch such a price in bartered goods here that it is unbelievable, except that all sorts of merchandise that are lacking here, even needles that are sold in the shops here for the price of one *stuyver* a piece. There is no meat to be sold, butter cannot be shipped, and tallow must be bartered along with salted hides because salt is sold for £8 copper [money] per Bristol barrel. As such the trade must in future be done here not with money but by barter.

If your honour therefore has further trade goods to send to this place for goods, if your honour thinks it advisable, I wish to venture my ¼ with your honour & your honour will find great advantage from sending or shipping off of these native goods.

In exchange for [wine], brandy, salt, linen, lace, thread, fashions, etc., I request you to consider it and seek some advantage reciprocally and command me in what I can be of service to you. Who remains at the same time in the quality of [obscure]
Monsr

John d'herbe

[1] Jean Stalpaert (d.1720), a Flemish merchant originally from Ostend, was a prominent figure in Nantes' expatriate trading community, though by 1704 he was doing business in Cadiz (Rilat, *Ces messieurs de Nantes*, 5:293; L. Gilliodts-Van Severen, *Coutumes des pays et comté de Flandre. Coutume de la prévoté de Bruges* [Brussels, 1887], 100; Anne Mézin, 'La correspondance des consuls de France à Cadix', in Anne Mézin and Anne Pérotin-Dumon (eds.), *Le consulat de France à Cadix: Institution, intérêts et enjeux [1666–1740]* [Paris, 2019], 44, available at https://books.openedition.org/pan/464 [accessed 12 October 2024]).

[2] The editors wish to thank Wim Klooster and Timo McGregor for assisting with the translation of this letter but acknowledge responsibility for any remaining errors.

45. **John D'herbe, Limerick, to 'Monsr Phillippe van Tours,[1] March^t^ a Bruges', 25 September 1690. No. 52[2]**

Lymerijk adij 25 7ber 1690

D'heer Phillippe van Tours

Mijnheer

UE aengenamen dato 13 maije so well ontfangen onder couverte van [Hr] Jan Stalpaert van Nantes.[3] De hoppe die UE in Compagnie met Jan Batt Korreel gehadt heeft is vercocht, t' ghelt betaelt ten deelen in Silver ende ten deele in roet inde maent ofte van may ofte Junij 1689; t' roet heeft sij afgescheept. T' ghelt heft ontgetwijffelt syne wed^e^ dewelcke een edele vrauw is; maer van t' geslaghten van d' inwoonders van t' graefschap van Connaugh geen satisfactie en behouft UE te verwachten so lancq als den oorloogh deurt: soo de wetten hier waeren als a costij alles waere well; considereert de saeke & de gelegentheijt van dit lant dewyll wy alhier voor Lymeryk hebben genootsaekt geweest te onderstaen de miserabelsten beleghering die oyt soo ick geloove ins' menschens gedenkenisse bedoncken can worden voor den tyt van 21 daghen, in dewelcke wij soo den vyant ons overcommen hadden: wij allegader sonder genade vermoort souden sijn geweest. Deselve vyanden syn vertrocken van dese stadt sonder slagh te leveren maer laeten deselve erger door hun bombardeeringen als Oudenarde[4] in @ 83: gestelt was. Ick magh UE geen voorder nieuws geven, voorder clarissem^{nt} wegens Ald^{m} Rostert meer dan ick hier vooren gest. hebbe can ick niet geven: desaeke van haer is sleght gestelt, dewyl, wanneer ick haer in rechte betrocken hadde sy valsche borghe voor haere adminisdrad^{ie} ingestelt heeft, can icke UE heenighen dienst alhier doen commandeer mij; ick sall UE oorders soo verre mij het mogelyck is naer de wetten vervolghen. Soo daedelicq compter tydinghe dat in dese reviere een schip van Dunq^{e} gearr. is met tobacq dat veel gelt weerdigh is, hoppe alluyn meecrappe &a. dat [*illegible word*] cargasoen is ingevallen dat maer goederen daer voor can gecocht werden welcke niet getwijffelt wort daerom soo UE eenigh inclina[tie] hebt omme deser weghte negotieren gelijk als d' heer Coppenolle[5] doet, ende waer in ick UE dienst can doen commandeert,

Mijnhr,
[obscure]

John D'herbe

[p.s.] Hier is geen staet op pryssen van goederen te maeken dewijl geen te becommen is dan goet voor goederen daer in is yts te doen, Corcq is belegert alsoo den vyant dat neempt wy syn verlooren

Translation

Mr Phillippe van Tours[1]

Limerick, 25 September 1690

Sir,

Your honour's welcome [letter], dated 13 May, was well received under cover of Jan Stalpaert of Nantes.[2] The hops your honour had in company with Jan Batt Korreel have been sold, the money paid partly in silver and partly in tallow in the month of May or June 1689. They have shipped the tallow. The money is undoubtedly with his widow, who is a noble woman. But for the slaughter of the inhabitants of the county of Connaught, your honour need not expect satisfaction as long as the war continues: if the laws here were as with you, all would be well. Consider the cause and the situation of this country while we in Limerick have had to endure, for twenty-one days, the most miserable siege that can be recalled in living memory, so I believe, in which we, if the enemy had overcome us, would all have been murdered without mercy. Those enemies have departed from this city without giving battle, but leave the same

worse because of their bombardments than Oudenaarde[4] in 1683. I cannot give you further news, [or] provide further clarification regarding Alderman Rostert beyond what I told you before. Their cause has been handled poorly since; when I engaged them legally, they established false surety for their administration. If I can be of service to your honour in this regard command me. I shall follow your honour's orders as much as possible within the laws. We have presently received tidings that a ship from Dunkirk has arrived in this river with tobacco that is worth a lot of money, hops, alum, and common madder. Goods can undoubtedly be bought for that cargo, therefore if your honour has any inclination to trade these away, just as Mr. Coppenolle[5] does, and in whatever I may be of service to your honour, command me, My lord,
[obscure]

John D'herbe

[p.s.] The prices of goods cannot be relied upon here because merchandise can only be obtained for goods that are in demand. Cork is besieged. If the enemy takes it we are lost.

[1] For Phillippe van Tours, see Ambroïse Keelhoff, *Histoire de l'ancien couvent des ermites de Saint Augustin, à Bruges* (Bruges, 1869), 132.

[2] The editors wish to thank Wim Klooster and Timo McGregor for assisting with the translation of this letter but acknowledge responsibility for any remaining errors.

[3] For Jan Stalpaert, see Letter 44, note 1.

[4] Oudenaarde, a city in Flanders, lies along the Scheldt River south of Ghent.

[5] François van Coppenolle (1633–1701) was a Brussels textile entrepreneur and dealer in fine tapestries (Koenraad Brosens, Klara Alen, and Astrid Slegten, 'Claiming Commerce, Quality and Credit: *Raisons d'être* of the Antwerp and Brussels tapissierspanden [Sixteenth–Eighteenth Centuries]', *Textile History*, 49:1 [2018], 14–15).

46. **Samuel Taverner, Limerick, 'To John & Edm^{d} Gould, Merchants In Rochell', 25 September 1690. No. 57; bill of lading, 25 September 1690. No. 78**

Limericke 7mo 25th 1690

Esteemed ffriends

Its a Longe time since I receaved Any from you neither have I wrote you for want of ocation[.] the present troble is to desire you will take into your care the contents of the Enclosed bill of Ladeing and dispose of the goods to ye most advantage of the concerned. I have Loaden twentie hogsheads of Tallow In wch I am Interested two thirds and Zacharie Holland one third two Tun of salmon fish and the one third of 198 sault hydes, and twelve sault hydes by themselves those goods Compleats one fourth of the Tunage being my parte, pray dispose of those goods for my best advantage and place the neat proceeds to my Credit, y^{ts} to say the neat proceeds of two thirds of the tallow, of one third of 198 salt hydes, of two tun of the Salmon and of the 12 ox hydes, wch are by themselves, and reload 3 qrt^{rs} of the ship for the acompt of Tho Pearce Zach Holland, and my Selfe, with Sixteen hogsheads of Choyce Coniack whyte wine, sixteen caskue brandie, I mean quarter caskues, and ye rest in Sault aplying one third of the cost to Each mans particulr Acompt[.] send alsoe on the same triple Acompt 60 reams of paper, one third ordinary shop paper, and the other two thirds good writeing paper of 2 or 3 sorts[.] furnish the master if hee wants it as far as fortie Crowns on ye ships Acomp^{t}, aplying a third to Each mans acomp^{t}[.] a fourth more must bee p^{d} him on James Cravens[1] Acomp^{t} who hath a fourth of ye ship, and hath some talloe on board as ye m^{r} can direct[.] I desire ye master may have all possible dispatch and advise mee ye needfull In reference to trade[.] when my goods are sould and their neat proceeds in cash, remitt ye ballance unto my wife Prudence Taverner at ye house of Joseph Scriven Linen Draper, at ye seyne of ye ragged Staff and beare In watling Street In London[.][2] but if shee should bee come for Irland, keepe it in your hands for my further orders hartily wishing you well, I take Leave, and remaine Your Verrie af^{ect} friend

Samuel Taverner

[p.s.] James Craven gives directions about Loading his 4th of ye ship

BILL OF LADING

Shipped by the Grace of God in good order and well conditioned, by *Samuel Taverner, Zachary Holland, and Thomas Pearce* in and upon the good Ship called the *Amity* whereof is Master under God for this present Voyage *John Michel* and now riding at Anchor in the *Pool of Limerick*, and by Gods grace bound for *Nants, or Rochel, or Bordx* to say *foure hundred fifty six sault hydes, fifty one dry hydes*[,] *forty two tierses of salmon fish, and twenty hogs heads of tallow* being marked and numbered as in the Margent, and are to be delivered in the like good order and well conditioned, at the above said Port of *Nants, Rochel, or Bordux* (the danger of the seas only excepted) unto *Patrick Rirdan of Nants or John & Edmond Gould of Rochel* or to *their* Assigns, he or they paying freight for the said Goods *nothing* with Primage and Avarage accustomed. In witness whereof the Master or Purser of the said Ship hath affirmed to *3* Bills of Lading all of this tenor and date; the one of which *3* Bills being accomplished, the other *two* to stand void. And so God send the good Ship to her desired Port in safety. Amen. Dated in *Limerick ye 25th Sep^{tr} 1690.* [signed] *John Mitchell*

[1] For Alderman James Craven, see Letter 33, note 8.

[2] 'The Bear and Ragged Staff' was a tenement in Watling Street near St Paul's Church (Henry A. Harben, 'Bear and Ragged Staff [The] - Beche [La]', in *A Dictionary of London* [London, 1918], British History Online https://www.british-history.ac.uk/no-series/dictionary-of-london/bear-and-ragged-staff [accessed 23 December 2024]).

47. Samuel Taverner, Limerick, 'To Patrick Rirdane, Merchant In Nants', 25 September 1690. No. 7

Limericke 7mo 25th 1690

Patrick Rirdan

My Last was the 20th Curr^{t} wch goes by this Conveyance To wch I reffer thee, and this is to advise that I have Loaden twenty hogsheads of Tallow In wch I am Interested Two thirds and Zachary Holland one third two Tun of Salmon fish and the one third of 198 Sault hydes, and twelve sault hydes by themselves, those goods compleats one fourth of the tunage being my parte[.] pray dispose of those goods for my best advantage and place the neat proceeds to my Credit that is to say the neat proceeds of two thirds of the 20 hogsheads of Tallow, of one third of 198 hydes, of Two tun of the Salmon, and of the 12 ox hydes, and reload three Quarters of the ship for the Accomp^{t} of Tho Pearce, Zacharie Holland, and my selfe, with sixteene hogsheads of Anjou wine,[1] choyce, and whyte, sixteene quarter caskue of Brandie and the rest In Sault aplying one third of the Cost to Each mans particulr Accompt[.] Send alsoe on y^{e} same triple Acompt sixty reams of paper one third ordinary shop paper, and y^{e} other two thirds good writing paper of 2 or 3 sortes[.] furnish the master if he wants it, as farr as fourtie Crownes, on y^{e} ship Acompt, aplying a third to Each mans part, the widow Lee, will furnish $^{4}/_{1}$ [sic] on James Cravens Acompt[.] I desire thee will give the master all possible dispatch, with my heartie repects To thy Selfe[,] I remaine

Thy verry Lov friend

Samuel Taverner

[p.s.] when all my goods are Sould, and In cash, remitt the full ballance of my Acompt to my wife In London or if shee should bee come for Irland, y^{l} remitt all to Rich^{d} haynes[2]

[1] For Anjou wine, see Letter 43, note 2.

[2] For Richard Haynes, see Letter 13, note 5.

48. Samuel Taverner, Limerick, 'To Prudence Taverner[1] at Joseph Scriven, Linen draper at the ragged staff and beare In watling street In London', 25 September 1690. No. 73

Limericke 7mo 25th 1690

My owne dearest hart

Thy most aceptable Lines of the 20th of ye 4th month Last are but newly come to my hands, and is ye first that I have receaved from thee, for these

Severall months past, but am over Joyed to hear of thy welfare wch is my harts desire may Longe continue, and that wee may have the Sweet felicity of Enjoying one another, once againe, I thinke all ye hardships and hazards that this uncertaine world, can impose on us shall never separate us more but will take our chance toogether[.] Let what will happen wee wil bee fellow sharers in prosperity, and adversity, and Leave all to providence, I could write much if it were convenient[.] I have shipt about two hundred pounds worth of goods to Nants, or Rochell, wch place the ship Can first make, if to Nants have ordred Patr Rirdane to remitt thee ye neat proceeds, and if to Rochell have ordred Edmond Gould to doe ye Same[.] I know not what Rirdane hath done, for I have noe Late Acompts from him, I ordred him Longe agoe to remitt thee mony, but I heare nothing from him, I heare my Cuz Ambrose Monihen is in this Countrie, I know not what will be done with Johny Craven,[2] I sent him hence, to bee ridd of him, not imagining twould bee thy hard fortune to bee perplexed with him, thee shouldst not have taken Any notice of him, but Left him to his brother but now it Canot bee helpt, I hope wee shal soone see Each other, my father mother, Broths &c are in health, but people dyes heare fast, the underneath are deceased within this Litle time[.] my Love to Sarah, and Hanah, with my verry deare Love to thy owne Sweet Selfe,

I am my dearest Hart[,]
Thy most afect husband untill death

Samuel Taverner

Samuel Berkley	John Hart	John Harts wife
Andrew Griggin	Tho Chambers	John Harper
Samuel Jacobs	Goody Moss	Hoel Jones wife
Nicholas Starky at my fathers	Captn Bentlys wife	Captn Lucas Daniel
Bowman Senior[3]	John Bayly Joynr	Walter hubbart
Hugh Montgomery	John foxon	John Cruce
Edw freeman	Margt Gore	Martha Martine
James Grubb	Thebaldys wife	Hanah Rumsay
Judith Clark	Tom hukmans wife	Betty Carr, als Martine
Henry Seymons	Mary Benet	Richd Cooper
Edwd wights wife	Aidn Warr	Jane Cooke
John Pappen	Richarde Abell	James Boulton
Martha Bowman[4]	Grumbly ye Excsman	

[1] Prudence Taverner (née Pearce), a native of Co. Limerick, married Samuel Taverner on 9 August 1680. She was the sister of Thomas Pearce, her husband's business partner ('Prudence [Pearce] Taverner', at https://www.wikitree.com/wiki/Taverner-197 [accessed 7 October 2024]).

[2] Johny Cravin was the son of James Cravin, Sr, a founding member of Limerick's Quaker Meeting. See Letter 33, note 8.

[3] Daniel Bowman, Sr, and Simon White served as sheriffs of Limerick City in 1684. 'Daniel Bowman, and Martha his wife, … obtained grants in St John's Parish, St Nicholas' Parish, in St Lawrence's Parish, in St Michael's Parish, and townlands in the South Liberties of Limerick' in the Restoration land settlement of 1666 (Lenihan, *Limerick*, 192, 704).

[4] For Martha Bowman, see above, note 3.

49. James Cravin, Limerick, 'To James Cravin, Junr, Merchant [London]', 25 September 1690. No. 70

Lymerick 25th September: 1690

Deare sonn

My Last unto thee was via Dunkirk by Jonathan Pery since thyne came to hand via Nantes pr Abr Bartely dated 20th Xbr last — Aboute 3 months since the Amitty arrived here Loaden with goods for S.T.[1] T.P.[2] & Patr Riwrdan Loaded my Quarter part for his owne Accot & writ att the same time unto S. Taverner that the charge of the redemption of My 4th pt came unto 400 Livres wch same I was willing to have discounted wth his brother John here out of this fraight inwards fraight being werth at Least five pounds pr tunn[.] but he would not alledgeing he had noe such order but to relade his 4th pt of again wch at this time I was willing not to contest but submitt unto In hopes his Bror Patrick will account & discount for the charges he hath been at for the said 4th pt & for the fraight due from himselfe the Widdow Lee & Sonns unto whom I have sent a Letter of Procuration[3] to that Purpose[.] I have sent a smale barell in her vizt one tunn of salmon & 12 or 13 hhds of tallow the wch I hope wth wt may be had from Patr Rirdan may Relade my pt back againe — we have had sad times here since thy departure[.] however God has preservd thy mothr Bros & sisters[.] Writ a line if Richard & John be well for I have not heard from them: not these 3 months[.] Thy onkle Trevor came to towne here & Ley sick wth us & dyed the 21st instant & thy Aunt Bennett the 19th or Friday before at Enish for wch our deare Loves to thee,

I remaine — Thy Loveing father

James Cravin

[p.s.] John Mitchell is still master of the Amitty — if this comes to hand in time write to Patr the needfull Remember our deare Love to Prudence[4] Johny[5] & all frends & Lett us heare from thee as often as thou canst

[1] Samuel Taverner.

[2] Thomas Pearce.

[3] Letter of Procuration: a document 'appointing a person with legal authority to act on one's behalf; the authority so delegated; (also) the authorized action of one's agent; the function of an attorney or representative' (*OED*).

[4] For Prudence Taverner, see Letter 48, note 1.

[5] For Johny Cravin, see Letter 48, note 2.

50. Zachary Holland, Limerick, 'To m^r^ Jos: Holland, Merch^t^ In Minehead',[1] 25 September 1690. No. 72

ye 25th Septr 1690

Dere Brother

I have not had the hapyness of hearing from you sence the trobles hapned[.] I hope this will finde you my sister and yor wife well, this goes by a small Vesle bound for ffrance[.] the chife Oration is to aquaint you of the welfaire of all our relacion, it has pleased [several words scratched out] god to perserve us in helth wch is a greatt Marcie[.] manie of our Nabo^rs^ are hackin away wth the Country decease[.][2] I have bene unfortunat^e^ in sendnig [sic] to Sea in a Vesle where one W^m^ fflaxson went in I had to the Vallue of £300[.] s^d^ fflaxson played the knave, I here from Carpent^er^[3] s^d^ ship was condemped, in England w^h^ is very hard to me that Tho Perse and I sent a smalle Barke for Ostend the cargo & Barke cost nere £400 p^od^[4] here[.] s^d^ Ship arriv^d^ safe but now feare he doth not desine to performe his promise[.] wee sent Tho fflaxson super cargoe he being Ingenious and macking [scratched out word] us great assurance of his retorning wch would be of greater advantage than I will mention[.] If you here of s^d^ parson pray aquaint m^r^ Thos & Jos Carpenter, that he may manadge that sparke,[5] I had great confidence in him, tho his Bro sarved me soe Ill

in the begennig of these trobles I sent goods to the value at least of £200 to m^r^ Abr Elton of Bristol[.][6] I orderd him to Remit of the produce £100 to m^r^ Tho & Jos Carpent^er^, who sence wrote me that he had not done it, wch I am much Concern^d^ for, I believe [indecipherable word] and Ab^r^ Ethan had Losses here, but I hope he is able for I have great dependence one what is in his hands, I will not Inlarge, but I wish I had the happyness of seeing you, the vesel I am concerned in the produce I have Ord^r^ to m^r^ Carpenter, I have order the master Mr Michel to adress you [here ?][.] you may send a Line to me in answer of this, I write not [indecipherable word], my ffather & Mother Bro & Sister Desires to be Rembred to you and yo^rs^[.] soe Doth Dr Brother him who is

Yo^r^ affectinat Brother

Zack Holland

[p.s.] wee have a report here that Bro Thomas went to the west Indies[.] lett me know theereof, keep what I write of Ethan to y^r^ selfe, lett me Know p^r^ ye bearer how he is

[1] Joseph Holland, the brother of one of the owners of the *Amity*, Zachary Holland, was a member of the Quaker Meeting in Minehead, a coastal town in Somerset, England.

[2] In this period, typically a reference to dysentery. Holland, however, mentions 'hackin' – coughing – suggesting a respiratory illness.

[3] For Joseph Carpenter, London, see Letter 22, note 1.

[4] Read: 'pounds'.

[5] Spark: 'A young man of an elegant or foppish character; one who affects smartness or display in dress and manners. Chiefly in more or less depreciatory use' (*OED*).

[6] For Abraham Elton of Bristol, see Letter 23, note 3.

51. **Robert Talbot, Limerick, 'To Patrick Cusacke, Chester', 26 September 1690. No. 47**

Limerick ye 26 of september 90

Deare Cousen

I prais god I am able now to goe a litlle and I am hartely glad to heare you are all safe landed[.] deare Coussen as for giving you an account of the seegh it were litle to tedious for me in ye condition I am in but I supose adam has given you account of all oure proceedings heare[.] I have been desperate^{ly} wounded in to two places but hopes to doe well, but be forced to goe on Cruchess a long tim before I recover the use of my legg but I am past danger[.] this being all from yor affectinat kinsman

Robert Talbott

[p.s.] my respects to Deare dowdall to my honnored my lady ales not forgeting yor deare selfe let me heare from you

52. **Adam Cusack,[1] Limerick, 'To Mr Mathew Rooth, or in his absence to Dr Patrick Cusacke[2] att m^{r} Gregory ffitzgerra^{lds},[3] March^{t} in Nantes', 27 September 1690. No. 45**

Limbrick ye 27th 7ber 1690

Deare S^{r}:

Although my acquaintance with y^{w} bee a suffitient pretense for the ambition I have had of presenting yow wth My lines since yower departure, yett the want of Conveniency occationed my long silence[.] butt finding this oportunity I Could noe longer delay giveing yow My humble respects as alsoe to lett yow understand that yower brother is in very good health; pray when next yow write to him desier him to stand my frind for hee is very great wth Dorrington[4] and on y^{t} acco^{t} Maÿ doe mee a very great Kindness, pray doe mee the favour as to write to mee p^{r} next Conveniencÿ and send the incloseds to My bro: & yo^{wr} Complyance heerein will oblige

Y^{r} Most Humble & affec^{t} Servant

Adam Cusack

[p.s.] Pray give my service to m^r^ ffi^tz^gerrald to m^r^ Browne & Conly to Mrs Aylwood[5]

[1] Adam Cusack served as an ensign in the King's Regiment of Infantry (D'Alton, *Army List*, 2:5).

[2] Dr Patrick Cusack was a Catholic priest. 'When, in 1690, King James [II] assumed to exercise ecclesiastical patronage in Ireland, he presented Dr. Patrick Cusack … with the vicarage of Saint Mary of Drogheda' (John D'Alton, *The History of Drogheda, with Its Environs*, 2 vols. [Dublin, 1844], 1:44–5).

[3] For correspondence between Gregory Fitzgerald, a merchant in Nantes, and John Aylward of Saint-Malo, see 'Aylward Papers', 6, 7.

[4] For William Dorrington, see Letter 26, note 1.

[5] Helena Aylward was the wife of the Saint-Malo merchant, John Aylward, a native of Waterford (Pizzoni, *British Catholic Merchants*, vii–viii; 'Aylward Papers', 1).

53. **Adam Cusack, Limerick, 'To the Reverend ffather in God Dr Patrick Cusack in Nantes or elsewhere', 27 September 1690. No. 46**

Limbrick the 27th Sep^ber^ 1690

Deare Life

The regreet I have for the absence of a Brother soe deare to mee as you must needs bee, makes me in writing to yow, seeke the Consolation I Cannot finde, of seeing yow, not that I mean to send yow an acco^t^ of all the transactions that hapened in this kingdom since yower departure, butt onely to let you understand that ouer Irish have behaved themselves gallantly and hope they have regained their Creditt, the Prince of Orrange Marched hither on the 9th of August with 28 thousand horse and foote and Continued his scene untill the 30th dittot[1] dureing wch time they gained three redoubts of ouers and fortified themselves soe well that they drew their trinches within 50 yards to oure pallessades, and then ye prince sent in a trompett that wee might surrender ye Citty and deliver up the keys and that wee should enioÿ ouer lives and liberties as wee did in King Charless time upon wch an answer was sent that the Keyes of the towne weare in St Germaine's[2] and that they would never bee surrendred without spesiall orders from the King of france[.] Moreover they placed 4 batterries within a muskett shott of the wall with 6 peeces of Cannon on each of them and Continued batterring the towne and walls for the space of three or fower days haveing fiered noe less than 15 hundred Shotts every day untill they Made a breach of forty yards breath and brought it soe low that a horse Man ridd out on itt with great ease, this beeing done they made Choyce of the best men in their whole army and Made a general attack, and on their Comeing into the pallessades[3] ouer men retreated out of pollissey[4] which gave incurradgm^t^ to the enemie to bee the More forward thinking that wee weare goeing to runn awaÿ, but when we saw Multitudes of them within ouer trinches, wee rallied and kill and wounded att least 4 thousands of them bisides what we distroyed another day that they attaced us, soe that I doe really think they have lost boath by the sword and sickness 10 thousand Men and I am Certain wee have not lost 200 Men and officers, Collonell David Barnewall [and] Collonell Patrick Dowdall[5] in ouer regiment are kiled and poore Ensigne Taffe[6] was shott by a Cannon balle goeing the streets; I hard letely from my ffather and Mother who are very well and lives quiettly as yett, all our friends in Paris are well onely that they weare plundered of all their goods[.] The enimie are now Marching to Corke and doe beleive ouer forces followes them suddenly,[7] ODonniell[8] who Comes lately from Spaine has 10 thousand vollunteers and rapperrees most of them well armed and likewise the Earle of Clancarty[9] has 7 or 8 thousand ditto aboute Corke soe that I doe really beleive that the king has above 50 thousand Men fitt for service, I beleive yow hard of Great searsfields[10] feates, whome God Allmightÿ I hope will preserve for the Good of our Nation; I hard not one word from my Lady Bath[11] since shee parted butt am tould that shee is att home, My uncle ffrank is att home and My uncle of ffleenstowne[12] is neere Gallway in good health, Barnewall of Archerstowne[13] died heere of a feaver, Dr Taffe and his familly are gon home soe is Cossen Geane Taffe, ffagan of Falltrim[14] was Kiled after Makeing his escape out of Goale by the rapperrees on his Jurney towards athlonne,[15] My Bro: Christy is Quarter Master[16] and is to bee Made Cornett within few dayes, I might bee advanced butt the Collonell desiered me to have patience and that hee will give mee a Companÿ very soone, I was ill with a splenter of a Cannon balle that struck mee in the back butt am now very well[.] My arm was in a sadd Condition after yow parted butt is now well[.] the Almighty bee praised, bee shure to send mee a Cupple of frinch hatts by the next conveniencÿ and a Cupple of ounces of Gould tread, & Case of pistalls[.] Pray give my Kind Salutes to my Cossen Dowdall and tell him that his bro: Nedd[17] is very well, give allsoe My humble respects to My Deare Lady Ales to m^rs Catty and to all the rest that inquire for Mee, and Make Mee hapy wth frequent advices of yor wellfare wch is the earnest request of D^r bro:

Yo^r most humble and affec^t Servt

Adam Cusack

[p.s.] I admier that I did not heere from yow since yor departure

[p.p.s.] Coll: Rob: Talbott[18] is wouned but will doe well

[p.p.p.s.] direct yor letter to Limbrick when yow write[.] pray give my service to Lif^t Roth[19] and tell him his bro: is well

[1] 'In or of the month already named; said month' (*OED*).

[2] Saint-Germain-en-Laye, the residence of James II just outside Paris.

[3] Read: 'palisades'.

[4] Read: 'policy'.

[5] According to a contemporary source, 'Captain Patrick Dowdall of the King's Regiment was slain a few days before [the Williamite assault on the breach in the walls of Limerick] in a sally'. His estates were among those attainted in 1691 (Gilbert, *Jacobite Narrative*, 116; D'Alton, *Army List*, 1:35, 2:4, 22.

[6] Ensign Mathew Taaffe served in the King's Regiment of Infantry (D'Alton, *Army List*, 2:4).

[7] A now obsolete sense of the word meaning 'Without delay, forthwith, promptly, immediately, directly, at once' (*OED*).

[8] Hugh Balldearg O'Donnell (d.1704), who claimed to be the true Earl of Tyrconnell, had been raised in Spain and achieved the rank of brigadier in the Spanish Army. O'Donnell arrived with troops at Kinsale a few days after the Boyne with a personal recommendation from James II. Following the lifting of the first siege of Limerick, O'Donnell's archrival, Richard Talbot (the acknowledged Earl of Tyrconnell), allowed him to raise a private army of thirteen regiments of infantry and one of cavalry from amongst the Ulster and north Connaught Gaels (Childs, *Williamite Wars*, 26–7; John Gibney, 'O'Donnell, Hugh Balldearg [Balderick, Balderock]', *DIB* [accessed 25 October 2024]).

[9] Donogh MacCarthy (1668–1734), 4th earl of Clancarty, was born in Blarney, Co. Cork. 'In March 1689 he received King James II on his arrival at Kinsale and was appointed … colonel of the 4th Regiment of Foot (subsequently "Clancarty's")' and made 'commander of the Jacobite army in Munster. … After the battle of the Boyne he was posted for garrison duty in Cork' and was captured after the city fell to Williamite forces under Marlborough. Clancarty was sent to the Tower of London but escaped in April 1694 and made his way to Saint-Germain-en-Laye (Éamonn Ó Ciardha, 'MacCarthy, Donogh', *DIB* [accessed 25 October 2024]).

[10] For Patrick Sarsfield, see Letter 6, note 5.

[11] Lady Bath (Jane Wyche, d.1692), 'daughter of Sir Peter Wyche, a wealthy London merchant', married Sir John Grenville, first earl of Bath, in 1652 (Victor Stater, 'Grenville, John, first earl of Bath [1628–1701], nobleman', *ODNB* [accessed 25 October 2024]).

[12] There are two townlands of this name in Co. Meath, Fleenstown Great and the adjacent Fleenstown Little, both south of present-day Ashbourne.

[13] The Barnwells took the side of James II in the Williamite War. Their family seat, Archerstown in Co. Meath, was forfeited following the Jacobite defeat in 1691 (Dataw Historic Foundation, 'John Barnwell (1672–1724)', at https://www.datawhistory.org/2022/01/09/ [accessed 12 October 2024]).

[14] For the Fagans of Feltrim, see Hickson, *Selections from Old Kerry*, 233.

[15] Read: 'Athlone'.

[16] Christopher Cusack served in the infantry regiment commanded by Christopher Fleming, Lord Slane (D'Alton, *Army List*, 2:339).

[17] Edward Dowdall served as quartermaster in Lord Abercorn's Regiment of Horse (D'Alton, *Army List*, 2:21).

[18] For Robert Talbot, see Letter 51.

[19] For Mathew Rooth (a variant of Rothe, a prominent Kilkenny Jacobite family) and his brother, Michael Rothe (1665–1741), see Letter 27, note 14, and Letter 52.

54. **Robert Hannan, Limerick, 'To Madam Lee and Company, Merchants In Nantes', 28 September 1690. Nos. 30 and 31**

Lym^{rk} 28 7^{ber} 1690

Madam Lee & Company

My last was 25 Cur^{t} on the new subject desireing yo^{u} to fraight a vessell on my act^{tt} thither & back to yo^{u} from 40: to 80:^{tts} or 100:^{tts} or 140:^{tts} & thereon to loade 8:^{tts} brandy ½ in pipes ½ in q^{r} Casques 3:^{tts} best canery or angy wine, 6 or 8:^{tts} of the best Burd^{x} Clarett wine[.] want thereof y^{e} quantity of the best Clarett or red wine yo^{u} can finde & two hox^{tts} of Cullering red wine, four dozen of the best black French hatts of 4^{lt} p^{rs} 4$^{\text{[obscure]}}$ weight [illegible] £400^{Cl} of Casteele Sope[1] one hundred weight of well cutt whelebone two Bar^{lls} of Tarr, ten or 12:^{tts} wheate & if y^{e} ship exeeds 100:^{tts} loade 20:^{tts} thereof to be baged & laid in y^{e} ships sterne, ten p^{s} kintin[2] of 24 § p^{r} @ & ten p^{s} d^{o} of 18 § p^{r} @ 56 @ lining of 26§ p^{r} @ a 28§ to make new shurts one pound of fine white tread,[3] halfe a pound d^{o} finer 50: Reams best pantalleone paper five hundred or one thousand or one thousand pound [sic] of leafe tobaco al pure cut[.] want thereof ye quantity in roule tobacco, one hox^{tt} of malloses,[4] one a two hundred of limons if cheape, a smale Casque anchioves, 12^{lt} tur^{s} worth of sweete meates of severall sortes, 20 @ fationable drugett sad cullerd of 26 to 28 § p^{r} @ mixed with a little silck 10: or 12 @ fationable lively cullerd striped silck of several mixtures of cullers therein not exceeding 40 a 50 § p^{r} @ its for a particler freind, ye rest of ye vessels loadding to be in ye whitest coarse salt & y^{r} to insure all to and froe on my acc^{tt}[.] in ase ye cannot gett a vessell att reasonable rate to fraight pray by[5] one for me from 50 to 120:^{tts} to loade the desired goods wch yo^{u} are to insure to & froe as well as ye cost of ye goods on my acc^{tt}, I recommend to yor care to choose & by a vessell & above all things to dispatch in sending me one as afore s^{d} att a reasonable fraight or to by one for that I have severall goods on my hands to be shiped of & by friends in Cevile[6] meanes hitherto prevented from being taken away for to pay french men for corne they brought in, I have an ord^{r} to keepe myne & by what I please but all will avail me nothing if y^{u} don't comply in sending ye vessell[.] I pray write me often via Brest by ye packett boate that comes to Gallowey & other Conviencys from Rochell & St Mallo. I am

Madam

I am most hum^{ble} S^{er}

Robert Hannan

[p.s.] butter for y^{r} governm^{t} must be deere wth yo^{u} for that youl not have much thereof from this Kingdom now — I am rid & cleared of m^{r} Wm Creagh ye man that Clampered[7] wth me — pray send me one pound of Nutmegs whole[.] Favor me as to send ye inclosed ad^{r} of m^{r} Tho: McNamara for my q^{r} parte of a

Cargo sent to Lixbone p^{r} the Speedewell & y^{u} to receave it if in mons^{r} Clarck & Quinns hand, if not let me know to whom they remitted it & how much all was[.] Pray deliver Mr Patrick Rirdan ye inclosed in proper hands & faver me as to forward ye rest p^{r} post & inclosed in yo^{rs} that for Mr James Power of Rochelle & that for Mr James Rice of Rouen & lett me know if they both receaved them — alsoe inclose this for m^{r} Dan^{ll} Arthur & let me know if he rec^{d} it — I recommend to y^{u} if y^{u} did not already fraight or by a vessel for me that y^{o} doe it wth speede & to insure all to & froe[.] I thanck God I am rid & cleered of that troublesom man Wm Creagh

[1] A fine hard soap made with olive-oil and soda. There are two kinds, the white and the mottled. Called also '*Spanish soap*' (*OED*).

[2] Read: 'kenting'.

[3] Read: 'thread'.

[4] Read: 'molasses'.

[5] Read: 'buy'.

[6] Read: 'Seville'.

[7] Clampered: 'To put together hastily or clumsily; to botch, tinker, or patch up, literal and figurative' [1545] or 'To tread heavily and clumsily' [1808] (*OED*).

55. **Robert Hannan, Limerick, 'To m^{r} James Hannan, Studint In Potyers',[1] 28 September 1690. No. 34**

Limerick 28 September 1690

Son James,

I writ yo^{u} severall letters since yor being att Potyirs, I had none from yo^{u} since yor departure there but one from Nantes att wch I admir & if yo^{u} writt for Nantes & Rochell inclosed to friends there they would have forwarded yo^{rs} to me but I believe yo^{u} naver did it, Dont neglect it for ye future nor above all things yo^{ur} carefull stoody — I gave an acc^{tt} of late of ye stoute defence wee made heere ag^{t} ye Prince of orange who for 21^{ds} beseidged upon John gates side & ye wall leadeing to Pennywell[2] battered our walls & made a breach of 40 foott long theron & atacked it[.] wee beate them of 3 or 4 severall tymes to att leest their loss of 9000: men whereof there was a Considerable noumber of his best officers & nobility[.] they were in great Confusion forced to raise ye sidge & the Duke of Berwick & Coll. Sarsfield Pressed & often prayed the Duke of Tyrconnell that the D: of Berwick & ye s^{d} Coll. should follow them wth our army but ye D: of Tyrconnell & Conul De Lazon[3] would not admitt it, had it bin allowed our people would have cutt them to peeces but p^{r}haps y^{u} may heare ye reason & accusations there[.] now they both are gon of — My respects to yor Rector,[4] your Mother & B^{rs} are all well tho wee had a great bomb & severall lardge Cannon balls fallen in our house[.] I thanck God none of our servants or family recaved ye least harme — I am

Your Loveing father

Robert Hannan

[p.s.] mynde well yor stoody & be sure I receave often from y^u^ & by this ship called the Recovery[5] of this place

[p.p.s.] Yo^r^ Mother giveth y^u^ [h]er Blessing —

[1] The Irish Jesuit College at Poitiers was established under letters patent granted by Louis XIV in April 1674. Although it remained a relatively small institution with never more than a few dozen students, the Irish College served as a continental base for the Jesuit mission to Ireland following the suppression of Catholicism in the wake of the 1691 Treaty of Limerick. The *Parlement de Paris*, under whose jurisdiction the college at Poitier fell, ordered the closure of Jesuit colleges throughout France in 1762 (Liam Chambers, '"Une maison de refuge": The Irish Jesuit College in Poitiers, 1674–1762', in Mary Ann Lyons and Brian Mac Cuarta [eds.], *The Jesuit Mission in Early Modern Ireland, 1560–1760* [Dublin, 2022], 227–50; Thomas O'Connor, 'The Domestic and International Roles of Irish Overseas Colleges, 1590–1800', in Liam Chambers and Thomas O'Connor [eds.] *College Communities Abroad: Education, Migration, and Catholicism in Early Modern Europe* [Manchester, 2018], 102; P. Boyle, 'Irish Colleges, on the Continent', *The Catholic Encyclopedia*, vol. 8 [New York, 1910], available at https://www.newadvent.org/cathen/08158a.htm [accessed 7 October 2024]).

[2] In the late seventeenth century, Pennywell was a suburb of Limerick due east of Irishtown on the Dublin Road.

[3] For the Comte de Lauzun, see Letter 8, note 10.

[4] William O'Ryan, S.J. (1628–1700), a native of Co. Kilkenny, served as rector of the Irish Jesuit college in Poitiers from 1679 to 1691 (Chambers, '"Une maison de refuge", 236; 'Irish Jesuit Archives: Item 1951 - Fr William O'Rian SJ', available at https://www.jesuitarchives.ie/fr-william-orian-sj [accessed 14 November 2024]).

[5] See Letter 43, note 7.

56. Robert Hannan, Limerick, 'To m^r^ James Power,[1] In Rochell,' 28 September 1690. No. 35

Lymerick 28th Sepr 1690

m^r^ James Power

S^r^

My last was 25th Cur^t^ since have none of y^rs^[.] I pray fraight as I therin writt moitaily twixt yo^u^ & I hither & back to y^u^ a vessell of 30 to 60:^tts^ & to loade on her eight Tuns of brandy ½ in pipes & ½ q^r^ Casq^s^ 10:^tts^ wheate, 8:^tts^ ¾ of the best Burd^x^ Clarett — 3 dozen fationable black french hatts, of 4:^lt^ p^r^ 2^[obscure]^ Casteele sope [illegible] two hundred pounds weight one hundred pounds weight of whalebone — 40 @ lining of 28 § p^r^ @ for shurts one pound fine white tread to sew them & halfe a pound d° finer, one thousand pound of roule tobacco, one Tuñ vinigar in qr Casques, 12 @ fationable striped silck of severall mixt cullers of 40 to 50 § pr @ — 20 @ fationable sad cullered drugett wth a litle silck mixed therin & the rest of ye vessels loading to be in ye whitest all coarse salt[.] insure all to & froe & if youl not be cuvered lett all be on my acctt & insure to & froe; and in case you send wth a biger vessell, then I limit fraight lost after thou faile, in case ye cant gett one at a reasonable fraight pray by one on my acctt to loade as aforesd & lett her be of 50 to 100:tts yor insureing her hither & back & the like to & from wth all ye goods yu loade on my acctt[.] in this I pray yor speedy care & dispatch for that I have severall goods on my hands & have obtained tolleration from the govrnmt to by more tho other men heere had their goods seized on, butter weyl be in demand wth yu litle may yu expect hence thereof I have 250: Casques thereof in rediness by me — lett me know if yu want 100 Casques on my acctt pr the Ranconter of Rochell wch aldn Edward Loftus sent yu by my ordrs 2/3 for Mr James Rice Fra: & 1/3 me — I lost 3000£ ster as things fell out by mr Patr Rirdans sending my vessel for London quiet contray to my ordrs for wch I beg to make him pay, he writ wethal ye Hopewell went for Lixbone from mr Degrave of London[.][2] it would be but honeste & civyl of him to arrest & send me her in regard & he writt me in his letters thus (that I writ touching to ye ordrs & that mr Degrave is to save me harmlese)[.] pray minde him of this & if he arests her lett him gett her loaden att Lixbone on my acctt wth salt 10: boxes limons & 10: boxes of oranges hither & one thousand pound of St Domingo tobacco[3] or som other tobacco[.] if he please he insuring ye rest of sd goods & 4000lt tur in ye ship — of this I writt him, I pray yr care & answur hereto & if mr Rivers of Lixbon payes[.] if not pray press him to it — lett me know what yu are owing yor mr Thomas & who yu found[.] writt me yr letter pr Capn Richard Creagh[4] & if it be not in ye supscription the very hand either Monsr Walsh & Gaull it being exactly like the supscription of their letters – I pray resolve me herein wch yu hitherto pass by silently, pray hasten to freight or by a vessell as I desire, & for want of ye Burdx Clarett loade the quantity in ye best & strongest maran Clarett[5] wine — yor mother & friends are well, I am Sr

Your afft Cou & sert

Robert Hannan

[p.s.] I prey write me often via Paris, Nantes & St Mallo — either by any ships bound hither or Galloway &ct — pray Send me a pound of nutmegs

[1] For James Power, see Letter 40, note 3.

[2] For John Degrave of London, see Letter 19, note 2.

[3] Tobacco from the Spanish Caribbean colony of Santo Domingo transshipped through Lisbon, Portugal.

[4] Richard Creagh, 'born in France, was son of John Creagh of Kilmallock, Co. Limerick; Richard had been captain in a French regiment and was now [by the 1690s] a merchant settled in La Rochelle' (Walsh, 'O Neills in Exile', 61).

[5] Wine produced in the neighbourhood of Marans, a town northeast of La Rochelle, in the Poitou-Charentes region of western France.

57. **Robert Hannan, Limerick, 'To Sr Daniel Arthur Kn^t^, In Paris',[1] 28 September 1690. No. 36**

Lym^{r} 28 7^{ber} 1690

S^{r}

ffavor me I pray as to deliver the inclosed into the Ld Bis^{p} Mollony's[2] hands & to pray him to give y^{u} his answer wch pray inclose to Madam Lee of Nantes & she will send it me by a vessell thats att Nantes bound hither, I am S^{r}

Your most hum^{ble} ser^{t}

Robert Hannan

[1] For Sir Daniel Arthur, Irish banker in Paris, see Letter 13, note 6.

[2] For Bishop John O'Molony, see Letter 58, note 1.

58. **Robert Hannan, Limerick, 'To the R^{t} R^{d} father in God John Ld Bisp. of Lymerick & Killaloe,[1] In Paris', 28 September 1690. No. 37**

Lymerick 28th Septemb^{r} 1690

My L^{d},

I writt yo^{u} not long since acquainting the death of y^{r} good nephew Cap^{n} Dan^{ll} Mollony[2] at our seidge here who behaved him selfe gallantly[.] y^{e} L^{d} have mercy on his good soule, besides y^{e} 20:$^{£}$ I first p^{d} him to wch I have yor Ldshipps aprobacion I gave him later on his & Doctor Mollonys[3] bond 30:$^{£}$ to furnish him & his Company y^{e} s^{d} Doctor being bound that y^{u} would be well satisfied wth my doeing it[.] if yo^{u} are not pray lett me have yor Ldships answer in tyme that I mey consult Dr Mollony to repay the same[.] there is a vessell att Nantes of this place by wch this goeth & pray write me by her yor resolution herein & let yor letter be inclosed to Madam Lee & Company of Nantes who will inclose it me & in regarde tymes are troublesom here & not knowing how long Dr Mollony or any man may be in a condicion its fitt I have yor result[4] herein wth all speede, I am my L^{d}

Your L^{d}ships most
aff^{t} hum^{ble} ser^{t}

Robert Hannan

[p.s.] the vicar gen[ll] Father Mathew Mollony was att me to pay this 30:[£] to accomodat Cap[n] Mollony & his company who were really in a sad condicion if not paid them —

[1] John O'Molony (1617–1702) was bishop of Limerick during the Williamite War but spent 1690 in France. For more information on Bishop O'Molony, see also Introduction, 32–3.

[2] Capt. Daniel Molony, nephew of Bishop Molony, 'may be presumed to have been of the Cuiltonan or Kiltannon Molonys, and his estates in Clare were, in 1703, sold by the Commissioners of the Forfeitures to Thomas St John of Ballymull Castle in the same county' (D'Alton, *Army List*, 2:700).

[3] 'Very Reverend Mathew Molony' benefited from a Malony family endowment at the Irish College in Paris dedicated to the training of family members for the priesthood. The undated fragment of his tombstone at Kilquane, Co. Kerry, reads 'Here lieth ye Body of Doctor Mathew Molony who was Vicar General of ye Diecess of Limerick and Killalowe for 32 years Parish [priest of Tomevara, Co. Tipperary]' (Lenihan, *Limerick*, 220–21n4).

[4] Result: 'An impulse, inclination, or prompting'; and 'A decision, a resolution' (*OED*).

59. **Robert Hannan, Limerick, 'To m[r] James Rice Francis, Merchant In Rouen', 28 September 1690. No. 38**

Forward this letter sealed to Mr Degrave & pray let me have from you what he doth with my vessell or if instead I should have her.

Lymerick 28th Sep[r] 1690

m[r] James Rice Francis

S[r]

My last was 13th Cur[t], since have none of y[rs][.] I long since gave orders att severall times to m[r] Patrick Rirdan to give yo[u] 1200:[lt] tur to pay it m[r] W[m] Clayburn & on paym[t] to gett the dischardge I sent y[o] signed by him & to recorde it in Paris in som court or office soe as it wil not stand above two or three Crownes[.] keepe y[u] for me the dischardge he signed and I signed one or two I sent y[u] for him – lett me know if yo[r] ord[rs] receaved 60 Casques butter I Shiped on the Compt De Lauzun of S[t] Mallo John Kely m[r] y[e] bill of loadeing signed by Mons[r] aufrey[.][1] y[e] s[d] Butter was marked R & [indecipherable] y[e] bill of loadeing being mencioned for y[r] acc[tt][.] they are for myne as I then writt[.] y[e] s[d] butter weighed here 112[Cl]:1[qr]:12[l] — let it not be sould under 36:[lt] pC or att least 30:[lt][.] it cost here 4:[£] in brass mony — pray let me often receave from yo[u] theres word bringing of Rouen goods hither[.] what best to remit here is anie brandy whete & salt — My Mother is dead[.] what you were oweing her make it me good & let me know it — wee made a gallant defence here when beseedged by y[e] P: of O:[.] I am troubled that I don't know what m[r] Degrave will doe for m[r] Rirdan in sending me my vessel — I am att least 3000£ ster a sufferer by my veseles goeing for London as tymes happened, I heare yt Degrave sent her for Lixbone on his acctt — I am well served — I pray indeaver wth him & mr Rirdan that I have my vessell or to sell her I will not, & if mr Rirdan liveth I will make him sensible of his doeing herein to me, I am Sr

Yours att all Comand

Robert Hannan

[p.s.] I sent yu two bills of loadeing for ye within 60: Casq: butter att two severall tymes[.] pray advise price of our goods, Monsr Aufrey that signd ye bill of loading is a strang slipery man[.] if yu dont get ye 60 Casq buttr shew him he writ from Galloway wth ye ffrench fleete he will be in Paris & I thinck Monsr De Laue of Paris or about the court if Concerned wth him, sd Aufrey was concerned wth Monsr Alexandre the French Treasurer.[2] Do call to sd Aufrey for 18:£ in brass mony he oweth me remaining of 121:£ I lent him for wch I desyerd gold or silver there or att least as an proclamation putt forth for every pistoll in gold to allow but 28[obscure] ps[.] let him pay it yu soe & want of his compleaine indeavor to see I have my due of him & rather then faile let me have a billett from him on any of his friends here to pay me ye sd 18:£ in brass money — it was unjust of him to goe away without paying me & Sir John Kirewan of Galloway[3] called to him for it often & sd he would pay it & neaver did

[1] Auffroy was a French army contractor. For his extensive report on the French military expedition to Ireland, see 'Memoire concernant l'Irlande donné par le sieur Auffroy', in Mulloy, *Franco-Irish Correspondence*, 1:215–22 #628.

[2] Pierre Alexandre, Commissary and Treasurer for French troops in Ireland (Mulloy, *Franco-Irish Correspondence*, 1:255 #669).

[3] John Kirwan, a merchant in London, was a native of Galway. The Kirwans operated the greatest of the Galway trading enterprises in the era of the Williamite War – and the one with the most extensive international reach. In the late 1670s, they laid the foundation of London's thriving Irish merchant community where they maintained a presence lasting 140 years (Cullen, 'Galway Merchants in the Outside World', 169–70, 178–9; W. L. Grant, James Munro, and Almeric W. Fitzroy [eds.], *Acts of the Privy Council, 1680–1720*, 6 vols. [London, 1908–1912], 2:97; O'Shea [ed.], *Letterbook of William Hovell*, 31, 33).

60. **Robert Hannan, Limerick, 'To Madam Lee & Company, Merchants In Nantes', 28 September 1690. No. 42**

Lymerick 28th Sepr 1690

Madam Lee & Company,

I writt yo this day by this Convyaunce John Mitchell mr of the Recovery[1] of this place desiring to fraight on my acctt hither & back to yu a vessel of 40: to 80tts or more — & I mean to load eight Tuns brandy ½ in pipes & ½ in qr Casques 3tts

of the best angy or canery wine, 6: or 8:^{tts} of the best Burd^{x} Clarett wine for want thereof s^{d} q^{ty} in ye best Clarett or red wine yo^{u} can gett & two hox^{tts} of Cullering red wine, 4 dozen fationable bl[ack] french hatts of 4^{lt} pr^{s} four hundred weight of Casteele sope, one hundred weight of whalebone well cutt, two Bar^{lls} of Tarr, one tun vinegar in q^{r} cas^{q}:, ten or twelve tuns of wheete & if the ship exceeds 100:^{tts} to loade 20:^{tts} thereof all to be baged & laid in ye ships sterne, 10: p^{s} kintin of 24 § p^{r} @, 10 d^{o} of 18 § p^{r} @, 56 @ linins of 26 § p^{r} @ for shurting, one pound of fine white tread to sew shurts & halfe a pound of d^{o} finer, 50: Reams best Pantalleone paper[,] 500:[1] or one thousand pound of good leafe tobacco[.] want thereof ye quantity in ye best roule tobacco, one hox^{tt} in all other & the rest of ye ships loadeing in salt, one or two hundred of limons if had cheape, Ten pound weight of anchioves, 12:^{lt} tur worth in sweete meates 20:[1] capers 20: @ fationable sad cullered drugetts of a little mixture of silck of 26 to 28 § p^{r} @, 12 @ fasionable silck of several mixed cullers of 40: to 50 § p^{r} @ & to insure ye rest of all s^{d} goods to & froe on my acc^{tt} & in case y^{u} cant fraight a^{tt} a reasonable rate I desire you by a vessell on my acc^{tt} to loade ye desired goods from 50 to 120:^{tts} yo^{u} insureing her cost to & froe as well as ye goods y^{u} loade for my acc^{tt}, I recommend expedition in either of al^{t}[2] y^{u} doe for that I have severeall goods on my hands to loade of wch I thank God & friends indeavers are not seazed on as others was & I have tolleration to by & ship of w^{t} goods I please, I recomend againe therefore expedition to y^{u} advise price of ours and yor goods & write me often via Rochell, Brest & St Mallo & y^{r} owne towne
I am Madam

Your most af^{ft} hum^{ll} ser^{t}

Robert Hannan

[p.s.] I hereby forward a lardge packet of letters for y^{u} & Burdeux inclosed herein — Madam Lee[,] but it may be more my advantadge to buy a vessel then to fraight[.] that I leave to y^{u} & I pray expedition what ever yo^{u} doe

[1] See Letter 43, note 7.

[2] Read: 'alternatives'.

61. **Robert Hannan, Limerick, 'To m^{r} James Power,[1] Merchant In Rochell', 28 September 1690. No. 61**

Lymerik 28th Sepr 1690

Mr James Pow^{r}

S^{r}

I writt yo^{u} this day desireing to fraight moitaily on yor & my acc^{tt} a vessell from 30 to 60^{tts} & to loade thereon the foll^{g} goods & now confirme y^{e}

same, eight Tuns of brandy ½ in pipes & ½ in q^{r} Casques, 10^{tts} of wheate to be baged up & laid in ye ships sterne, 8^{tts} ¾ best Burd^{x} Claret[.] want therof ye quantity in ye best Maran clarett wine, 3 dozen fationable bl[ack] hatts of 4^{lt} tur p^{s} two hundred pounds of Casteel sope, one hundred pounds of well cutt whalebone, 40 @ lining of 28 § p^{r} @ for shurts one pound of fine white tread to sew the same & halfe a pound finer, one thousand pound of leafe or roule tobacco, one tun vinegar in q^{r} Casques, 12 @ fationable striped silck of severall mixtures of 40: to 50 § p^{r} @ 20 @ fationable sad cullored drugett mixed wth a litle silke & the rest of ye vessells loading to be in the whitest all coarse salt and to insure my moity to & froe, & in case you will not be concerned I pray that you fraight & loade all on my acc^{tt} getting the rest of all s^{d} goods insured to & froe on my acc^{tt} —

and in case y^{u} cant gett a vessel att a reasonable rate to fraight pray by a vessell on my acc^{tt} from 50 to 120^{tts} & loade the desired goods & insure the cost of s^{d} vessell to & froe as alsoe ye cost of ye goods to & froe on my acc^{tt} — which of the two y^{u} doe pray be nemble for that I have severall goods on my hands — wch I thanck God & friends in Court werent or any parte of them seazed tho four of my neighbors were & I have an ord^{r} to by & ship of what goods I have & will by — its much out of my wey & purs that y^{u} did not as y^{u} s^{d} y^{u} would freight last season — thats over now & I pray yor complioance in what I now desire & pray mind if but its [more?] advantageous to by a ship then fraight wth if both sail here I shall be satisfied & pray ofer all expedition possible — I thank God I am rid of w^{m} Creagh w^{m}[.] I writt y^{u} lately via Nantes under Madam Lees Cover, & if the bearer putts in to y^{rs} faver me by to forward a packet of Letters of myne he hath for Madam Lee — m^{r} Pa: Rirdan writes me that ye Hopewell was sent by m^{r} Degrave for Lixbone[.] if s^{d} Rirdan doth the s^{d} Degrave ad^{vs} to send him here news of for Sending her to London without any ord^{rs} its but Just & honest of m^{r} Rirdan to arrest ye vessell att Lixbone & send her me wth salt & 10: boxes limons & 10: of oranges & one thousand pounds of tobacco if cheape[.] y^{r} goods to be insured & 4000: l^{t}tur on s^{d} ship of all[.] this pray write m^{r} Rirdan for me

S^{r}, I am af^{t} Hum^{bl} Srv^{t}

Robert Hannan

[p.s.] I pray writt me often via Nantes Brest & St Mallo

[1] For James Power, see Letter 40, note 3.

62. **Ellen Lee,[1] Kilrush, 'For Her Loveinge Husband Nicholas Lee in Nance[2] In Franc', 28 September 1690. No. 44**

Killrush ye 28 of 7^{ber} 1690

Deare Husband

finding this convenience by m^{r} Mitchell have sent yo^{u} these feow lines acquainteinge yo^{u} y^{t} I am in good helth & ye Children onely my youngest guirl Anstus is verry sick & ye Little boy Thomy is ded[.] things goes verry hard wth me[.] I desire you to ma^{ke} hast home for I am sure you can doe better then if yo^{u} stay there[.] Cap^{tin} Sober is Coll^{r} in Dublin[.] I desire yo^{u} to let me here from yo^{u} by ye verry first conveniency if yo^{u} doe not co^{m} speadily y^{r} selfe[.] being all at p^{r}sent from yor Everlovenige wife

Ellen Lee

[p.s.] I desire yo^{u} to bringe som Papor wth yo^{u} for it is scarce her[.] rember to bring som fine thred & som pins for ye guirls work

[1] For Ellen Lee, see Letter 1, note 1.

[2] For Nicholas Lee (Jr) of Nantes and Limerick, see Letter 1, note 3.

63. **Ducorail, infantry major, Limerick, to unknown, 28 September 1690. No. 54**

A Lesmericq le 28 7bre 1690

Mon Cher monsieur Je nay le temps que de vous priere de vous lestres auriez la bonte darester Les Incluze de mon beau perre et de mons^{r} de Callinand a Tournay[1] et de vous assurez que Je veux vite finir La guerre de Ce roiaulmes auparavand que de quitter Le porteur de La presantes vous dira Les bonnes et meschantes nouvelle dirlandes naiand pas le pety monmand pour vous en nentretenire que Ce Luy de vous marquer que quelques destine quy marive que Je serray toustes ma vie, c[her] Monsieur vostre humbles et tres affectionne serviteur

Ducorail

[p.s.] Sy Jay Laventages de recevoires de vos nouvelle Ceste a ducorail Majorre en Cheffe de M^{r} guilleaume Thutes brigadier des armes du roy et Colonelle dinfantery a Lesmericq

[p.p.s] Je vous prier dassurer Melle vostres Cher maistre et toutes vostres famille de mes respets et beau baissamens et aussy mes Complimand au bonne amie de Monsieur Cavillier mon beaufrere ayand perdu toutes mon equipages a dradrat et Les adresse que vous mavies donne tous deux pour vous escrirre

Translation

In Limerick, 28 September 1690

My Dear Sir,

I only have time to beg you for your letters – be so kind as to send the enclosed for my father-in-law and M. de Callinand in Tournay[1] – and to assure you that I wish soon to be finished with the war of this kingdom, so I can quit it. The bearer of this letter will tell you the good and the bad news of Ireland, I having not a moment to tell you about it other than to say that, whatever my fate, I will be all my life, Dear Sir, your humble and very affectionate servant

Ducorail

[p.s.] If I have the good fortune to receive news from you, it should be addressed to Ducorail, major-in-chief of Mr Guillaume Thutes, brigadier of the king's army and colonel of infantry at Limerick.

[p.p.s] I beg you to assure Mademoiselle, your dear master, and all your family of my respects and salutations, and also my compliments to the good friend of Monsieur Cavillier my brother-in-law (having lost all my gear at Drogheda, and the addresses the two of you gave me to write to you).

[1] Likely, Tournai, on the River Scheldt in modern-day Belgium.

64. Nicholas Gerraldin, Jr,[1] Limerick, 'To ye Widdow Lee & Comp^{e} In Nantes', 1 October 1690. No. 25

Limmericke ye first 8^{ber} 1690

D^{re} ant

I arived in ye river just now, & have oneley ye tyme to writt a few leynes to my poore wife, who has not heard from mee sence my departure[.] wherfore pray forward hir ye inclosed & y^{w} wil oblidge mee, I have tyme to enlarge father oneley y^{t} I am to y^{w} & familey D^{re} ant

y^{r} most aff^{te} nephew & serv^{t}

Nicholas Gerraldin
Junior

[1] Capt. Nicholas Gerraldin, Jr (b.1658), master of *Le Soleil* of Saint-Malo, was a native of that city where he served as mayor between 1713 and 1716. Active in Saint-Malo privateering, Nicholas, Jr, was the son of Nicholas Geraldine, Sr (1623–1693), originally from Waterford. Nicholas, Sr, was a prominent merchant in Saint-Malo and the English Consul in 1689. Geraldine, Sr, was the brother of Madame Marie Lee, merchant in Nantes (Rilat, *Ces messieurs de Nantes*, 4:145; Mulloy, *Franco-Irish Correspondence*, 3:158 #2010; J. S. Bromley, *Corsairs and Navies* [London, 1987], 148; Lyons, 'The Irish in Saint-Malo').

65. Nicholas Gerraldin, Jr,[1] Limerick, to Madame Gerraldin[2] at 'Monsr Nicolas Gerraldin, Lejeune, Merch^{t} a s^{t} malo', 1 October 1690. No. 28

ye Loer end of ye river of Limmericke
ye first October 1690

My D^{re} Life

I have writt y^{w} from baltimore & from Corcke, wher I was to proceed had not ye ennemys Lay^{d} shidge[3] by sea thertow,[4] wch compelled mee to Come hidther, I bles god for my happy escape from ye ennemys who have surrounded wth thire mighty fleete ye kingdome, our vessel sayles mighty well, wch has deliverd us god bee blessed & praysed, I have not tyme to relate y^{w} anny thing tutcheing ye kingdome in relation to newes or to my owne particular Consernes[.] I meane abouth ye shipps Cargo, I hope I may make a saveing voyadge in soe unhappie a Conjoughture[5] wch will bee very mutch, & if I can possible shall goe abouth Irland comeing whom[6] wherby to meete wth Some pryse[7] y^{t} may in Some manner recompence ye owners, for I have noe mynd to Come whom butt wth Spoyle as ye tartars doe Soe as pray bee not in anny trouble for my delaye from y^{w} sence I advise y^{w} my desine wch if takes effects will bee some what tedious, though very secure; I doe protest y^{w} y^{t} all my trouble is to bee separated from y^{w} & ye aprehention I have of y^{r} beeing troubled in mynd greeves mee more y^{n} anny thing in this woorld, I was never better in health y^{n} I am att present & I assure y^{w} y^{t} I take aspesiall care of my selfe more to please y^{w} y^{n} anny Inclination to preserve my selfe, I have not tyme to writt m^{r} Duhoux nor ye others Conserned of anny thing ye vessel being under sayle present my hum^{e} respects to my father & uncle Doud & to my sisters & rest of frends & give my bennediction to my d^{re} babes[8] & assure your selfe of my ever beeing D^{re} hearth,

Your ever aff^{te} husband & ser^{vt}

Nicholas Gerraldin Junior

[p.s.] they goes via nantes under my ant^{s} Cover

[p.p.s] our shipps crew are all in health

[1] For Capt. Nicholas Gerraldin, see Letter 64, note 1.

[2] Anne Gerraldin (née Malbranck) and Capt. Nicholas Gerraldin were married on 7 September 1684 (Rilat, *Ces messieurs de Nantes*, 4:145).

[3] For the siege of Cork (21–29 September 1690), see Childs, *Williamite Wars*, 267–72.

[4] Read: 'thereto'.

[5] Read: 'conjuncture'.

[6] Read: 'home'.

[7] Saint-Malo, the home port of Capt. Nicholas Gerraldin, Jr, was the center of French privateering during the Nine Years' War (1688–1697). The 'cité corsair', with a population of less than 20,000, 'was preeminent among French ports' (Bromley, *Corsairs and Navies*, 139–46, 279).

[8] Four of Nicholas and Anne Gerraldin's eight children had been born before the 1690 siege of Limerick (Rilat, *Ces messieurs de Nantes*, 4:145).

66. Laughlin Cleere,[1] Limerick, 'To m^rs^ margaret Walsh,[2] alias Cleere, In s^t^ Malo', 1 October 1690. No. 29

Limericke River ye first day october '90

My Dere,

Since my parting you had nevr more wories haveing beene mett in the middle English fleete yesterday[.] butt God be praised skaped them — have been in Baltimore these 25 dayes expecting to goe to Corke to discharge which was hindred by reason said place is beseeched these five days by sea and lande this towne defended itt selfe well, and killed the enemies tenn thousand men, doe nott know what good may doe heere as yett nott haveing beene ashoare, nor spoke to any butt the bearer who is a master of a vessell bound to nanse[.][3] my love to sister June and Brother Ja: & his wife nott forgetting yourselfe with whome I longe with great impatience to be[.] nott else butt remaines

your Lo: husband till death

Laughlin Cleere

[p.s.] excuse hast for am under saile, goeing into the harbor, & this vessell goeing away

[1] Laughin Cleere was a privateer captain licensed by James II and Louis XIV to prey on English and Dutch merchant shipping in the Channel. Cleere was part a group of privateers operating out of Saint-Omer (Eoghan Ó hAnnracháin, 'Munster Galley Slaves', *North Munster Antiquarian Journal*, 45 [2005], 12).

[2] Margaret Walsh, alias Cleere, had kinship ties to Philip Walsh, founder of a notable Franco-Irish family. Philip Walsh had settled at Saint-Malo in 1685 where he engaged in ship-building (including men-of-war for the French government), privateering, and the slave trade. Walsh commanded the vessel that returned James II to France following the Battle of the Boyne (Richard Hayes, 'Biographical Dictionary of Irishmen in France, Part XXI', *Studies: An Irish Quarterly Review*, 36:143 [Sept. 1947], 349).

[3] Read: 'Nantes'.

67. **Pierre Charié, Limerick, to his wife, care of Pierre Charié de Senaserre, in the river of Nantes, 2 October 1690. No. 53**

En La Riverre de Limericq, L^{e} iime du mois doctobre 1690

ma Cher fame se Ligne sont pour vous faire scavoir Letat de ma scantez La quelle Et bonne dieux mercy Je pry dieux que En Sy soit Et de vous Et de Nos En fans Je vous pry de faire mes bessemain a mon perre Et a mes seur Et a tous mes a my de par de La Nous Esperons a pres Nostre de Charge de torner En Entez sy plait a dieux autre chosse Je ne puis mander Sy Non que Je demeure vostre marit

pierre Charié

Translation

In Limerick river, 2 October 1690

My dear wife,

These lines are to let you know the state of my health which is good, thank God. I pray God it is the same for you and for our children. I pray you to give my respects to my father and my sisters and to all my friends on the other side. We hope after our discharge to return to Nantes, if it pleases God. I have nothing else to report except that I remain your husband,

Pierre Charié

68. **Guillaume Nau, Limerick, to his mother in Pornic,[1] 2 October 1690. No. 64**

Le iime doctobre 1690
En La Rivier de Limericq

ma tres cher mere se Lingne sont pour vous faire savoir Letat de ma scantez La quelle Et bonne dieu mersy Je pry dieux que En soit de vous Et de mes fraire Et tous Nos a my de par de la pierre Reinbaux il vous pry de faire se baisse Main a sa fame Et a sa fille Et a son perre Et a sa merre Et a tous nous a my de par Et pry dieux pour Leur scantez Jaque boisserpe il vous pry de faire se baisse Main a sa merre Et pry dieu pour sa santez outre Chosse Je Ne puis mander sy Non que Je demeure vostre tres huble fils guillaume Nau

[On the back] soit donne a Renne Le prou a pornicq

[Enclosed in another paper] soit donne a ivonne guerein a pain beuf[2] pour faire teneir a Reneié La — cordonne a porneicq

Translation

2 October 1690
In the river of Limerick

My very dear mother, these lines are to let you know the state of my health, which is good, thank God. I pray God it is likewise for you and my brothers and all our friends. By request of Pierre Reinbaux: he begs you to give his greetings to his wife, and to his daughter, and to his father, and to his mother, and to all our friends thereabouts, and that he prays God for their health. Jacques Boisserpe, he begs you to give his respects to his mother and that he prays God for her health. I have nothing more to report except that I remain your very humble son,

Guillaume Nau.

[On the back] To be given to René le Prou at Pornic.[1]

[Enclosed in another paper] To be given to Yvonne Guerein at Paimbœuf[2] to hold for René La — shoemaker at Pornic.

[1] Pornic is a town on the French Atlantic coast located near the Loire Estuary.

[2] Paimbœuf, in western France, lies on the south bank of the Loire upriver from Saint-Nazaire on the passage to Nantes. Communities such as Paimbœuf provided mariners for the Atlantic trade of Nantes.

69. Thomas Pearce, Limerick, 'To Joseph Scriven, linnen draper in Watling street, London', 6 and 7 October 1690. No. 5

Lÿmerick y^{e} 6th 8^{ber} 1690

Deare Cosine

I wrote thee by way of Dublin y^{e} 25th past & then advised of 300$^{\pounds}$ to be p^{d} Amos Strettell[1] & y^{t} if thee thought fit to draw it into thy hands — I allso advised y^{t} on y^{e} 24th 7^{ber} I shipt in y^{e} Amity of Lymerick burd 36^{tts} John Michell m^{r} bound for Nants, Rochell or Burdoux in france three tuns of Salmon fish, in eighteen caskue one hundred eighty nine salt hydes & fifty one dry hydes consign^{d} on Patrick Rirdan at Nants, John & Ed^{m} Gold at Rochell &c^{t} who are to sell for ready mony & remite y^{e} produce to thee or thee to draw on them, as I compute it will yeald 300$^{\pounds}$ if goes safe, but haveing opportunity am willing y^{t} 100$^{\pounds}$ or 200$^{\pounds}$ be insured by y^{e} best insurers on my ¼ part of s^{d} ship & y^{e} above goods — just now I heare from Thomas fflaxon[2] who writes me his hard fortune & gives satisfaction of his honesty so y^{t} w^{t} I wrote before y^{t} he went from Ostend to London was on a false reporte he is in Midlebrough,[3] as he writes he sent ye rabbet skins from Dower[4] to London so I hope they are in thy custody & y^{t} he will do ye best he can & returne for Irland so y^{t} I desire ye inclosed for him may be forwarded; we have just now from Joan Cooke[5] from Barnett[6] she writes of your wellfare wch I pray God to continue to you all, & now deare Cosine I am very sorrowfull to informe thee y^t my poore ffather is on a sick bid & so weake y^t I greatly feare his recovery, how God may dispose of him I know n^t but we are a sorrowfull house & shall greatly want him[.] I may say he have been a tender father to me & we so lived together y^t its hard to part[.] I know it will be sorrowfull news to thee & my Poore sister & all his friends, but Gods will be don[.] we must shortly follow & I pray God y^t we be prepared for y^t rest where conserne and sorrow seases; I have but little time ye messenger goeing back; if my father recovers this time I shall soon let thee heare from thy sorrowfull kinsman

Tho: Pearce

[p.s.] I told my father I had wrote thee[.] he desires wth all deare affections to be remembred to thee &c^t

[p.p.s] tusday ye 7th I thought y^t ye above should a been sent last night but ye opportunity staying untill this morning I have only to write y^t my poore father this morning between ye 5th & 6th houre expired this life[.] I am well satisfyed of his honest & harmless life y^t gives me hopes is well wth him; he will be much lamented after as well as mist by his Wife Children & friends[.] I hope thy affections will desent to his ofspring, who have been much obliged to thee as is Deare Kinsman thy very

Tho: Pearce

[1] Amos Strettell (1657–1729) was a Quaker merchant and linen draper on Back Lane, Dublin. Strettell was a prominent figure in Dublin's Quaker community and, together with John Burnyeat, was the author in 1688 of *The Innocency of the Christian Quakers Manifested* (P. Beryl Eustace and Olive C. Goodbody [eds.], *Quaker Records, Dublin: Abstracts of Wills* [Dublin, 1957], 4, 6, 13, 29, 35, 64; Wight and Rutty, *A History of the Rise and Progress of the People Called Quakers*, 262; Greaves, *Dublin's Merchant-Quaker*, 54, 113–14, 146–52).

[2] For Thomas Flaxon, see Letter 34, note 1.

[3] Middelburg, a port in the Dutch Republic.

[4] Dover, Kent.

[5] Joan Cooke (1653–1737) was active in Limerick's Quaker ministry ('Quaker Queries & Archives', at https://sites.rootsweb.com/~quakers/qq4-99.htm [accessed 19 October 2024]).

[6] Barnet, Middlesex, located to the northwest of London.

70. **Thomas Girard, Limerick, to his wife in Saint-Malo, care of de La Riviere, surgeon, Champs au vers,[1] Saint-Malo, 9 October 1690. No. 27**

De La riviere de Limeric Le 9 octobre 1690

apres avoir eu bien des peines et des traverse et apres avoir esté obliges de quiter nos Cables et ancres et panser nous perdre plusieurs fois nous sommes enfin arives icy sans fortune Je Croy que ce sera avec Joÿe que Lon entendra de nos nouvelles Je prie dieu que ces Lignes vous trouve en sante et tous nos amis pour cequy est de La mienne elle est fort bonne grace a dieu et Celle de nos gens de S^t^ malo dont je vous prie de le faire scavoir a Leur amis vous feres mes baisse mains a mon frere La garde & a sa famme & Comme Je ne Scay pas Come^nt^ Ces que les affaires irons pour La brase monnoye ces Ce quy fait que Je ne vous en parle pas Jy faire tout mon possible pour La passer a quelque pris que ce soit pourveu que m^r^ gerardin[2] puisse profiter Je suis contant car cest un homme quy merite davoir du bien & une personne Selon dieu Je finis & suis vostre mary & amy

Thomas girard

[p.s.] mes baise mains a mad^le^ gerardin[2] & a mes enfans & a tous mes amis Le moyne que Je vous aves dit est mort 12 Jour apres nostre sortie adieu ma chere famme pries dieu pour nous

[c/o] Monsieur de La Riviere
girard chirurgien au Champs au vers[1] a St Malo.

Translation

From Limerick river, 9 October 1690

After having many difficulties and adversities, and after being obliged to cut our cables and anchors, and believing ourselves lost on several occasions, we finally arrived unluckily here. I believe our news will be heard with joy. I pray God that these lines find you in health, and all our friends. As for my own, it is very good, thanks be to God, and those of our people of Saint-Malo, about whom I pray you to inform their friends. Pay my respects to my brother Lagarde and to his wife. And as I do not know how business will go on account of the brass money, I have nothing to say about it. I will do everything I can to get it accepted at whatever valuation it may be. Provided that Mr. Gerardin[2] profits, I am happy, because he is a man who is well deserving and righteous. I conclude and am your husband and friend,

Thomas Girard.

[p.s.] My respects to Miss Gerardine[2] and to my children and all my friends. The monk whom I mentioned to you died 12 days after we left. Adieu my dear wife. Pray to God for us.

[c/o] Mr de La Rivière [for] Girard, surgeon at Champs au vers[1] in Saint-Malo

[1] Likely, Champs-Vauverts, a district inside the old city ramparts of Saint-Malo after which a part of the fortifications were named, the Cavalier des Champs-Vauverts.

[2] Presumably, Gerraldin. For the Gerraldins of Saint-Malo, see Rilat, *Ces messieurs de Nantes*, 4:145–6.

71. **René Lelieur, Limerick, to his father and mother in Saint-Malo, care of Dupremorin, merchant at Saint-Malo, 9 October 1690. No. 26**

Du bas De la River DLemeriqu Le 9e obr

Monsieur,

Mon tres cher pere et mere ces ligne seront pour vous faire a scavoir Letat Demasante La quel est fort bonne Je prie Dieu quinsoit Delavostre et De celle De nos amis engeneral pour Des nouvelle Je vous endire point sinon que nous avon eu La chage[1] plusieurs navire Mais Dieu mercie nous sommes bonn voile a Dieu mon tres chere pere Je vous prie De faire mes bessemains a monsr Duvalle et tout Lemen
vostres humble serviteur
Renelelieur

Translation

From the mouth of the river of Limerick, 9 October [1690]

Sir,

My very dear father and mother, these lines will make known to you the state of my health, which is very good. I pray God it is likewise with you and our friends in general. As for news, I have none for you except that we escaped capture[1] by several ships. But, thank God, we made good sail. Goodbye my very dear father. I pray you to give my respects to Mr Duvalle and everyone.
Your humble servant,

René Lelieur

[1] Probably 'nous avons eu lâchage'. The writer might possibly mean that they were stopped and released by several ships, or conceivably that they were abandoned by other ships with which they were sailing. (Lelieur's spelling and syntax are very approximate.)

72. Jacques Mahon,[1] Scattery Island, to Jacques Souchay and François Bouchaud, bankers,[2] Nantes, 12 October 1690. No. 56

Le 12e 8bre 1690

Messrs Souchay & bouchaud – Scattery[3]

Messrs La presante est pour vous donner advis de mon arrivé Icÿ ce soir de s^{t} domingo avec mil et quelque rolles tabac et 10 bariques feulle et un tiercon et un Cart d'indigo pour les quels Jay signe quatre Connoissances que Jay laisse entre Les mains de mons^{r} Pichard au Cap[4] Lamané me presse pour monter Lariviere Je suis de Ceux

Messrs Vostre tres humble serviteur

Jacques Mahon

Translation

the 12th of October 1690

Messrs Souchay & Bouchaud[2] – Scattery[3]

Sirs, this is to give you notice of my arrival here this evening from Santo Domingo with a thousand odd rolls of tobacco, 10 casks of leaf, and a keg and a quarter of indigo, for which I signed four bonds which I left in the hands of Mons. Pichard at Cap [Français][4] Lamané presses me to go up river.
I am one of those Sirs

Your very humble servant

Jacques Mahon

[1] Capt. Jacques Mahon was a shipmaster from Nantes with trading connections in the west of Ireland in 1690 (Mulloy, *Franco-Irish Correspondence*, 2:125 #1063, 3:159 #2010).

[2] Jacques Souchay and François Bouchaud, sieur de la Foresterie, were prominent merchants in Nantes with investments in sugar refining and other enterprises. Bouchaud was a magistrate [échevin] of the city from 1690 to 1693 (Guy Saupin, *Nantes au XVIIe siècle: Vie politique et société urbaine* [Rennes, 1996], 219–20, 223, 225–8).

[3] Scattery Island, near Kilrush, in the estuary of the River Shannon.

[4] Cap-Français, the chief port of the French colony of Saint-Domingue, now known as Cap-Haïtien, Republic of Haiti.

73. Zachary Holland 'To Mr Tho & Jos Carpenter, at the Blackamores head, In Alderman burr^{e}, London', 7 December 1690.[1]

Limericke ye 7th Dec^{br} 1690

Mr Tho & Jos Carpent^{r}

My Last to you was ye 29th 8^{ber}, advisnig [sic] that in ye Amity John Michel Master I was one forth concerned, in herr I shipped 189 Ox hides 12 barels of Salmon two tones of tallow, and if she Arrived safe would have at least produced £300 str of wch I desired you would Inshure £150, but have no account wheather you did it, but yesterday had ye bad newes of her benig [sic] tackin into Millford,[2] if thay should Indevor to macke her a prise, it would be the greatest harship in the world, for its Impossible for us to send Ships where wee please, I understand you apear^{d} for me & am Shure y^{r} Indevors will not be wanting[.] I hope in God I may live to macke you sutable retornes for your manie favors to me, had not I great hopes by giving some monie you may gett her of, it would very much discomposse me, having great dependance one that Concerne and what I shiped of sence these trobles was Lost, Ostend is a good market for ye hyds and salmon[.] ye ship is new and stronge & ye opportunity that m^{r} scriven writes to his Cozen, Let me here of thy concerne as also what became of ye Butter in ye Jamie[3] and wheather m^{r} Ab^{r} Elton[4] observd my Ord^{r} to you wch is all I desire to here Except ye welfaire of you and yo^{rs} and ye rest of Our frinds[.] I nead not Inlarge, you know how to manadge shuch a concerne[.] m^{r} scriven will asist you benig [sic] concern^{d} for his relacions here that is concern^{d} in her[.] ye bearer in hast therefore will not Inlarge

I am Sr^{s} Yo^{r} Most Humble Ser^{t}

Zach Holland

[p.s.][5]

189 ox Hydes	[illegible]
12 barels Salmon	[illegible]
2 tunns Tallow	[illegible]
I Judge ye Value to be	[illegible]
1/4 Pte[6] Shipp	[illegible]

ye 3^{d} Jan^{ry} 90 recomended to m^{r} Hen^{y} Syms att m^{r} Riverston oekes att ye Hal & four In Clonmell[7]

[1] This letter was not included among the documents seized aboard the barque *Amity* but filed with the *Amity's* papers by the Prize Court (TNA, HCA 32/15).

[2] The 35-tun barque *Amity* of Limerick (John Mitchell, master) was captured by an English warship, the 36-gun HMS *Nonsuch* (Captain Robert Sincock, commander) off Milford Haven in October 1690.

[3] The ship *Jamie* is mentioned in Letter 23.

[4] For Abraham Elton, merchant of Bristol, see Letter 23, note 3.

[5] Postscript is not in Zachary Holland's hand. It appears that whatever was written originally was written over and deliberately obscured.

[6] Read: 'part' or 'part of'.

[7] Clonmel, Co. Tipperary.

74. Thomas Pearce, Limerick, 'To Joseph Scriven, In London', 18 December 1690.[1]

X^mo^ 18th 1690

Deare Cozen

my Longe Silence, I can In noe wise Excuse, but sorrow and misfortunes makes mee forgett my selfe, but indeed I never ought to bee forgetfull, of the greatest of obligations In your Extraordinary kindeness to my Dearest wife, but with all gratefull acknowledgment I shall Ever owne them, but doe never Expect to bee capable of discharging them, wch if I Ever am shal make it my full Endeavors, to serve thee, or any of thine, to ye utmost of my power.

I understand the Amity is carryed Into England, as a prize I hope shee will bee gott of, If not Its a most severe thing, that wee should Loose on Every side, wee canot have Liberty to send else where, and when wee doe send wee are forct to give seccurity to returne goods from franc hither, will not your Governm^t^ consider, that wee Canot doe what wee would doe, If our goods were safe heare wee would send nothing awaÿ, those perillous times sure I hope they will consider our condition, I am sure in justice they ought to doe it,[2] If the ship and goods be recovered, my L^rs^ will show what my Intrest in her was[.] Ostend will bee the best market for her to bee sent unto, I desire from y^u^ the Issue, with my Deare Love unto thy Selfe, and my shee, Cosen I am

Thy verry afect Coz

[1] This letter was not included among the documents seized aboard the barque *Amity* (TNA, HCA 32/15).

[2] For the fate of the *Amity* of Limerick in the High Court of Admiralty, see pp. 33–4.

Appendix I

William III's proclamation restricting trade with 'rebellious subjects' in Ireland

6 June 1689

A PROCLAMATION

WILLIAM R.

Where as the French King hath lately caused Our Kingdom of Ireland, in an Hostile manner, to be Invaded by a great number of Officers, Soldiers, and others, and hath Raised and Carried on a War against Us in our said Kingdom, and Furnished our Rebellious Subjects there with Arms, Ammunition, and Money, to the apparent Danger and Hazard of that Our Kingdom; We have therefore thought fit, and by and with the Advice of our Privy Council, We do, by this our Royal Proclamation, strictly Prohibit and Forbid all and every Our Loving Subjects, and all other Persons whatsoever, within these our Dominions, to Trade or traffick with any Person or Persons whatsoever in Our said Kingdom of Ireland, without Our Leave first Obtained in that behalf, or Correspond or have Communication with any Person any Parts or Places within the same, except such as are in Obedience to our Government, upon pain of our utmost Displeasure, and of being proceeded against as Persons holding Correspondence with Rebels and Enemies. And we do here by Require and Command all and singular Justices of the Peace, Mayors, Sheriffs, Bayliffs, Constables, and other Our Officers and Subjects, to use their Endeavours in and for the Discovery and Apprehending of all Offenders herein, to the intent, that they may be Prosecuted and Punished according to the utmost Rigour and Severity of Law.

Given at our Court at Hampton-Court the Sixth Day of June, 1689. In the First Year of Our Reign.

Source: *London Gazette*, 13 June 1689.

Appendix II

English 'Act for Prohibiting all Trade and Commerce with France' (1689)

I. Mischiefs from Importation of French Commodities and Manufactures.

Importation of French Commodities prohibited for Three Years; such Importation a common Nuisance.; Such Commodities may be seized and carried to the King's Warehouse.; Persons claiming such Goods shall give Security to answer Penalty, otherwise such Goods deemed to be imported; and after Security given, Claim and Security to be registered.; on Default of giving Security and making Claim within a Time limited, Goods deemed imported.; If Security given, the Importation shall be tried in the Exchequer.; Jury may judge of the Quality of Goods on Taste or View, and ascertain what are French Commodities.; If Jury find the Goods to be French,; then such Goods shall be destroyed.; Certificate of Destruction of Goods.; Saving such Goods.; Penalty.

Forasmuch as your Majestyes upon just and honourable grounds have beene pleased to declare an actuall Warr with France and to enter into severall Confederacies for carrying on the same and that it hath beene found by long experience that the Importing of French Wines Vinegar Brandy Linnen Silks Salt Paper and other the Commodities of the Growth Product or Manufacture of France or of the Territories or Dominions of the French King hath much exhausted the Treasure of this Nation lessened the value of the native Commodities and Manufactures thereof and greatly impoverished the English Artificers and Handycrafts and caused great detriment to this Kingdome in generall Bee it therefore enacted by the King and Queens most excellent Majestyes by and with the advice and consent of the Lords Spirituall and Temporall and Commons in this present Parlyament assembled and by the authoritie of the same That from and after the foure and twentyeth day of August in the yeare of our Lord one thousand six hundred eighty nine none of the Commodities aforesaid or any other Goods or Commodities whatsoever of the Growth Product or Manufacture of any of the Dominions or Territories of the French King or any Goods Commodities or Manufactures made of or mixed with Silke Thread Wooll Haire Gold Silver Leather or other Goods or Commodities being of the Growth Product or Manufacture of any the Dominions or Territories of the French King shall dureing or within the Terme of three yeares to be accounted from the said foure and twentyeth day of August or at any time or times before the end of the first Session of

Parlyament next after the Expiration of the said three yeares be brought in by Land or shall be imported in any Shipp or Shipps Vessell or Vessells whatso-ever into any Port Haven Creeke or other Place whatsoever in the Kingdoms of England or Ireland the [Dominion] of Wales or Towne of Berwicke upon Tweede or Isles of Jersey Guernsey Alderney Sarke or Isle of Man from any place or Port whatsoever either mixt or unmixt with any Commodity of the Growth or Product of any other Nation Place or Country whatsoever And that all and every Importation and Importations vending or selling or uttering or retailing of any French Wines Vinegar Brandy Linnen Silks Salt or Paper or other Com[m]odities imported contrary to this Act or any of them shall be and is hereby declared and adjudged to be a common Nusance to this Kingdome in generall and to all their Majesties Subjects thereof And that if any French Wines Brandy Vinegar Linnens Silks Salt Paper or other Commodities whatsoever (mixt or unmixt) shall be imported contrary to this Act the same soe imported in whose Hands or Custodie or in what place soever they shall or may remaine or be found or kept shall and may be forthwith seized and carryed by any person or persons whatsoever into their Majestyes Warehouse of the Port or place where such Goods shall be seized or to the Warehouse of the next Port Member or Creeke to the place of such Seizure And if any person or persons shall make any Claime to all or any part of the said Goods soe seized and brought in as aforesaid he shall be obliged to tender good and sufficient Security to answere the Penalties of the said Act and to make the said Claime within twenty dayes after such Seizure to the Collector or Customer or his sufficient Deputie where noe other Collector is established or to the Commissioners of the Customs in time of Vacation or within ten dayes in Terme time by delivery of a Bill to such Officer subscribed with his Name Addition and place of abode together with the particulars of the respective Goods by him soe claimed and date of such Claime and the Names of two or more such sufficient persons whome he shall propose and tender to be security with him to answere the Penalties of the said Act and every one of them being worth five hundred pounds at the least and to be ap-proved of by the said Commissioners Collectors or Customers to whome the persons are alsoe to be tendred at the same time and if approved to give Bond unto their Majestyes in the penall summe of double the value of the Goods and the Penalties in this Act to answere the Value of the Goods and other Penalties in this Act and after such Security given the said Claime with the Names of the persons giveing such Security and the Summe and Date of the said Bonds to be registred in a Booke herein after mentioned to be kept in the Warehouse for that purpose and subscribed by the said Claimer and Collector or Customer to whome such Bill shall be delivered And in case Default shall be made in give-ing such Security and makeing such Claime within the times limitted as afore-said That then and in every such case the said Goods shall be adjudged deemed and taken to all intents and purposes to be imported contrary to this Act and to be forfeited to their Majestyes and shall within seven dayes after such default be destroyed in such manner as is herein after appointed but in case such Security shall be given and Claime made in manner as aforesaid an Information thereof shall the next Terme or sooner as soone as the Method and Course of Proceedings will admitt be exhibited into their Majestyes Court of Exchequer and all the Barons and Officers of the said Court of Exchequer are hereby required and strictly enjoyned to cause due speedy and effectuall Prosecution in the said Court of every such Information and not to grant any Writt of Delivery or Restitution for such Goods or any of them on any Security or pretence whatsoever untill the Cause shall be finally determined in Law by or upon the Verdict of a Jury of twelve good and lawfull Men to be returned by the proper Officers in the presence of a Commissioner of the Customs in London and in the presence of the principall Officer in such Out-Port where the Goods soe seized shall be brought and lodged as aforesaid Which Jury upon the Taste or View of any of the Commodities seized or stayd as aforesaid or upon proofe before them made shall and may judge the Quality and Value thereof and whether any of the Commodities soe seized and which of them were of the Growth Product or Manufacture of any of the Dominions or Territories of the French King or mixed with any Goods or Commodities of such Growth Product or Manufacture or were imported contrary to this Act and in what Shipp or Shipps Vessell or Vessells the same were imported and by whome the same were imported or vended retailed or sold and in whose Custodie they were at the time when the said Seizure or Stay was made and whether the said Commodities or any of them or any part of them were of the Growth Product or Manufacture of any of the Territories or Dominions of the French King or mixed with any Goods or Commodities of such Growth Product or Manufacture and in case the said Jury shall finde and returne their Verdict upon their Oaths that the Commodities soe seized or stayd or any of them or any part of them or any of them were of the Growth Product or Manufacture of any of the Dominions or Territories of the French King or mixed with any Goods or Commodities of such Growth Product or Manufacture that then immediately Judgement shall be passed upon the Goods soe found and the Judgement executed accordingly (to witt) That all such Wines Vinegar and Brandies or other liquid Commodities soe found whether single or mixt shall in some River Streame or Sea neare the place where they were soe seized or shall remaine in the Warehouses as aforesaid be there staved and spilt and destroyed and the said Linens Silks Salt or Paper and other Commodities soe found by the said Jury (whether mixed or unmixed) shall be publickly burnt and destroyed in the open Fields or Streets neere the place where they were soe seized or shall remaine in the Warehouses as aforesaid in the presence of one of the Sheriffes of the City of London in the Port of London the Chiefe Magistrate in every other Port or place who are hereby required upon Notice of the Chiefe Officer of the Customs in such Port to be present at and assisting in the destruction of the said Goods to prevent all Abuses

Hindrances or other Disturbances or Frauds in the destruction of the same as alsoe to open view taste and examine the said Commodities as to kinde quality and quantity according to the first Entry made in the Warehouse Booke and to joyne with the Collector Customer or his sufficient Deputy who are alsoe required to be present at the destruction thereof in a Certificate of the same to be entred in the said Booke under their Hands as aforesaid on the day of the destruction thereof And that noe person or persons whatsoever doe presume to take up or save any of the said Com[m]odities soe adjudged to be spilt burnt or destroyed under the penalty of forty shillings over and above the value of the said Goods

II. Importing Goods.

Penalty.; Having such Goods in Custody.; 1st Offence. Penalty.; 2d Offence.; Penalty.; Selling, &c. such Goods.; Penalty.; Onus probandi to lie upon Importer, &c.; And in Default of Proof, Judgment.; Informer acting by Collusion.; Penalty, £500. All Officers to aid in executing this Act.; Such Goods to be put into the King's Warehouse.; Where and by whom they are to be viewed, registered, and accounted for.; Seizures, Examinations, &c. to be entered and subscribed by Officers.; Copies of Entries, &c. and Certificate of Destruction of Goods, to the Commissioners of the Customs.

And moreover it is further enacted That every person and persons that shall have imported the same shall forfeite the full value thereof according to the Rates and Prices hereafter in this Act respectively mentioned and every person and persons in whose Custodie the same shall be found at the time of such Seizure or Stay or that shall sell utter or retaile within the Kingdoms of England or Ireland Dominion of Wales or Towne of Berwicke upon Tweede or the Isles of Jersey Guernsey Alderney Sarke or Isle of Man any of the Commodities imported contrary to this Act shall for the first Offence forfeit the full Value thereof according to the Rates and Prices hereafter mentioned and for the second Offence (after Conviction for such first Offence) shall forfeit double the full value thereof according to the Rates aforesaid and shall alsoe after Conviction of such second Offence stand and be disabled and be incapeable in Law to beare or execute any Office or Employment for or concerning or relateing to the Collection or Managery of the Customs or any part of their Majestyes Revenue or any other Office or Publick Employment whatsoever And if any of the Commodities aforesaid whether they be single or mixt with any Commodity of the Growth or Product of any other Nation Country or Place whatsoever imported contrary to this Act shall dureing the said Terme of three yeares or before the end of the Session of the next Parlyament after the end of the said three yeares upon any pretence whatsoever be vended sold retailed or uttered or be found or remaine within the Kingdoms of England or Ireland Dominion of Wales or Towne of Berwicke upon Tweede or Isles of Jersey Guernsey Alderney Sarke or Isle of Man the same shall and may be seized by any person or persons whatsoever in whose Possession or Custodie soever they shall or may be found and like Informations thereof and Judgement and Execution for the destruction of them shall be had made and given as is before expressed And moreover every person in whose Custody or Possession they shall be found or that shall vend sell retaile or utter the same shall incurr the Forfeitures and Penalties aforesaid to be recovered as herein is mentioned And if any Question Dispute or Doubt shall arise whether any of the Commodities aforesaid seized sold found or uttered as aforesaid or any part thereof either single or mixt were of the Growth Product or Manufacture of any of the Territories or Dominions of the French King or were imported contrary to this Act the Proofe shall be incumbent onely upon the Importer Claimer Owner Proprietor Seller and Retailer or such person or persons with whome the said Goods shall be found respectively and not upon the Informer And for default of such Proofe that then a Judgement thereupon shall be given for the destruction of the said Commodities and for Recovery of the aforesaid Forfeiture and Execution of such Judgement shall be immediately granted and awarded according to the true intent and meaning of this Act without any stay or delay whatsoever And if any Informer or other person or persons shall take upon him or them to seize or prosecute any Goods or Commodities or any person or persons upon or by virtue or meanes of this present Act shall by Fraud or Collusion desist or delay the prosecution of the Condemnation of any the Commodities aforesaid after seizure or stay of the same or the Prosecution of any person or persons for any Offence against this Act he and they soe desisting or delaying shall for every such Offence upon due Conviction thereof forfeit the Summe of five hundred pounds And all Customers Searchers and other Officers belonging to the Customs And all Sheriffes Mayors Bailiffes Constables and other Officers shall be and are hereby strictly injoyned and required to be aiding and assisting in the due Execution of this Act in reference to the Commodities aforesaid which are to be destroyed or disposed of as aforesaid And noe Commissioner or Commissioners Customer Surveyor Generall or Surveyor or other Officer or person whatsoever relating to the Customs shall signe suffer or allow of any Warrant free Warrant or Order for passing or delivery of any Goods prohibited by this Act either to any person or into any place whatsoever other then into one of their Majesties Warehouses there to remaine in safe Custody untill a Judgement or Condemnation in Law upon or touching the said goods be given and passed according to the true intent and meaning of this Act nor shall any Surveyor of the Land Waiters nor [Surveyer] of the Tyde Waiters or Kings Waiter or Land-Waiter or other Officer or person whatsoever relateing to the Customs either by vertue colour or pretext of any Warrant or Order whatsoever take up or deliver any of the Goods prohibited by this Act or carry them or suffer them to be carryed to any other place then one of their Majestyes Warehouses there to remaine untill a Judgement or Condemnation upon or touching the said Goods be given and passed according to the true intent of this Act And all such Goods soe as aforesaid brought into any of their Majestyes Warehouses shall be forthwith viewed opened or examined in the presence of two or more principall Officers of that Port whereof the Collector Customer or Customers Deputy to be one and the Marks Numbers of each Vessell or Package and the Nature Kinde Quality Quantity and true Contents of the said Goods together with the time when they were soe brought in and the time of their delivery out of the said Warehouses shall by speciall direction of the Commissioners or other Chiefe Officers that shall have the Managery Direction or Collection of the Customs be fairly registred in a Booke to be kept for that purpose and for entry of the Claimes as is herein before directed and for noe other purpose whatsoever And every such Entry of each Seizure with the time of viewing opening and examineing thereof to be duely entred and subscribed by the Officers aforesaid and by the Warehouse-keeper or Surveyour where noe Warehouse-keeper is established Which Examination [alsoe shall] be repeated and entred in manner aforesaid by the said Officers after Condemnation of the said Goods at the time of the delivery out of any the said Goods to be destroyed or otherwise disposed of and to be diligently compared with the first Entry to prevent any Fraud Change or Imbezelment And in case any shall be found upon such Examination or after delivery upon the destruction of the said Goods the same to be entred and subscribed in the said Booke by the principall Officer of the said Port not haveing Charge of the said Warehouse and true Copies of all the said Entryes and Examinations with the Claimes as aforesaid as alsoe a true Certificate of the destruction of the said Goods signed as aforesaid be from time to time transmitted by the Collector of the said Port unto the Com[m]issioners Farmers principall Officers or other persons haveing the Managery of their Majestyes Customs for the time being together with the monthly Abstracts of the said Ports which shall be carefully filed and a distinct accompt kept thereof by the Register of the Seizures in the Port of London

III. The Goods not to be delivered out of the Warehouse till Judgment, except for Production at Trial.

And bee it further enacted That the said Goods or any of them be produced at any Tryall that shall be had for and in order to the Condemnation or destruction of the said Goods or touching the unlawfull importing thereof or for the Recovery of any Forfeiture or Penalty incurred by reason of the importing of such Goods contrary to this Act nor shall such Goods be delivered out of any of the said Warehouses by any Officer whatsoever relateing to the Customs untill a Judgement or Condemnation shall have beene given and passed upon or touching the said Goods other then to be produced at such Tryall as aforesaid according to the true intent and meaning of this Act

IV. Person, not being a Merchant, &c. selling such Goods

Punishment.

And forasmuch as the Commodities and Manufactures of the Territories and Dominions of the French King prohibited by this Act are often sold by persons not being knowne Merchants Vintners or Shopkeepers Bee it enacted by the authoritie aforesaid That if any person not being a knowne Merchant Vintner or Shopkeeper shall from and after the first day of September one thousand six hundred eighty nine sell or expose to sale or be found to have sold or exposed to sale any of the Commodities or Manufactures soe prohibited as aforesaid (and shall be thereof lawfully convicted by Indictment Information or otherwise in any of their Majestyes Courts of Record) shall over and above the penalties aforesaid suffer twelve months Imprisonment without Baile or Mainprize

V. Ship importing, forfeited; and also Lighters, &c. employed. Master, Seamen, &c. importing; Penalty, £500 and Punishment.

Seamen, Carmen, &c. assisting in unshipping and conveying such Goods; Punishment. Carts, &c. bringing such Goods, forfeited. Master, &c. of Ship letting go such Goods; Penalty, £500 and Imprisonment.

And to the end the Prohibition and Restraint of Importation of the Commodities aforesaid hereby intended may be more effectually putt in Execution It is hereby further enacted That all and every Shipp or Vessell with all her Guns Tackle Apparell and Furniture in which any of the said French Wines Vinegar Brandy Linens Silks Salt Paper or other Commodities before mentioned shall after the said twenty fourth day of August and dureing the said Terme of three years or before the end of the next Session of Parlyament after the said three yeares be imported And alsoe all and every Barke Hoy Lighter Barge Wherry Boate Shipp or other Vessell whatsoever out of which the same or any of them shall be putt on shore shall be forfeit And moreover the Master Purser Boatswain or other person takeing care of such Shipp or Vessell for the Voyage or out of which any of the Commodities shall be unshipt into a Hoy Boate or Vessell or landed or putt on shore shall forfeit the Summe of five hundred pounds and alsoe being apprehended by Warrant of any one or more Justices of the Peace of the County City or Burrough where such Importation or Landing shall be or where the person or persons offending shall or may be found Which the said Justices of the Peace are hereby anthorized to issue and to examine Witnesses upon Oath concerning such Fact and the same being proved by the Oath of two Witnesses shall and may be by such Justice of the Peace committed to the next Goale there to remaine without Baile or Mainprize for the space of twelve months And all and every the Seamen Mariners Watermen Carmen Porters Labourers or other persons whatsoever assisting in the unshipping landing takeing up carrying or conveying of any of the said Com[m]odities either by

Land or by Water shall upon Examination and Proofe as aforesaid be subject to like Imprisonment or be publickly whipt at the discretion of the Justice of Peace before whome such Conviction shall be And all and every the Carts Wains Waggons Carriages Ploughs Teams Horses or Oxen made use of assisting carrying or moveing in the Carriage or Conveyance of any of the said Goods or Commodities hereby prohibited to be imported shall and may be seized and stayd and upon proofe made before some Justice of the Peace of the County where the same shall be soe seized by the Oaths of two credible Witnesses (which Oaths the said Justice of the Peace is hereby impowered and required to administer) That the said Carts Wains Waggons Carriage Ploughs Teams Horses or Oxen respectively were made use of assisting carrying or moveing in the Carriage or Conveyance of any the said Goods and Commodities hereby prohibited to be imported the same shall be forfeited one halfe thereof to be disposed of to the use of the Poore of the Parish where the same shall be soe found and seized and the other halfe to his or their owne use that shall soe seize the same And if the Master Purser Boatswain or other person belonging to any Shipp or Vessell laden or part laden with any of the Commodities aforesaid shall after the said foure and twentyeth day of August unshipp or discharge or wittingly or willingly permitt or suffer any of the said Goods hereby prohibited to be unshipt or discharged either at Sea or in any Harbour Creeke or Bay of the Kingdoms aforesaid into any lesser Vessell Lighter Barge or Boate shall forfeit the Summe of five hundred pounds and suffer like Imprisonment as aforesaid

VI. All Brandy, &c. prohibited; Penalty.

And bee it further enacted That noe sort of Brandy Aqua vite or other Spirits or distilled Waters of any Kingdome Country or place whatsoever shall after the said foure and twentyeth day of August be imported into the Kingdoms of England or Ireland aforesaid Dominion or Islands aforesaid under paine of forfeiture thereof as alsoe of the Shipp or Vessell wherein the same shall be imported

VII. The Value of Goods to be according to the Book of Rates; 12 Car. II. the Goods not there settled to be valued by a Jury, except Wine, which is £30 per Tun, and Brandy £40.

In case of Condemnation, the Value of the Goods to be determined by a Jury.

And it is hereby further enacted That where any Forfeitures or Penalties are given by this Act upon the Value of the Goods hereby prohibited that the Values and Prices of the said Goods and Commodities although the same are to be destroyed are to be and shall be reckoned stated and esteemed as followeth (that is to say) The value and price of every Ton of Wines thirty pounds the value and price of every Ton of Brandy forty pounds and soe after that Rate for a greater or lesser quantity And that the value and price of all other the Commodities aforesaid which are rated in the Booke of Rates made in the twelfth yeare of the Raigne of his late Majestie King Charles the Second shall be esteemed according to the Rate Price or Value at which they are valued in the same Booke of Rates And that the value and price of all other the Commodities aforesaid not rated in the said Booke of Rates shall be enquired and determined by the Jury that shall try the Cause or which shall be impannelled to inquire whether the said Goods were of the Growth Production or Manufacture of the French Kings Dominions and the Values above stated and those returned by the said Jury which shall be esteemed according to the Value the said Goods would have borne if they were not to have beene destroyed shall be the stated Values thereof And in case of Condemnation by Default the Value to be enquired and determined by a Jury to be returned before the Mayor or Bayliffe of the City or Towne Corporate or before the next Justice of the Peace of the County where the same Goods shall happen to be brought and the Forfeitures imposed by this Act upon any person or persons relateing to the Values of any of the said Goods shall be reckoned accordingly

VIII. Third Part of the Value given to Prosecutor.

And for the Encouragement of all such whether Officers of the Customs or others that shall effectually putt in Execution the Prohibition hereby intended by seizing and prosecuteing the Goods aforesaid to Condemnation and Destruction and alsoe by prosecuteing all or any other the Offences or Offenders against this Act It is hereby further enacted by the authoritie aforesaid That all and every such person and persons soe prosecuteing shall be recompensed and rewarded with one third part of the value of all the Goods by him or them soe prosecuted to Condemnation and Destruction as aforesaid to be paid unto them by the Owners and Proprietors of the said Goods soe imported

IX. Division of the Part of Penalty not before disposed of.

Prosecution to be at the King's Charge.

And it is hereby further enacted That all the Residue of the Forfeitures and Penalties before in this Act mentioned and provided (and not before distributed and disposed of) shall be divided into three severall parts two third parts thereof to their Majestyes their Heires and Successors and the other third part to such person and persons as shall seize or sue for the same by Bill Plaint or Information in their Majestyes Court of Exchequer or in any other their Majestyes Courts of Record wherein noe Essoigne Protection or Wager of Law shall be allowed The Charge of which Suite and Prosecution shall be borne by their Majestyes their Heires and Successors and issued by the Receiver Generall or Cashire of their

Majesties Customs by Warrant from the Commissioners of the Customs for the time being as there shall be occasion

X. Foreigner, &c. claiming to give Security.

And for the avoiding of Fraud Vexation and Delay in prosecuting the said Goods or Shipps to Condemnation by entring Claimes in false or unknowne Names or in the Names of absent persons It is hereby further enacted That noe Forreigner or other person be admitted to claime any of the said Goods or Commodities which shall be seized or stayed as aforesaid untill Security first given to the satisfaction of the Collector of such Port where the said Goods shall be brought and lodged as aforesaid to answere such Penalties or Forfeitures as shall be incurred by him as the Importer of the said Goods or which the Owner Importer or Possessor of the said Goods or Commodities as shall or may be subject or lyable to by force or vertue of this Act or the true meaning thereof

XI. Officer conniving at Importation; Penalty £500. Punishment.

And bee it further enacted That if any Officer or person of or belonging to the Customs shall by Fraud or Corruption connive at the Importation of any of the Commodities aforesaid contrary to the true meaning of this Act he shall not onely forfeit the Summe of five hundred pounds to be recovered as aforesaid but be made incapeable of any Office or Employment under their Majestyes their Heires and Successors and alsoe forfeit the Penalties of such Bonds wherein they stand obliged to their Majestyes for the true performance of their Trust as Officers of the Customs

XII. Person authorized may search any House, and break open Doors, &c.

And for the more effectuall discovery and seizure of any of the Commodities aforesaid It shall and may be lawfull to and for any person or persons whatsoever authorized by Writt of Assistance under the Seale of their Majestyes Court of Exchequer to take a Constable Headburrough or other publick Officer inhabiting neare unto the place and in the day time to enter and goe into any House Shopp Cellar Warehouse or Roome or other place and in case of Resistance to breake open Doores Chests Trunks or other Package there to seize and from thence to bring to their Majestyes Warehouse any of the Commodities aforesaid prohibited by and imported contrary to this Act

XIII. Attorney General, or any Person seizing the Commodities, may prosecute.

Action for executing Act.; General Issue.; Treble Costs.

And for the more speedy and effectuall Prosecution of the Offences and Offenders against this Act Bee it enacted by the authoritie aforesaid That it shall and may be lawfull to and for their Majestyes Attourney Generall and all and every other person and persons that shall seize or stay any of the Goods or Com[m]odities aforesaid or prosecute any of the Offences or Offenders against this Act to lay his or their Information or Action and to try the same in such place or places and to use such and the like Method and Course of Proceedings in prosecuteing and condemning of the Goods or Commodities aforesaid as is in this Act directed are have beene or may be used in or about the seizing trying condemning or prosecuteing of any Goods or Commodities for Non-payment of Customs or other Duties or any person or persons for offending against any the Laws or Statutes relateing to the Customs and that if any Action or Suite shall be brought or prosecuted against any person or persons for what he or they shall doe in or about the Prosecution or putting in Execution this present Act or any of the Powers therein It shall and may be lawfull to and for the Defendant or Defendants in such Action or Suite to plead the generall Issue and to give the speciall Matter in Evidence And if the Plaintiffe or Plaintiffes in any such Action or Suite shall discontinue or delay the prosecution thereof or shall become Nonsuite or that a Verdict or Judgement shall passe against him or them that then the Defendant and Defendants in every such Action or Suite shall recover his and their treble Costs and shall have Judgement and Execution for the same in such sort and manner as Defendants by any the Laws and Statutes of this Realme shall or may have for Costs

XIV. Goods prohibited not to be imported from Guernsey, &c.

Penalty.

And bee it further enacted by the authoritie aforesaid That from and after the first day of September one thousand six hundred eighty nine none of the Goods Commodities or Manufactures prohibited by this Act shall be imported from the Islands of Guernsey Jersey Alderney Sarke and Man or any of them into any of the Ports Creeks or Havens of England Ireland Dominion of Wales or Towne of Berwicke upon Tweede under the Penalties and Forfeitures contained in this Act

XV. G. Heathcote and Arthur Shallot, &c. licensed to import not exceeding 200 Tuns of Brandy.

Affidavits on such Importation.

Provided alwayes and bee it enacted by the authoritie aforesaid That Gilbert Heathcote and Arthur Shallott of London Merchants or either of them have leave to import into the Port of London any Quantity of Spanish Brandy not exceeding two hundred Ton at most paying to their Majestyes all Dutyes payable for the same before this Session of Parlyament importing the same at or before the five and twentyeth of March one thousand six hundred and ninety and not lesse then fifty Ton thereof in any one Vessell and produceing a Certificate and Testimoniall from the Governour of Catalonia and the English Consull there together with an Affidavit of the Distiller made before the said Governour that it is all Brandy made of Wine of the Growth of Spaine and likewise the severall Affidavits of the Master Mate and Purser of such Shipp and Shipps as shall import the said Brandyes that the same was taken in at Sallow one of the Sea ports of the Province of Catalonia aforesaid any thing contained in this Act to the contrary notwithstanding

XVI. Rate of French Wine settled.

First Offence, Penalty £5.; Every succeeding Offence £10.

Provided that noe person shall sell at or demand a greater Price for any French Wines or Wines soe reputed or other Wines mixed with any French Wines from and after the tenth day of September one thousand six hundred eighty nine to the tenth day of September one thousand six hundred and ninety then twelve pence by the Quart and from and after the said tenth day of September one thousand six hundred and ninety the Summe of six pence the Quart and noe more and soe proportionably for a greater or lesser quantity upon penaltie of forfeiting for every Quart for which a greater price than what is above mentioned is either demanded or taken the Summe of five pounds for the first Offence to the Informer and the Summe of ten pounds for the second and every other Offence to the Informer to be recovered by Action of Debt Bill Plaint or Information in any of their Majestyes Courts of Record wherein no Protection or Wager of Law shall be allowed or any more then one Imparlance

XVII. Retailers to sell Wine in Pewter Measures sealed. Penalty £5.

And it is hereby enacted That from and after the tenth day of September one thousand six hundred eighty nine noe Vintner or Retailer of Wines whatsoever shall sell or utter any Wines by Retail other then by and in Measures made of Pewter and sealed according to the Statute under the paine and penaltie of five pounds for every such Offence to the Informer to be levyed and recovered in any of such Courts and in such manner as aforesaid

XVIII. Selling sophisticated Wine; Penalty £300.

And for the preventing of the Mischiefs which may be occasioned by the sophisticating corrupting and adulterating of Wines dureing such time as they are by this Act allowed to be sold Bee it enacted That if any Merchant Vintner Wine-Cooper or other person selling Wine by Wholesale or Retaile shall corrupt sophisticate or adulterate any Wine or shall utter or sell any Wine corrupted sophisticated or adulterated such person shall forfeit the Sum of three hundred pounds for every such Offence the one moyety thereof to their Majesties and their Successors and the other moyety thereof to such person as shall sue for the same by Action of Debt Bill Plaint or Information wherein noe Essoigne Protection or Wager of Law or more then one Imparlance shall be allowed and alsoe shall suffer Imprisonment by the space of three months without Baile or Mainprize.

Source: 1 William & Mary c. 34 (1688) in *Statutes of the Realm*: Volume 6, 1685–94, (s.l, 1819), 98–103. British History Online https://www.british-history.ac.uk/statutes-realm/vol6/pp98-103 [accessed 2 June 2024]. Using the modern system of dating in which 1 January rather than 25 March is considered the first day of the year, the statute was passed in 1689 not in 1688. The heading of Appendix II reflects this.

Appendix III

Irish 'Act for the Advance and Improvement of Trade, and for the Encouragement and Increase of Shipping and Navigation' (1689)

Whereas, this kingdom of Ireland, for its good scituation, commodious harbours, and great quantity of goods the growth product, and manufactury thereof, is, and standeth very fit and convenient for trade and commerce with most nations, kingdoms and plantations; and several laws, statutes and ordinances, having heretofore been made, and enacted, from time to time, prohibiting and disabling the king's subjects of this realm, to export, or carry out of this kingdom, unto any other the kings islands, plantations, or colonies, in Asia, Africa, or America, several of the goods, wares, merchandizes, and commodities of this nation; or to import into this kingdom, the goods or merchandizes of the said plantations, colonies and islands, without landing and discharging in England, Wales, or the town of Berwick upon Tweed, under great penalties and forfeitures, not only to the decay of the king's revenue, but also to the very great prejudice and disadvantage of all the inhabitants in this kingdom, as well subjects as strangers; and which hath in a high measure contributed to impoverish this kingdom, and discouraged several merchants, traders, and artificers, to come from abroad, and dwell, and trade here: and whereas, the encrease of shipping, and the encouragement of navigation, under the good providence of God, and the careful protection of his sacred majesty, are the best and fittest means and foundations, whereon the wealth, safety and strength of this island and kingdom, may be built and established.

[s. 1] Be it therefore enacted, by the king's most excellent majesty, with the advice and consent of the lords spiritual and temporal, and commons, in this present parliament assembled; and by the authority of the same, that it shall, and may be lawful, to and for his majesties subjects of this realm of Ireland, and to and for every other person and persons, of what nation soever, residing and inhabiting here, during the time of such residence, freely to trade into, and from all and every his majesties plantations, colonies and islands, in Asia, Africa, and America, and to export from this kingdom, and carry unto all and every the said plantations, colonies, and islands, and there sell, dispose of, and barter all sorts of goods, wares, merchandises and commodities, as well of the growth product, or manufactury of this kingdom, as of any other part of Europe, commonly called, European goods, and import, and bring into this kingdom of Ireland, all sorts of goods, wares, merchandizes, and commodities of the growth product, or manufactury of all or any the said islands, colonies and plantations, without being oblidged to land or unload in England, Wales, or the town of Berwick upon Tweed, or entring all or any such goods, wares, or merchandizes there; but as herein after is expressed, and without being oblidged upon shipping, or taking on board, in the said plantations, colonies, or islands, the said commodities, to enter into any bond, to bring the said goods into England, Wales, or town of Berwick upon Tweed, and to unload and put the same on shoar, any act, statute, ordinance, law, sentence, or judgment, at any time heretofore made, given, or in force, to the contrary notwithstanding:

[s. 2] provided always, that the master or owner of all and every such ship and ships, vessel or vessels, so trading, from this kingdom, unto all or any the said islands, colonies, or plantations, his or their agents or factors shall, and do before such ship or ships, vessel or vessels, sail from any part of this kingdom, towards the said islands, colonies, or plantations perfect, and enter into a bond, with one sufficient security, to the use of the king, and to be perfected to the collector, or chief custom-house officer of such port or place, whence such ship or vessel is to sail, in such a reasonable sum, as such collector, or custom-house officer, shall require, regard being had to the value of such cargoe, as the said ship or vessel shall export, with condition to bring the goods, wares, and merchandizes, which such ship or vessel shall take in, at all or any the said plantations, colonies, or islands, into England, Ireland, Wales, or town of Berwick upon Tweed, and to no other place, and there to aboad and put the same on shoar, the danger of the seas only excepted:

[s. 3] be it likewise enacted, by the authority aforesaid, that all goods and merchandizes whatsoever, which shall be carryed, conveyed, or exported out of this kingdom of Ireland, to the said islands, colonies, and plantations, shall be lyable, and pay to the king's majesty, his heirs and successors, in the said islands, plantations and colonies, the same or so much customs, excise, or other duties, as the like goods or merchandizes being exported out of England, into all, or any the said plantations, colonies, or islands, and all goods or merchandizes imported into this kingdom, out of all or any the said islands, colonies, and plantations, (tobacco and sugar only excepted) shall pay in this kingdom to the use of the king's majesty, his heirs and successors, the same or like duties, custom and excise, and no more or other, and in such manner, and at such time, and subject to such penalties and forfeitures, for non-entry, undue entry, or non-payment of duties, as in the like acts of parliament made in this kingdom, in the fourteenth and fifteenth years of the reign of the late King Charles the Second; the one, entituled, an act for settling the subsidy or poundage, and granting of subsidy of tunnage, and other sums of money unto his royal majesty, his heirs and successors; the same to be paid upon merchandize, imported and exported into, or out of the kingdom of Ireland, according to a book of rates hereunto annexed; and the other, entituled, an act for the settling of the excise, or new im-post, upon his majesty, his heirs and successors, according to the book of rates therein incerted, and as in the said book of rates, and as in the rules, orders, and directions, to the said acts and books of rates annexed, are contained and specified:

[s. 4] and whereas, the duties, and custom, and excise on tabacco, of the king's majesty's plantations, imported into this kingdom, amount to no more, according to the said two late acts of parliament in this kingdom, and books of rates to them annexed, but to two pence per pound, which is too small a duty. Be it therefore enacted, by the authority aforesaid, that all tobacco of the growth, or product of all or any his majesties new plantations or islands, or any plantations belonging to his most Christian majesty, imported into this kingdom, out of all or any the said plantations and islands shall from and after the eighteenth day of July, 1689. be charged, and lyable to pay unto his majesty, his heirs, and successors, the sum of five pence, sterl. for each pound, custom, and excise, (that is to say) two pence for each pound custom, and three pence for each pound excise, and no more, provided always, that Spanish and Brazill tobacco, shall pay the same duty of custom, and excise, as formerly; and that likewise, tobacco of that growth or product of the kings plantation, or any of the foreign plantations belonging to his most Christian majesty, imported into this kingdom out of England, or any other part of Europe at any time, from and after the eighteenth day of July, 1689. shall pay and satisfy unto the kings majesty, his heirs and successours, the sum of two pence, sterl. custom, for, and out of each, and every pound, and the sum of two pence, half penny, sterl. excise, for, and out of each pound, and no more. And, that sugars, indicoe, log-wood, imported into this kingdom out of England, shall pay, and satisfy unto the kings majesty, his heirs and successours, (viz.) white sugar coming from England, ten shillings custom, and ten shillings excise, for every hundred weight, and no more; brown sugar, the sum of two shillings, six pence sterl. custom, and the like sum of two shillings, six pence sterl. excise for each hundred weight, and no more; indicoe, the sum of two pence per pound excise, and two pence custom for each pound, and no more; and log-wood, five shillings, sterl. excise, and five shillings, sterl. custom, for each hundred weight, and no more; the said duties, customs, and excise to be paid in such manner, and under such pains and forfeitures, and with such allowances, as in the aforesaid two acts and books of rates, orders and directions are expressed and contained.

[s. 5] And for the further encouragement and advance of the said plantation trade, and for maintaining a greater, and more firm correspondence and kindness between the subjects of this kingdom, and the planters, and inhabitants of the said plantations and islands; be it enacted, by the authority aforesaid, that whatsoever goods or commodities of the growth, product, or manufactury of the said islands or plantations, shall be at any time hereafter unloaded, or landed, in any part of this kingdom, and shall pay or secure to be paid, the customs, duties, and excise on the said goods, due and payable, that at any time hereafter, within the space of one whole year, to commence from the day of such landing, it shall, and may be lawful to and for the merchant, owner or proprietor of such goods and commodities, his or their agents or factors, to export and carry out of this kingdom into any other nation, dominion or country, such and so much of the said goods and commodities so landed, as he or they shall think fit; and that upon such exportation the whole excise of such goods, which was before paid, or secured to be paid for the same, and one half of the custom of the said goods before paid or secured to be paid, shall be re-paid or allow'd to such merchant, owner, proprietor, his or their factors or agents so exporting, and that within twenty days next and immediately ensuing the date and time of such exportation, tobacco only excepted.

[s. 6] And for the more encouragement of building good and serviceable ships, be it enacted by the authority aforesaid, that any person or persons who shall within the space of 10 years to commence the 24th of June, 1689. build, or cause to be built within this kingdom of Ireland, any ship or vessel above twenty five tun, and under one hundred tun burthen, shall and may for the first three voyages any such ship or vessel shall make out of this kingdom, upon the said ship or vessels return from such voyage back into this kingdom, have, receive, or be allowed to his and their own proper use one eighth part of the duties of customs and excise which shall be due or payable to the king, his heirs, or successors, for and out of all the goods and commodities so imported in such ship or vessel upon the said three first returns, which such ship or vessel shall make into this kingdom. And likewise, that any person or persons, who shall within the said space of ten years commencing, as aforesaid, build or cause to be built in this kingdom any ship or vessel exceeding in burthen an 100 tun, shall for the first four voyages such ship or vessel shall make out of this kingdom, and upon the said ship or vessels return from the said voyages back to this kingdom, have and receive to his and their own proper use one eighth part of the duties of custom and excise, which shall be due or payable to the king, his heirs or successors, for or out of the goods and commodities so imported into such ship or vessel upon the four first returns such ship or vessel shall make out of this kingdom.

[s. 7] And to the end that masters of ships, sea-men, mariners, ship-wrights, carpenters, rope-makers and block-makers may be encouraged and invited to come and dwell in this kingdom, and that thereby navigation may improve and increase, be it further enacted by the authority aforesaid, that all and every masters of ships, and ship-wrights, ship-carpenters, sea-men, mariners, rope-makers, and block-makers, who are at present residing within this kingdom, or who shall or do at any time from henceforth come and reside in this kingdom of Ireland, and shall pursue and follow his trade or calling, shall and may for the time and space of ten years after his or their so coming into this kingdom, be freed, exempted and discharg'd of, and from all sorts of taxes, and cesses, watch, ward, and quarterings of soldiers and officers in and throughout this kingdom: and shall likewise have and be allowed his and their freedom gratis in any town, city, sea-port, corporation or borough, where he or they shall please to reside, and pursue his or their calling and trade.

[s. 8] And be it further enacted by the authority aforesaid, that in the respective cities and towns of Dublin, Belfast, Waterford, Cork, Lymerick and Gallway there shall be established, erected and setled, before the first day of December, 1689. in each of the said towns and cities, and so continued for ever hereafter, a free school for teaching and instructing the mathematicks, and the art of navigation; in every of which schools there shall be placed and continued one or more able and sufficient master or masters for teaching and instructing the said arts: and that every of the said towns and cities shall out of the publick revenue and stock to them belonging, or otherwise, settle and secure a reasonable pension and stipend for such master or masters, to be paid them quarterly during his and their continuance in such employment or employments:

[s. 9] provided always, and be it further enacted by the authority aforesaid, that the said duties of custom and excise of tobacco of the growth or product of his majesties plantation, shall be and continue payable to his majesty, his heirs and successors, during the time, and so long as the now duties in England of custom and excise on tobacco, amounting to five pence per pound, shall and do continue, and so long as this kingdom of Ireland shall have a free and open trade to and from the kings said foreign plantations, and no longer; and whensoever the said duties of five pence per pound custom and excise shall cease and determine in England, that then the duties of custom and excise, payable for tobacco imported in this kingdom before the making of this act shall remain, and be payable for ever thereafter to his majesty, his heirs and successors, and no more or other, and this present duty to cease and determine. Provided likewise, that it shall and may be lawful to and for all and every person or persons so importing tobacco from time to time, and at all times hereafter, to export and carry out of this kingdom into any other nation or kingdom all or any part of the said tobacco imported, and that upon such exportation out of this kingdom, the whole duty of excise of the said tobacco, and three half pence per pound of the custom shall be allowed and re-paid the merchant, owner or proprietor, his or their agents or factors so exporting the said tobacco; so that there shall be and remain to his majesty, his heirs and successors, but one half penny per pound custom for the said tobacco so exported.

Source: James II's Irish Parliament, c. 29 (1689) in John Bergin and Andrew Lyall (eds.), *The Acts of James II's Irish Parliament, 1689* (Dublin, 2015), 83–7.

Appendix IV

High Court of Admiralty

Documents in the proceedings against the Barque Amity of Limerick, 1690

John Mitchell M^{r}, Amity of about 35 tuns laden with salt hydes tallow salmon & bound from Limerick for Nantz or Bordeaux seized by the Nonsuch Capt. Robert Sinthock Command^{r} at or near Milford Haven

Source: TNA, IND 1/9013

♦

CLAIMS

The Amity, John Mitchell Ma

Claimes Given by Wm Smith 19 Novr 90

The Claime of Samuell Taverner, Thomas peirce, Zachary Holland, and James Craven of Limrick, merchants being Protestants and subjects of their Matie^{s} King William and Queen Mary for the said Ship, Tackle and Furniture, and for the Lading of the said ship consisting of Tallow, Hides, and Salmon, except the Goods hereunder naimed.

The Claime of the said John Mitchell for thirteen Cask of Butter, and eighteen hides and a halfe of tann'd Leather, and thirteen Dozen of Calves Skins.

The claime of John Reordon and Patrick Reordon of Limerick merchants for forty one Cask of Tallow.

Source: TNA, HCA 32/1851/19.

EXAMINATIONS [30 October 1690]

The Examinations of John Mitchel Master of ye barque called the Amity of Limbrick, Mathew Nesbett Samuel Davis John Williams [and] Patrick Caroll saylors belonging to ye said barque Deposed & taken the thirteenth day of October Anno Dom 1690 before Walter Middleton Esqr & Richard Evans gov^{d} by Virtue of A Comission to them & others directed as followeth

Captain John Mitchell

The Examin^{t} John Michell haveing taken his oath upon ye holy Evangelists deposeth & sayth, that ye said Barque hath been called ye Amity for ye space of about A year or more & that she was called by ye name ye Ann and Mary before ye present owners bought her, & that he ye say^{d} examin^{t} were Master of her and that he was apointed to be master of her by Patrick Reading an Irish merch^{t} in Nants, & y^{t} there is noe other Master besides & y^{t} ye say^{d} Barque was built in Ireland.

And further ye examin^{t} deposeth & sayth that Samuel Taverner of Limbrick Merch^{t} owneth a quarter part of ye say^{d} Barque, & Thomas Peirce Merch^{t} of Limbrick a quarter part & Zachary Holland of Limbrick aforesay^{d} one other quarter part & James Corven of Limbrick ye other quarter part & that he say^{d} owners have lived in Limbrick for ye space of seven years & some of them longer.

And further ye examin^{t} deposeth & sayth that the say^{d} Barque was laden, & full freighted in Limbrick with Tallow hides & Salmon, and bound for Nantz, Rochell or Bordeaux In ye kingdom of ffrance

And further ye Examin^{t} deposeth & sayth that all ye goods laden aboard the say^{d} barque belonged to the say^{d} owners, except 13 Casks of butter & 18 hides & half of tanned leather, & 13 dozen of Calves Skinns, which was the Examinants and 41 Casks of Tallow which belonged to Patrick Reding A Merch^{t} in ffrance, & shipped by John Reding his brother A Roman Catholick

And further ye examin^{t} sayeth y^{t} he was born in Kinsale in ye kingdom of Ireland, & y^{t} his usuall place of residence is at Galloway, & y^{t} that he hath lived there these two years last past, & that he was Educated in ye Prostes^{t} profession & soe Continueth.

And further ye Examin^{t} deposeth & sayth that he had Bills of ladeing & other papers & french letters aboard when the say^{d} Barque was seized, & that he had delivered all to Captain Robert Sinthock Com^{dr} of theyr Mat^{ies} frigott Nonsuch before the time of his seizing ye say^{d} Barque, And that had noe other papers aboard, nor any double dockets. And further ye Exam^{t} deposeth not.

[signed] John Michell

Mathew Nesbett

The Examination of Mathew Nesbett taken as aforesaid, ye day & ye oure[1] aforesaid

The Examin^{t} deposeth & sayth y^{t} he hath known ye s^{d} Barque in question for ye space of six months & y^{t} shee was called by ye name of the Amity & that John Michell was Master of ye said Barque, & y^{t} he hath heard ye said Barque was built in Ireland, & ye burthen, between 30 or 40 tunne, & y^{t} ye owners lived in Limbrick.

And further deposeth y^{t} ye said Barque was laden full & freighted at Limbrick with hides, Tallow & Salmon, and that ye said Master when he shipped him told him his design was for England, otherwise he ye examin^{t} had refused to goe with him, & deposeth y^{t} he was born in Glasgow in Scotland & a Subject to ye King of England.

And further ye Examin^{t} deposeth that he saw severall papers & french Letters aboard ye said barque but ye Contents, or to whom they were directed or from whom, ye Examin^{t} knoweth not, but beleiveth that they were delivered to ye Com^{dr} of their Mat^{ies} frigott Nonsuch or at least some of them, & further sayeth not

[signed] Mathew Nisbett

◆

Philipp Lepeulire

The Examination of Philipp Lepeulire, Captain in ye Regiment de la Marsh & passenger in ye Barque Amity from Limbrick for france. The Examin^{t} deposeth & sayth That he was ordered by Collonell Darington governour of Limbrick to goe passenger in ye Barque Amity now in question for ffrance, And y^{t} ye said Barque was bound for Nantz Rochell or Bourdeaux, and y^{t} ye say^{d} Barque had traded from Limbrick to ffrance these last six Months, transporting Butter, Tallow &c, & importing Salt, wine &c., And further deposeth, That he had A lett^{r} from Mr John Rowland[2] A Councellor in Limbrick to be deliverd to his sonn & y^{t} he ye Examin^{t} meeting his said sonn aboard the same Barque Amity delivered it to him, but what became of it afterwards the Examin^{t} knoweth not, & deposeth y^{t} both ye said John Rowland & his sonn were Roman Catholicke, & y^{t} ye same Lett^{r} is not to be found.

[signed] Lepeulire

[1] Read: 'hour'.

[2] Read: 'Ronan'.

James Ronan

The Examination of James Ronan taken as aforesay^{d}, the day & yeare aforesaid. The Examin^{t} deposeth that, he was A passenger in the say^{d} Barque Amity bound for ffrance, And y^{t} ye Cargo laden aboard ye said barque belonged to Samuel Taverner of Limbrick & partners, and that ye say^{d} Barque had formerly traded between Limbrick & ffrance these six months, transporting & importing Comodities, & further sayeth not

[signed] James Ronan

Source: TNA, HCA 32/1851/19.

Appendix V

Port of Limerick

Customs ledger fragment
April–July, 1691

April 21st 1691

John Snow Ma^{r} of the St John Bapst of Limerick bur^{d} 50^{tts} Outvoyces his s^{d} ship for Nantes with

278 dry hydes
384 Salt Oxe & Cowe Hides
1 Caske of Tallow
23 bags of Wooll, more five salt Hydes

John Leonard, James England, Dom: Terry, & Robt Hannan, M^{rts}

Cleared outwards this 10th day of June 1691

♦

Ditto 22nd

John Stafford Ma^{r} of the Diligence of Rochelle bur^{d} 100^{tts} Outvoyces his s^{d} ship for Rochelle with:

Forty five Caskes of Tallow
Thirty Caskes of Salmon
Sixty six salt Hydes
Two hundred thirty six dry hydes
Nine sackes of Wooll [Loaded by] Piers Moroney
32 Caskes of Tallow
12 Caskes of Butter
17 packes of Wooll
38 Tand Hydes
8 smale Caskes of Tallow [Loaded by] Jasper White
22 packes of Wooll
21 Caskes Butter [Loaded by] Thomas Curtis
37 tan'd Hydes
30 bundles of Bazells [Loaded by] Saml England
12 packes of Wooll [Loaded by] Robt Hannan
5 Packes of Wooll [Loaded by] Piers Moroney, M^{rts}

Cleared Outward the 22nd day of April 1691 John Stafford

April 25th 1691

John Player Mas^{r} of the Edmond of Nantes bur^{d} 40^{tts} Outvoyces his s^{d} Ship for Nantes wth

723 Salt Hydes
650 salt Hydes
96 dry hydes
5 Caskes of Tallow

John Martin & John Rirdan M^{ts}

Cleared Outward the 2^{d} July 1691 John Player

◆

June the 1st

Charles Sable Mas^{r} of the Rene of Morlis [Morlaix] bur^{d} 40^{tts} Outvoyces his s^{d} ship for Burdeax wth

20 bags of Wooll
20 packes of tan'd Leather
6 Tierces of Salmon
20 dry hydes

Cleared Outwards this 20th day of June 1691 Charles Sable

◆

June the 6th

Capt Fran^{s} Le Peppe Commander of the La Maria Victory of Rosco bur^{d} 120^{tts} Outvoyces his s^{d} ship for Burdeaux wth

26 Bags of Wooll	Charles Robord	
15 Bags of Wooll	Robt Hannan	M^{rts}

Cleared Outwards this 6th day of June 1691 François Le Peppe

Source: Limerick customs ledger, April–July 1691, in Archives of the Archbishop of Westminster (London), B6, folder 92, Henry Browne Papers.

Index of Personal and Mercantile Names

General Index